THEY
LOOKED LIKE THIS
(EUROPE)

THEY
LOOKED LIKE THIS
(EUROPE)

*An Assembly
of Authentic Word-Portraits
of Men and Women in
European History, Art and Literature
over 1900 years*

COMPILED BY
AVRIL PEDLEY
AND
GRANT UDEN

BARNES & NOBLE, INC. · NEW YORK
PUBLISHERS · BOOKSELLERS · SINCE 1873

PRINTED IN GREAT BRITAIN

So that you need not bestir yourselves . . .
His very person.
                    —Luis de Gongora y Argote

I remember your name perfectly, but I
just can't think of your face.
                    —attrib. to the Rev. W. A. Spooner

INTRODUCTION

The earlier volume in this series was concerned with the appearance of characters in English history and literature. Our brief for its successor has been the rest of Europe, though our frontiers have been fairly flexible and we have included some extraterritorial characters because of their temporary incusions into, or influence on, Europe.

Translations from a number of languages have been involved, and for these we are greatly indebted to Valerie Blackton, Peter Hoy, John Mundy, Betty Parr and J. Robinson. As ever, our obligation to our librarian friends cannot easily be measured, and we must make particular acknowledgement to Dr. Tim Pedley, who has rendered constant service throughout the preparation of this book.

A.P. and G.U.

ACKNOWLEDGEMENTS

The authors and publisher wish to thank the following for permission to reproduce copyright material from the sources shown:

ABELARD-SCHUMAN SERVICES LTD for the extract from *Kepler* by Max Caspar

ALLEN & UNWIN LTD for the extracts from *Memoirs of the Duke of Saint-Simon* translated by Bayle St John and *Life of Mendel* translated by E. and C. Paul

W. H. ALLEN & Co for the extract from *Memoirs of Alexandre Dumas* translated by A. F. Davidson

EDWARD ARNOLD LTD for the extracts from *My Memoirs* by Henri Stephan de Blowitz

BATSFORD LTD for the extracts from *Memoirs of Horace Walpole* edited by Matthew Hodgart and *Memoirs of the Reign of George the Second* by Lord Hervey

MRS MARY BENNETT for the extract from *An Unfinished Autobiography, 1940* by H. A. L. Fisher

D. C. BENSON & CAMPBELL THOMSON LTD for the extract from *Victorian Gallery* by Merial Buchanan

BLACKIE & SON LTD for the extracts from *Dr Charles Burney's Continental Travels, 1770–1772* edited by C. H. Glover

GEOFFREY BLES LTD for the extract from *My Life in the Russian Theatre* translated by John Cournos

THE BODLEY HEAD for the extracts from *The Reminiscences and Recollections of Captain Gronow* edited by John Raymond, *Constantine, King and Traitor* by Demetra Varka and *Recollections of a Court Painter* by H. J. Thaddeus

BURNS & OATES LTD for the extracts from *The Augustians* by E. A. Foran and *The Mirror of Perfection* translated by Constance, Countess de la Warr

CAMBRIDGE UNIVERSITY PRESS for the extract from *Memoirs, Diaries and Correspondence* edited by N. Rich and M. H. Fisher; and THE HAKLYUT SOCIETY for the extract from *Travels in Europe and Asia 1608–1667* by Peter Mundy

JONATHAN CAPE LTD for the extract from *Carl Linnaeus* translated by Alan Blair

CASSELL & CO LTD for the extract from *Memories of Forty Years* by Princess Radziwill

GEOFFREY CHAPMAN LTD and FIDES PUBLISHERS INC for the extract from *Saint Jerome* translated by Ronald Matthews

CHATTO & WINDUS LTD for the extract from *The Noble Savage* by L. and E. Hanson

THE CLARENDON PRESS for the extract from *Letters of Sidonius* edited by O. M. Dalton

WILLIAM CLOWES & SONS LTD for the extract from *The Army Quarterly*, January 1921

COLLINS PUBLISHERS AND LITTLE, BROWN & CO. for the extract from *Renoir, My Father* translated by R. and D. Weaver

COLUMBIA UNIVERSITY PRESS for the extracts from *A History of Deeds done beyond the Sea* translated and edited by E. Atwater Babcock and A. C. Krey, *The Conquest of Constantinople* edited by E. H. McNeal, *The Deeds of Frederick Barbarossa* translated and edited by Charles C. Mierow and *Adam Mickiewicz, Poet of Poland* edited by Manfred Kridl

CONSTABLE PUBLISHERS for the extracts from *Personal Recollections of Vincent Van Gogh* translated by Katherine S. Dreier and *Personal Recollections of Wagner* translated by Edith Livermore

CURTIS BROWN LTD for the extracts from *The Spanish Royal House* by Sir Charles Petrie and *Queen Victoria's Relations* by Meriel Buchanan

J. M. DENT & SONS LTD and E. P. DUTTON & CO LTD for the extracts from *Tacitus* translated by A. Murphy, *The Prince* translated by W. K. Marriott and *Memoirs of Benvenuto Cellini* translated by A. Macdonell

J. M. DENT & SONS LTD and W. W. NORTON & CO INC for the extract from *Schubert* translated by Eric Blom

ANDRE DEUTSCH LTD for the extract from *Leaves from a Journal* by Queen Victoria

GERALD DUCKWORTH & CO LTD for the extract from *Auguste Rodin* translated by Clementina Black

ELSEVIER PUBLISHING CO for the extract from *Nobel, the Man and his Prizes* edited by the Nobel Foundation

ENCYCLOPAEDIA BRITANNICA INTERNATIONAL LTD for the extract from *Michel Eyquern de Montaigne, the Essays* translated by Charles Cotton

FABER & FABER LTD for the extract from *Italian Journal* edited by J. R. Hale

GILL & SON LTD and THE NEWMAN PRESS for the extract from *The First Jesuit* by Mary Purcell

VICTOR GOLLANCZ LTD for the extracts from *Peace in their Time* by Emery Kelen

HAMISH HAMILTON LTD and THE MACMILLAN CO for the extracts from *The Memoirs of Catherine the Great* translated by Moura Budberg and edited by D. Maroger

HAMISH HAMILTON LTD and THE VIKING PRESS INC for the extract from *Mirabeau, Voice of the Revolution* translated by Antonina Vallentin

HARVARD UNIVERSITY PRESS for the extract from *The Letters of Peter Paul Rubens* edited by Ruth S. Magurn

WILLIAM HEINEMANN LTD, J. C. and R. G. MEDLEY for the extract from *Confessions of a Young Man* by George Moore

DAVID HIGHAM ASSOCIATES LTD for the extracts from *The Bourbons of Naples* by Harold Acton and *Memoirs of Napoleon I* edited by Somerset de Chair

LAURENCE POLLINGER LTD and LITTLE BROWN & CO for the extract from *Emperors, Angels and Eunuchs* translated by E. and C. Paul

LIBRAIRIE ERNEST FLAMMARION for the extract from *Pages from the Goncourt Journal* edited by Robert Baldick

HUTCHINSON PUBLISHING GROUP LTD for the extracts from *The Life of Cesare Borgia* by Rafael Sabatini, *Nearing the End of Imperial Russia* by George T. Marye and *The Real Rasputin* translated by Arthur Chambers

LONGMANS GREEN & CO LTD for the extracts from *The Life of St Thomas Aquinas* by Kenelm Foster, *Saint Bernadette Soubirous* translated by John Joyce, *Letters and Recollections of Mazzini* edited by G. M. Trevelyan and *Farewell My Youth* by Sir Arnold Bax; and HARPER & ROW PUBLISHERS INC for the extract from *Life of Saint John of the Cross* translated by Kathleen Pond

MCGRAW-HILL BOOK CO for the extract from *Drawn from Life* by S. J. Woolf

JACKSON SON & CO LTD for the extract from *An Itinerary* by Fynes Moryson

MACMILLAN & CO LTD for the extract from *Life, Letters and Works of Louis Agassiz* by Jules Marcou

MACMILLAN & CO LTD, HARCOURT, BRACE & WORLD INC and THE TRUSTEES OF THE ESTATE OF THE LATE LORD KEYNES for the extract from *The Economic Consequences of the Peace* by J. M. Keynes

DAVID MAGERSHACK ESQ for the extract from his translation of *Ivan Turgenev, Literary Reminiscences and Autobiographical Fragments*

MEREDITH PRESS for the extracts from *Royal Portraits* by Princess Marie Bibesco

METHUEN & CO LTD for the extracts from *Medieval People* by Eileen Power and *More English Diaries* by A. Ponsonby

THE UNIVERSITY OF MICHIGAN PRESS for the extract from *The Life of Charlemagne* translated by Samuel Epes Turner

MILLS & BOON LTD for the extract from *A Mystic on the Prussian Throne* translated by Gilbert Stanhope

VALENTINE MITCHELL & CO LTD for the extract from *Heinrich Heine* translated by Joseph Witriol

JOHN MURRAY for the extract from *Gustav Mahler, Memories and Letters* translated by Basil Creighton; and VANGUARD PRESS INC for the extract from *Effie in Venice* by Mary Lutyens

SIR HAROLD NICOLSON for the extract from his book *Some People*

ODHAMS BOOKS LTD for the extracts from *Great Contemporaries* by Winston S. Churchill

PENGUIN BOOKS LTD for the extracts from *Pliny's Letters* translated by Betty Radice and *Marco Polo, Travels* translated by Ronald Latham

PHAIDON PRESS LTD for the extract from *Rembrandt, Paintings, Drawings, Etchings* by Ludwig Goldscheider

WILLIAM REEVES for the extract from *Musical Memories* by William Spark

ROUTLEDGE & KEGAN PAUL LTD for the extracts from *Historical Memoirs of Alexander I and the Court of Russia* by Choiseul-Gouffier, *Musicians of Today* by Romain Rolland, *Vita de Michelangelo Buonarroti* translated by Elizabeth Hall, *Travels into Spain 1691* edited by R. Foulché-Delbose, *Discovery and Conquest of Mexico* translated by A. P. Maudslay, *Dostoevsky Portrayed by his Wife* translated by S. S. Koteliansky, *The Vespasiano Memoirs* translated by William George and Emily Waters and *Liudprand of Cremona, Works* translated by F. A. Wright

ROYAL HISTORICAL SOCIETY for the extract from *The Transactions of the Royal Historical Society*, 1907, I

RUTGERS UNIVERSITY PRESS for the extract from *The Life of Christopher Columbus* translated by Benjamin Keen

Secker & Warburg Ltd and Putnams and Coward McCann for the extracts from *The French Revolution* translated by R. Graves

John Sherratt & Son for the extracts from *Shakespeare's Europe* edited by Charles Hughes

Society for Promoting Christian Knowledge for the extract from *Life of Otto, Apostle of Pomerania* edited by Charles H. Robinson

The College of Arms for the extracts from the document at the College of Heralds

Van Nostrand Co Inc for the extract from *Louis Philippe and the July Monarchy* translated by Paul Beik

The Viking Press Inc for the extracts from *Three Exemplary Novels* translated by Putnam

The authors and publisher have made every effort to clear all copyright material, but in spite of their efforts, it has been impossible to trace the holders of some of the extracts. In the event of any unforeseen infringements, they express their regrets, and would welcome any information which would remedy such oversight in future editions.

THEY
LOOKED LIKE THIS
(EUROPE)

ABDUL HAMID II (1842–1918), Sultan of Turkey; deposed and exiled, 1909; called 'the Damned'.

He was rather above the average height, of slight build, and almost thin; he had a brown skin, warm and dry-looking, his beard was black, well-groomed, and rather short and thick. His mouth was energetic, but sad; his nose a regular Turkish nose, large, long and bony, with a slight deflection of the upper part of the nostril. His eyes were black, rather large, resolute, thoughtful, and penetrating, but not gentle-looking; they were set deep in the orbit, and as the light fell on one side of his face, leaving the other side in the shade, his eyes appeared to be remarkably deep-sunk. His forehead was wide and straight, of medium height, and slightly furrowed. The black hair which was visible on his temples, between the fez and the beard, was short and almost close-shaven. Abdul Hamid was then forty-one years of age, but he looked more, particularly as he had lost an upper tooth on the left side near the middle. He spoke in a louder voice than his subjects; his language was sonorous, his words distinct, and his phrases lengthened out and terminated without hesitation.

SOURCE: Henri Stephan de Blowitz, *My Memoirs*, Edward Arnold, 1903, pp. 288–289.

And then, after a short, breathless silence, a blast of silver trumpets, and the open carriage with the Sultan Abdul Hamid II. A solitary, round-shouldered figure, his plain black frock-coat unadorned by any jewels or decorations, his brilliant red fez making him look pale and yellow. A grim, evil, sullen face, a big hooked nose, a short henna-dyed beard, and deep-set eyes, casting a quick look at the balcony where we stood, a look which seemed to take in all the details of our appearance, and to express in its malevolence, his deep, unutterable hatred not only for us but for the European countries we represented.

SOURCE: Meriel Buchanan, *Victorian Gallery*, Cassell & Co., 1956, pp. 94–95.

AGASSIZ, JEAN LOUIS RODOLPHE (1807–1873), Swiss naturalist, geologist and teacher.

Agassiz was a little above the average height, although not tall. He was squarely built, with broad shoulders and a powerful and well-proportioned body, and with remarkably large, and at the same time well-formed, hands, which he always used most skilfully. They were the hands of an artist or of a naturalist, ready to use the pencil, the hammer, the scalpel, or the microscope, and his manner of shaking hands was very cordial and friendly. He stood firmly, though his feet were rather small in comparison with his herculean structure, and seemed formed for walking; indeed, he was all his life a capital pedestrian, both on level ground and among the Alpine mountains.

His head was simply magnificent, his forehead large and well developed; and his brilliant, intelligent and searching eyes can be best described by the word fascinating, while his mouth and somewhat voluptuous lips were expressive, and in perfect harmony with an aquiline nose and well-shaped chin. His hair was chestnut colour and rather thin, especially on the top of his head; indeed, after he was thirty-six years old he showed signs of baldness, which greatly increased after his fiftieth year. The only part of Agassiz's body which was not in harmony with the rest was his short neck, which gave him the appearance of carrying his head on his shoulders, —a defect which he possessed in common with Napoleon Bonaparte. It was his weak point, and the part which failed first . . .

Fine clothes never attracted him. He was, on the contrary, rather inclined to wear the most common and unbecoming suits and a slouch hat during winter and summer, and I do not believe that during his whole stay in America he ever wore a silk hat. At Neuchâtel, his dress was most ordinary, notwithstanding the rather formal society in which he moved. But in Paris, during his long visit of 1846, he was obliged to follow the customs of other savants, conformed to ever since the time of Cuvier and Humboldt, viz. a black frock coat, white cravat, and high hat. Alexander von Humboldt affected to wear such ceremonial dress even when he explored the Ural Mountains and Central Asia, and Leopold von Buch, as well as Élie de Beaumont, did the same during their geological excursions. It was not becoming to Agassiz, however, and he was delighted when he arrived in America to find that every one dressed as he pleased, without any ceremony or convention of any sort. He very seldom wore gloves, never carried a cane, except an alpenstock, and very seldom used an umbrella. When in Neuchâtel at official meetings, he wore over his coat the ribbon and cross of the Red Eagle of Prussia, but after leaving Neuchâtel he wore no decorative ribbon of any kind, notwithstanding that he possessed that of knight and officer of the Legion of Honour of France, besides the Prussian order. On the whole, Agassiz was extremely simple, and did not like to make an appearance different from that of ordinary people in his neighbourhood.

SOURCE: Jules Marcon, *Life, Letters, and Works of Louis Agassiz*, Macmillan & Co., 1896, Vol. II, pp. 217–220.

AGRICOLA, GNAEUS JULIUS (37–93), Roman general and governor of Britain.

As to his person, about which in future times there may be some curiosity, he was of that make and stature which may be said to be graceful, not majestic. His countenance had not that commanding air which strikes with awe: a sweetness of expression was the prevailing character. You would have been easily convinced that he was a good man, and you would have been willing to believe him a great one.

SOURCE: Tacitus, *The History, Germania and Agricola*, trans. Arthur Murphy, Everyman edition, J. M. Dent & Co., Vol. II, p. 384.

B

ALBUQUERQUE, AFFONSO DE (1453–1515), Portuguese captain General and governor of India, 1509–1515; known as the 'Portuguese Mars'.

This great captain was a man of middle stature, with a long face, fresh coloured, the nose somewhat large. He was a prudent man, and a Latin scholar, and spoke in eloquent phrases; his conversation and writings showed his excellent education. He was of ready words, very authoritative in his commands, very circumspect in his dealings with the Moors, and greatly feared yet greatly loved by all, a quality rarely found united in one captain. He was very valiant and favoured by fortune.

SOURCE: Walter de Gray Birch, edit., *The Commentaries of the Great Afonso Dalboquerque*, Vol. IV, Hakluyt Society, 1884, p. 199.

ALEXANDER I (1777–1825), Emperor of Russia; succeeded, 1801.

The Emperor Alexander, at the time of which I speak, was thirty-five years old, but he looked much younger. I remember asking Count Tolstoi how the health of the Emperor could stand these long journeys. 'Look at him,' said the count, 'and you will cease to wonder.'

Notwithstanding the regularity and delicacy of his features, the brightness and freshness of his complexion, his beauty was less striking, at first sight, than that air of benevolence and kindness which captivated all hearts and instantly inspired confidence. His tall, noble, and majestic form, which often stooped a little with grace, like the pose of an antique statue, already threatened to become stout, but he was perfectly formed. His eyes were blue, bright and expressive; he was a little short sighted. His nose was straight and well shaped, his mouth small and agreeable. The rounded contour of his face, as well as his profile, resembled that of his august mother. His forehead was somewhat bald, but this gave to his whole countenance an open and serene expression, and his hair of a golden blond, carefully arranged as in the heads of antique cameos or medallions, seemed made to receive the triple crown of laurel, myrtle and olive. He had an infinity of shades of tone and manner ... This prince in his early youth had had his hearing seriously impaired by the report of a discharge of artillery, in consequence of which his left ear was somewhat deaf, and he usually turned his right toward the speaker to hear better. No painter, without exception, has ever been able to catch the likeness of his features, especially the expression and refinement of his countenance.

SOURCE: Choiseul-Gouffier, *Historical Memoirs of Alexander I and the Court of Russia*, Kegan Paul, Trench & Trübner, 1904, pp. 81–83.

ALEXANDER (1876–1903); King of Serbia; succeeded his father King Milan in 1889. He and his Queen, Draga, were murdered in 1903.

I met King Alexander for the first time on the morning after his arrival in Biarritz. I met him on the beach, *à la Grande Plage* under the royal tent, adorned for the circumstance with new little Serbian flags fluttering brightly in the sun—red, white and blue.

He stood beside his radiant mother. He was a dark, sulky-looking little fellow with a little black mustache, of medium figure, badly clothed in a common white flannel suit with blue stripes, wearing an out-of-date, foolish little straw hat, with a string to keep it safe against the sea winds; and over his frowning black eyebrows, over his short-sighted small black eyes, half shut, he wore a disgraceful, a detestable pair of sunglasses fastened with a golden chain. I could have sobbed on the spot to find he was so ugly.

SOURCE: Princess Marie Bibesca, *Royal Portraits*, D. Appleton & Co., 1928, p. 11.

ALEXIUS MIKHAILOVICH (1629–1676), Tsar of Muscovy.

His Imperial Majesty is a goodly person, two months older than King Charles the Second, of a sanguine complexion, light brown hair, his beard uncut, he is tall and fat, of a majestical Deportment, severe in his anger, bountiful, charitable, chastely uxorious, very kind to his Sisters and Children, of a strong memory, strict in his Devotions, and a favourer of his Religion; and had he not such a cloud of Sycophants and jealous Nobility about him, who blind his good intentions, no doubt he might be numbered amongst the best and wisest of Princes . . . As for his Treasure of Jewels, I think no Prince doth exceed him, yet he hath many foul Stones . . . The fashion of the Emperor's clothes is like that of his Nobility but only richer.

SOURCE: 'An eminent Person Residing at the Great Tsar's Court at Moscow for the space of nine years' [Dr. Samuel Collins], *The Present State of Russia, In a Letter to a Friend*, 1671, pp. 44, 65.

ALFIERI, COUNT VITTORIO (1749–1803), the greatest Italian tragic poet.

Curious and strange was the character of that singular man: proud as Milton's Satan, and more choleric than Homer's Achilles. He esteemed himself far beyond his real worth, and very few were the poets or men of letters for whom he had any regard. He was proud of his reddish hair, which he always wore studiously curled and tended; of his fine and speckless apparel, and especially of his uniform as a captain in the Piedmontese infantry, which he donned for more solemn occasions; of his pure gold buckles for shoes and breeches, as then worn; of his handsome English horses, of which, counting together saddle and carriage horses, he had sixteen; and of his fine and elegant phaeton, which he generally drove four-in-hand, and went in pomp, taking the air in city and high-road.

SOURCE: Gaetano Polidori, his secretary from 1785; quoted *Dante Gabriel Rossetti, His Family-Letters*, edit. with a memoir by William Michael Rossetti, Ellis & Elvey, 1895, Vol. I, p. 27.

AMALRIC I (1136?–1174). See Amaury I.

AMAURY I (1136?–1174), fifth Latin King of Jerusalem; formerly Count of Jaffa and Ascalon, he succeeded his brother, Baldwin III (q.v.) in 1162.

He was of goodly height, taller than many although shorter than those of maximum stature. His features were comely and his bearing proclaimed even to strangers the dignity of a prince to whom reverence was due. He had sparkling eyes of medium size; his nose, like that of his brother, was becomingly aquiline; his hair was blond and grew back somewhat from his forehead. A comely and very full beard covered his cheeks and chin. He had a way of laughing immoderately so that his entire body shook. He loved to talk with wise and discreet men as well as with those who were familiar with far countries and foreign customs . . . Amaury was excessively fat, with breasts like those of a woman hanging down to his waist. Nature had framed his other members with a kinder hand, however, for these displayed not merely ordinary comeliness, but, in fact, a rather unusual beauty. Not even his enemies could deny that in the use of bodily nourishment he was moderate and in regard to wine most abstemious.

SOURCE: William, Archbishop of Tyre, *A History of Deeds done beyond the Sea*, trans. and edit. E. Atwater Babcock and A. C. Krey, Columbia University Press, 1943, Vol. II, pp. 298 and 300. William of Tyre (c. 1130–1185) was Archbishop of Tyre from 1175 to 1184 or 1185, and Chancellor of the Latin Kingdom from 1174 until his death.

ANDERSEN, HANS CHRISTIAN (1805–1875), Danish story-teller and novelist.

Suddenly . . . as we were seated in the living-room, there appeared in the doorway a very tall, elderly gentleman, dressed in a complete suit of brown, and in a curly wig of the same shade of snuff-colour. I was almost painfully struck, at the first moment, by the grotesque ugliness of his face and hands, and by his enormously long and swinging arms; but this impression passed away as soon as he began to speak. His eyes, although they were small, had great sweetness and vivacity of expression, while gentleness and ingenuousness breathed from everything he said . . .

The face of Hans Andersen was a peasant's face, and a long lifetime of sensibility and culture had not removed from it the stamp of the soil. But it was astonishing how quickly this first impression subsided, while a sense of his great inward distinction took its place. He had but to speak, almost but to smile, and the man of genius stood revealed.

SOURCE: Edmund Gosse, *Two Visits to Denmark*, 1911; quoted Monica Stirling, *The Wild Swan*, Collins, 1965, p. 341.

ANDREYEV, LEONID NICOLAIEVICH (1871–1919), Russian novelist; in 1894 he made an attempt on his own life as a result of which he suffered from a weak heart, which ultimately caused his death.

In the Autumn, on my way to the Crimea, at the Kursk railway station in Moscow, someone introduced us to each other. Dressed in an oldish overcoat, in a shaggy sheepskin hat tilted to one side, he looked like a young actor in an Ukrainian theatrical company. His handsome face struck me as not very mobile but in the fixed glance of his dark eyes gleamed the smile which so pleasantly irradiated his stories and light articles. I don't remember his words, but they were unusual, and unusual also was the construction of his agitated speech. He spoke hurriedly, with a dullish, booming voice, with a little crisp cough, his words slightly choking him, while he waved his hands monotonously as though he were conducting. He appeared to me a healthy, sprite-like, cheery man, capable of supporting with a laugh the woes of this world.

SOURCE: Maxim Gorki, *Reminiscences of Leonid Andreyev*, trans. K. Mansfield and S. S. Koteliansky, William Heinemann Ltd., 1931, pp. 3–4.

ANGELA, a young girl of Bologna, Italy, in the early seventeenth century.

In these last days of carnival, one night towards three o'clock in the morning there was brought into my house a mask, who both in her dress and in her face when unmasked, seemed an angel of Paradise—her head crowned with a wreath of laurel, her clothing white, of stuff most skilfully arranged, and bearing a trumpet in her hand, whereon she played certain notes as she entered the chamber where I was, with a natural virginal grace. She then spoke the verses I send you herewith, with so graceful gesture and speech that it seemed as though Poetry herself were come from heaven to delight me.

Since when I have been thinking to beg you to employ your own Muse in singing the praise of this young girl, of such extraordinary virginal beauty, exceeding the customary stature of women. She is fifteen or sixteen years of age and so eloquent, courteous and graceful that I have never seen her like, even on the stage, for the grace with which she recites her verses and the manner in which she fits her movements and gestures thereto... The name of the girl is Angela.

SOURCE: Letter of Lodovico Carracci to Ferrante Carlo, Bologna, February 15th, 1617; quoted Richard Friedenthal, *Letters of the Great Artists from Ghiberti to Gainsborough*, Thames & Hudson, 1963, p. 130. Lodovico Carracci (1555–1619) was the founder of the Bolognese school of painting and established the Academy of the *Incamminati*, those 'brought on to the right road'.

ANKER, BERNT (1746–1805), a native of Christiania in Norway. Anker was Chamberlain to the King of Denmark.

He had travelled much, and combined, in his manners, all the best characteristics of our own countrymen, with a good deal of French foppery, and that native heartiness of a Norwegian, which knows no bounds to its hospitality, but, as in Sweden, will carry its kind attention to strangers even to excess... Being Chamberlain to the King of Denmark, Bernard Anker wore the Danish court badge, —a large key and riband, fastened to the button of his coat behind. In his person he was above the common size, of athletic form, and well-looking. His hair, decorated in the old Parisian taste, was highly frizzled and powdered; and, during the whole of his conversation, he stood opposite a large mirror, attentively surveying and adjusting the different articles of his dress; but in all this there was nothing of mere vanity, or of affectation; it was evidently what among the French, would have been once considered the ease and gaiety of a well-bred fashionable beau: although to English eyes, such an air and manner might have been considered as bordering upon those of the *petit-maître*. However we soon found, in the conduct of this exemplary individual, a lesson against judging too hastily from outward appearances.

IN 1799.

SOURCE: Edward Daniel Clarke, *Travels in Various Countries of Europe, Asia and Africa*, Vol. VI (1823), pp. 34–35.

ANTONELLI, GIACOMO (1806–1876), Italian Cardinal; exerted a most unscrupulous influence in the struggle between the Papacy and the Italian *Risorgimento*.

The Cardinal is thin, although he has appropriated the fat of the States of the Church. His face is incredible to every one who has not seen him. You might confidently allow Antonelli to travel through the whole Catholic Germany, to enlist volunteers for a crusade for the Holy Father. Every believer would draw on one side, every *gendarme* would ask him for his passport. In our harmless, truthful world it would be considered a sheer impossibility that such a physiognomy could sit in the Sacred College, much more that it could conduct the affairs of Christ's representative on earth ...

Antonelli's face is divided into two halves, which must have been put together from different parts of creation. The upper half is Egyptian, Asiatic; two restless eyes roll in large circles under black hair. From a strictly physical point of view these eyes are fine, clear, light in the darkest ground, —much as the beast of prey of the desert has fine eyes; but their uncertainty and incessant motion, their permanent rolling, shooting, and piercing are so demoniacal, that one could not wish better eyes to the personator of Mephistopheles. They are the eyes of the sphinx, from which a human soul seems to look when there is none there; it is the mockery of advancing nature, which would gladly become man, but cannot get possession of a single attribute, and therefore is enigmatical, disquieting, uneasy. Just in the moment when you would embrace it with love as something congenial, you are icily touched by something most foreign, and you shudder.

The lower half of the face dates still further back by a few hundred thousand years. When this jawbone and mouth appeared, there were as yet no men on the earth: all was still gigantic amphibia, the organic existence an everlasting devouring. The motion of the facial muscles shows what was the employment of those oxygen-breathers, for they go regularly up and down, down and up, even when there is no booty at hand for the moment. The corners of the mouth are continually going half-way up to the ears and back again. Each time they go up you have a fresh alarm, for you see in the open hollow the remains of an elephant. The Cardinal has wonderful teeth, and he makes a regular show of them.

SOURCE: Gregorovius, *Dublin University Magazine*, LXXVII, p. 308 (March 1871); quoted William Roscoe Thayer, *The Life and Times of Cavour*, Constable & Co., 1915, Vol. I, pp. 181–182.

AQUINAS, SAINT THOMAS (1225?–1274), 'the prince of scholastic philosophers'; born near Naples; known as the 'Angelic Doctor'.

Concerning his appearance and physique some details have been preserved. He was tall and stout. He held himself erect, as men of an upright character do. His complexion was healthy, as of one who shunned excess of any kind; and in colour like ripe wheat. He had a large head, with a full development of the organs that minister to reason. He was somewhat bald. His body had the delicately balanced texture that goes with a fine intelligence; yet virile also, robust and prompt to serve the will, and trained never to shrink from any pain or peril by a soul that drew its confidence from God. It was, in short, a noble instrument for noble deeds, showing that God himself had designed it for this purpose. But in thunderstorms and tempests Thomas would fortify himself with the sign of the cross and say: 'God came to us in the flesh, He died for us and rose again.'

SOURCE: Bernard Gui's Life of Saint Thomas Aquinas, Chapter 35; included in *The Life of Saint Thomas Aquinas*, biographical documents, trans. and edit. by Kenelm Foster, Longmans Green & Co., 1959, p. 53. Gui's account was one of three lives of the saint written between 1318 and 1330 which drew on much common material at a time when many who knew Thomas personally were alive. The testimony given by the witnesses at the first canonisation inquiry held in 1319 bears out much of what Gui relates. 'Asked when he saw Thomas ill in the monastery he said it was about forty five years ago. He remembered him as a big stout man, with a dark complexion and bald. As for his age, he had seemed to the witness about fifty or sixty.' So runs the account of the testimony of Nicholas of Priverno, quoted Kenelm Foster (see above), p. 88.

ARISTO, TITIUS, a distinguished Roman jurist and friend of the Younger Pliny, he flourished under the Emperor Trajan who ruled from A.D. 98 to 117.

He is genuine and authoritative in conversation, and his deliberate manner is firm and dignified; there can be few questions to which he cannot provide a ready answer, and yet he often pauses to weigh up the many alternative arguments which his keen and powerful intellect derives from their fundamental source and then selects with fine discrimination.

Moreover, his habits are simple and his dress is plain, and his bedroom and its furniture always seem to me to give pictures of bygone simplicity. It has its adornment in its greatness of mind, which cares nothing for show but refers everything to conscience, seeking reward for a good deed in its performance and not in popular opinion . . .

His patience throughout his illness, if you could only see it, would fill you with admiration; he fights against pain, resists thirst, and endures the unbelievable heat of his fever without moving or throwing off his coverings.

SOURCE: Pliny the Younger, *Letters*, trans. Betty Radice, Penguin Books Ltd., 1963, pp. 55–56.

ARNIM, BETTINA VON (1785–1859). Born Bettina (in full, Elizabeth Katharina Ludovica Magdalena) Brentano, she became one of the outstanding women writers in modern Germany.

In 1840–7 she was living in Unter den Linden in a very smart house with a touch of poetic disorder, such as a big bunch of wild flowers and grasses arranged in an elegant vase. We often spent the evening with her. At dusk she became dreamy and talked about her memories; she sat curled up in an armchair, not on the seat, but on the arm with her feet on the seat, with an expression on her face like that of a gypsy fortune teller, her talk lit up with rockets of sarcasm like a female Mephistopheles.

SOURCE: Edward Weiss; quoted Arthur Helps and Elizabeth Jane Howard, *Bettina*, Chatto & Windus, 1957, p. 196.

Half witch, half angel; half priestess, half Bayadere; half seeress, half liar; half cat, half dove; half lizard, half butterfly; half morning dew, half fish-blood; half chaste moonlight, half wanton flesh; half flower, half toad; half Spinx, half Gurli; half Ganymede, half German student complete with riding whip and pistols; half intrigante, half lover; half Sybil, half Amazon; half child, half actress; half Mignon, half Philistine; half sylph, half rat; half diplomat, half innocent girl from the country; half dung-beetle, half nightingale; half Maid of Orleans, half Diogenes in the barrel; half Jacobine waving the flag of freedom; half Catholic with a rosary, half ranging maenad, half bluestocking; half commander-in-chief, half regimental drummer boy; half market woman, half king of the

Elves; half adventuress, half nun; half sleep-walker, half coquette; half inspired pantheist, half frivolous dancer.

SOURCE: Clemens; quoted Helps and Howard (see above), pp. 204–205.

AROUET, FRANÇOIS MARIE (1694–1778). See Voltaire, François Marie Arouet de.

ATTILA (406?–453), King of the Huns; called 'The Scourge of God'.

A lavish meal, served on silver trenchers, was prepared for us and the other barbarians, but Attila just had some meat on a wooden platter, for this was one aspect of his self discipline. For instance, gold or silver cups were presented to the other diners, but his own goblet was made of wood. His clothes, too, were simple, and no trouble was taken except to have them clean. The sword that hung by his side, the clasps of his barbarian shoes and the bridle of his horse were all free from gold, precious stones or other valuable decorations affected by the other Scythians ...

After the songs a Scythian entered, a crazy fellow who told a lot of strange and completely false stories, not a word of truth in them, which made everyone laugh. Following him came the moor, Zerkon, totally disorganised in appearance, clothes, voice and words. By mixing up the languages of the Italians with those of the Huns and Goths, he fascinated everyone and made them break out into uncontrollable laughter, all that is except Attila. He remained impassive, without any change of expression, and neither by word or gesture did he seem to share in the merriment except that when his youngest son, Ernas, came in and stood by him, he drew the boy towards him and looked at him with gentle eyes.

SOURCE: Priscus, *Historici Graeci Minories*, edit. Dindorf, trans. B. K. Workman, and included in *They Saw it Happen in Classical Times*, Basil Blackwell, 1964, pp. 204–205.

AUGUSTA WILHELMINA AMELIA LOUISE, PRINCESS OF MECKLENBURG-STRELITZ (1776–1810), became Queen Louise of Prussia, wife of Frederick William III.

Her beauty was truly royal. Though she was taller than most women, the proportions of her figure were perfect. Her shoulders, her bust, were incomparable, her complexion dazzling. Her hair was slightly auburn, her forehead noble, her eyes full of gentleness, her lips vermilion. Her neck and the movements of her head were of unequalled elegance. Possibly her teeth were not as brilliant as might have been wished, her hands, though white, were a little too powerful and her foot was rather bad. But these slight imperfections were more than redeemed by the majestic semblance of her person.

SOURCE: Princess Dorothea of Courland; quoted Constantin de Grunewald, *Baron Stein, Enemy of Napoleon*, trans. Charles Francis Atkinson, Jonathan Cape, 1936, p. 91. Princess Dorothea was the future Duchess of Dino and a friend of Talleyrand.

I think I see this Princess before me still, half-reclining on a sofa, a golden tripod by her side and a shawl of Oriental purple about her exquisite figure. There was in the tone of her voice so harmonious a beauty—in her words something so loveable and touching, in that way she held them—such grace and such majesty, that for a moment I would believe myself in the presence of a fairy-tale apparition.

SOURCE: General de Ségur; quoted ibid., p. 92.

AUGUSTINE, SAINT (AURELIUS AUGUSTINUS) (354–430), Numidian bishop of Hippo in preconsular Africa; philosopher.

His vesture, shoes and apartments were in accord with his moderate needs, neither too good, nor too mean; but men are inclined to treat such modesty with contempt and to avoid it, seeking rather themselves than that which is of Jesus Christ. But he, as I have shown, kept to the medium course, not inclining to the right or to the left. At table it was his custom to be frugal and sparing ... He was always hospitable, but at table he showed more delight in the reading and conversation than in eating and drinking.

SOURCE: Saint Possidius, *Life of Saint Augustine*, published in E. A. Foran, *The Augustinians*, Burns Oates & Washbourne Ltd., 1938, p. 23.

BACH, CARL PHILIPP EMMANUEL (1714–1788), second son of Johann Sebastian Bach; called 'The Bach of Berlin' or 'The Bach of Hamburg'.

I prevailed upon him to sit down again to a clavichord, and he played, with little intermission, till near eleven o'clock at night. During this time, he grew so animated and *possessed*, that he not only played but looked like one inspired. His eyes were fixed, his under lip fell, and drops of effervescence distilled from his countenance. He said, if he were to be set to work frequently in this manner, he should grow young again. He is now fifty-nine, rather short in stature, with black hair and eyes, and brown complexion, has a very animated countenance, and is of a cheerful and lively disposition.

SOURCE: Doctor Charles Burney, *An Eighteenth Century Musical Tour in Central Europe and the Netherlands*, edit. Percy Scholes, Oxford University Press, 1959, Vol. II, p. 219.

BALDWIN I (1172–1205), Emperor of Rumania. Count of Flanders and Hainaut; one of the most prominent leaders of the Fourth Crusade, during which he was elected first Emperor of Rumania, after the capture of Constantinople. He is here described at his coronation.

They [i.e. the leading lay and ecclesiastical nobility] took the emperor to a place apart in the church into a chamber. There they divested him of his outer garments and took off his *chausses* [long hose coming well up the thigh] and put on him *chausses* of vermilion samite and shoes all covered with rich stones. Then they put on him a very rich coat all fastened with gold buttons in front and behind from the shoulders clear to the girdle. And then they put on him the *palle*, a kind of cloak which fell to the top of the shoes in front and was so long behind that he wound it about his middle and then brought it back over his left arm like the maniple of a priest. And this *palle* was very rich and noble, and all covered with precious stones. Then over this they put a very rich mantle, which was all covered with previous stones, and the eagles on it were made of precious stones so that it seemed as if the whole mantle were aflame ... When the emperor was come before the altar, he knelt down and they took off first the mantle and then the *palle*, so that he was left in his coat, and then they unfastened the coat by the gold buttons in front and behind, so that he was bare from the girdle up, and then they anointed him. When he was anointed, they put on again the coat with its gold buttons and then they vested him again with the *palle* and then they fastened the mantle over his shoulder ... to serve as a clasp they hung about his neck a very rich jewel which the emperor Manuel had once bought for sixty-two thousand marks ... And the jewels which he was wearing were worth more than the treasure of a rich king would make.

SOURCE: Robert of Clari, *Chronicle*, edit. Edgar Holmes McNeal in *The Conquest of Constantinople*, Columbia University Press, 1936, pp. 115–117.

BALDWIN III (1130–1162), fourth Latin King of Jerusalem.

In vivacity of mind and brilliancy of speech he was superior to all the nobles of the realm. He was taller than the average man, but his limbs were so well proportioned to his height that no feature seemed out of harmony with the whole. His features were comely and refined, his complexion florid, a proof of innate strength. In this respect he resembled his mother and was not inferior to his maternal grandfather. His eyes were of medium size, rather prominent and sparkling. He had straight yellowish hair and wore a rather full beard on cheeks and chin. He was of somewhat full habit, although he could not be called fleshy like his brother or spare like his mother. In short, it may be said, that his whole appearance was so superior by reason of a certain remarkable dignity which shone forth from him that even strangers could not fail to recognise his innate kingly majesty.

SOURCE: William, Archbishop of Tyre, *A History of Deeds done beyond the Sea*, trans. and edit. E. Atwater Babcock and A. C. Krey, Columbia University Press, 1943, Vol. II, p. 137. For a note on William of Tyre, see under Amaury I, fifth Latin King of Jerusalem.

BALDWIN IV (c. 1161–1185), sixth Latin King of Jerusalem; known as 'the Leper'. He succeeded his father at the age of thirteen.

As he began to reach years of maturity, it was evident that he was suffering from the terrible disease of leprosy. Day by day his condition became worse. The extremities and the face were especially attacked, so that his faithful followers were moved with compassion when they looked at him. Nevertheless, he continued to make progress in the pursuit of letters and gave ever increasing promise of developing a lovable disposition. He was comely of appearance for his age, and far beyond the custom of his forefathers he was an excellent horseman and understood the handling of horses. He had a retentive memory and loved to talk. He was economical but always remembered both favours and injuries. In every respect he resembled his father, not alone in face but in his entire mien; even his walk and the tones of his voice were the same. His intellect was keen but his speech was somewhat halting. Like his father he listened eagerly to history and was well disposed to follow good advice.

SOURCE: William, Archbishop of Tyre, *A History of Deeds done beyond the Sea*, trans. and edit. E. Atwater Babcock and A. C. Krey, Columbia University Press, 1943, Volume II, p. 398. For a note on William of Tyre, see under Amaury I, fifth Latin King of Jerusalem.

BALZAC, HONORÉ DE (1799–1850), French novelist.

Balzac had nothing in his outward man that could in any way

respond to the ideal his readers were likely to form of the enthusiastic admirer of beauty and elegance in all its forms and
phases . . . The great enchanter was one of the oiliest and com-
monest looking mortals I ever beheld; being short and corpulent, with a broad florid face, a cascade of double chins, and
straight greasy hair. The only striking feature in that Friar
Tuck countenance was his eye; dark, flashing, wicked, full of
sarcasm and unholy fire.

Balzac had that unwashed appearance which seems generally
to belong to French *litterati*, and dressed in the worst possible
taste, wore sparkling jewels on a dirty shirt front, and diamond
rings on unwashed fingers. He talked little, but it was evident
that nothing escaped him, and that bright eye seemed almost
to read the secrets of the heart. No literary man, except perhaps
Alexandre Dumas, ever ran through so much money as Balzac.
The immense sums which he received for his writings were
spent in the most absurd attempts at aristocratic luxury, which
ended invariably in a steeplechase between the great author and
the bailiffs.

SOURCE: Captain Gronow, *Reminiscences and Recollections*, edit.
John Raymond, The Bodley Head Ltd., 1964, pp. 186–187.

BARBERI, DOMENICO (1792–1849), Italian, member of the
   Passionist movement; he became Provincial of the Passionists
   in England and worked to reconvert the country to the Roman
   Catholic faith.

He was not handsome, nor was he tall. He was short, and rather
stout of body, and his voice was squeaky, but he had an eagle
eye . . . In secular clothes he was a holy show. His coat was not
made in any style known to English tailors; it was neither clerical
nor secular; it fitted nowhere, and where it might fit it was
wrongly buttoned. He carried a watch when he travelled
which might well have served for a town clock amongst the
Lilliputians, and required to be arranged every five weeks at
least. His waistcoat seemed the cast off garment of some
itinerant hawker, and his pantaloons were evidently constructed

C

without any consideration for the length and circumference of the legs they enclosed. His shoes might have done service in the ark of Noah, so ancient, patched, and innocent of polish did they look. To crown all, he wore the meanest and most wretched hat that could be seen in England, out of the collieries. His gait was shuffling. His countenance appeared to be grieving and was often unshaven. The comical twinkle of his eye when he told a good story, and his grave demeanour when he spoke of heaven, made him seem a compound of all that was humble and sublime in human nature.

SOURCE: Monsignor Searle, secretary to Cardinal Wiseman; quoted Devine, *The Life of Father Dominic*, 1898, p. 181, and Denis Gwynn, *Father Dominic Barberi*, Burns Oates, 1947, p. 172.

BARRAS, PAUL FRANÇOIS JEAN NICHOLAS (1755–1829), French revolutionist.

In 1829, Barras was a very handsome old man of seventy-four years. I can still see him in his wheel-chair, his hands and head appearing to be the only animate part of him, though these seemed to have consolidated in themselves the life of the whole body—and wearing a little cap which never left him and which he never removed for anybody.

SOURCE: *The Memoirs of Alexandre Dumas* (Père), selected and trans. A. F. Davidson, W. H. Allen & Co., Calcutta, 1891, Vol. II, p. 316.

BASTIEN-LEPAGE, JULES (1848–1884), French painter of portraits and rustic subjects.

I saw before me a young man, plainly dressed, small, fair, and muscular; his pale face, with its square determined brow, short nose, and spiritual lips, scarcely covered with a blond moustache, was lighted up with two clear blue eyes whose straight and piercing look told of loyalty and indomitable energy. There was roguishness as well as manliness in that mobile face with its flattened features, and a certain cool audacity alternated with signs of sensitiveness and sparkling fun and gaiety.

SOURCE: André Theuriet, *Jules Bastien-Lepage and his Art. A Memoir*. T. Fisher Unwin, 1892, pp. 29–30.

BAUDELAIRE, CHARLES PIERRE (1821–1867), French poet.

His appearance was striking: he had closely shaved hair of a rich black, which fell over a forehead of extraordinary whiteness, giving his head the appearance of a Saracen helmet. His eyes, coloured like tobacco of Spain, had great depth and spirituality about them, and a certain penetration which was, perhaps, a little too insistent. As to the mouth, in which the teeth were white and perfect, it was seen under a slight and silky moustache which screened its contours. The mobile curves, voluptuous and ironical as the lips in a face painted by Leonardo da Vinci, the nose, fine and delicate, somewhat curved, with quivering nostrils, seemed ever to be scenting vague perfumes. A large dimple accentuated the chin, like the finishing touch of a sculptor's chisel on a statue; the cheeks, carefully shaved, with vermilion tints on the cheekbones, the neck, of almost feminine elegance and whiteness, showed plainly, as the collar of his shirt was turned down with a Madras cravat.

His clothing consisted of a paletot of shining black cloth, nut-coloured trousers, white stockings, and patent leather shoes; the whole fastidiously correct, with a stamp of almost English simplicity, intentionally adopted to distinguish himself from the artistic folk with the soft felt hats, the velvet waistcoats, red jackets, and strong, dishevelled beards. Nothing was too new or elaborate about him. Charles Baudelaire indulged in a certain dandyism, but he would do anything to take from his things the "Sunday clothes" appearance so dear and important to the Philistine, but so disagreeable to the true gentleman.

Later he shaved off his moustache, finding that it was the remains of an old picturesqueness which it was both childish and bourgeois to retain. Thus, relieved of all superfluous down, his head recalled that of Lawrence Sterne; a resemblance that was augmented by Baudelaire's habit of leaning his temple against his first finger, which is, as everyone knows, the attitude of the English humorist in the portrait placed at the beginning of his books.

Such was the physical impression made on us after our first meeting with the future author of 'The Flowers of Evil'.

SOURCE: Théophile Gautier, *Charles Baudelaire, His Life*, trans. Guy Thorne, Greening & Co., 1915, pp. 2–3.

... slim, elegant, a little furtive, almost alarming because of his attitude of one with a secret fear which could be discerned from time to time beneath an hauteur of manner softened by a grave courtesy. He had the irresistible charm of beauty in distress and carried himself with the air of a fastidious bishop somewhat fallen from grace who had donned an elaborate lay costume to go on his travels—His Eminence Monseigneur Beau Brummel.

SOURCE: Catulle Mendès; quoted Lawrence and Elizabeth Hanson, *Verlaine*, Chatto & Windus, 1958, p. 55.

BEAUMARCHAIS, PIERRE AUGUSTIN CARON DE (1732–1799), watch-maker, musician, playwright, business man, and secret diplomatic envoy; creator of Figaro, made famous in Mozart's opera. He assumed the surname Beaumarchais in addition to his original one of Caron.

I went to see him there [at his home] from time to time, and I saw nothing which did not confirm me in the first opinion I had formed of him. This man, so terrible when irritated, was in fact a very kindly soul. Full of domestic affection, adored by the family he in turn worshipped, he looked like a retired old soldier, an old soldier who is resting, although he is still in a condition to take up arms. Of all the writers then in repute, Beaumarchais was the one who most encouraged young people.

SOURCE: The contemporary dramatist Arnault; quoted Cynthia Cox, *The Real Figaro*, Longmans, 1962, p. 197.

BECCARIA, GIOVANNI BATTISTA (1716–1781), Italian physicist and early pioneer in electrical research.

[He] through choice, lives up six pair of stairs, among his observatories, machines, and mathematical instruments; and there does everything for himself, even to making his bed and dressing his dinner . . .

He is not above forty; with a large and noble figure, he has something open, natural, intelligent and benevolent in his countenance, that immediately captivates. We had much conversation concerning Dr. Franklin, Dr. Priestley, and others [i.e. Benjamin Franklin (1706–1790), American statesman and scientist, and Joseph Priestley (1733–1804), chemist and nonconformist minister].

SOURCE: Cedric Howard Glover, edit. *Dr. Charles Burney's Continental Travels, 1770–1772*, Blackie & Sons Ltd., 1927, pp. 22–23.

BEETHOVEN, LUDWIG VAN (1770–1827), German composer.

Beethoven was dressed in a jacket and trousers of long, dark goat's hair, which at once reminded me of the description of Robinson Crusoe I had just been reading. He had a shock of jet black hair (cut *à la* Titus) standing straight upright. A beard of several days' growth made his naturally dark face still blacker. I noticed also, with a child's quick observation, that he had cotton wool, which seemed to have been dipped in some yellow fluid, in both ears.

He did not appear at all deaf. . . His hands were covered with hair, and the fingers were very broad, especially at the tips.

AGED ABOUT 30.

SOURCE: Charles Czerny, *Autobiography*, published 1870 by the Keepers of Archives of the *Gesellschaft der Musikfreunde* at Vienna; quoted Dr. Ludwig Nohl, *Beethoven and his Contemporaries*, W. Reeves, 1880, p. 41.

During the last years of his life, I frequently saw Beethoven at a little Inn on Winter evenings.

He had entirely lost his hearing at that time. Everyone showed him the greatest respect when he entered the room. He was a sturdy looking man of middle height, with grey hair flowing like a mane from his truly lion-like head; he had a wandering expression in his grey eyes, and was unsteady in his movements, as if walking in a dream. He would sit down with a glass of beer and a long pipe, and close his eyes ... If one of his friends spoke, or rather bawled to him, he opened his eyes like an eagle started from its slumbers, smiled sadly, drew a pocket-book and pencil from his breast pocket, and, in the shrill voice peculiar to deaf people, bid his visitor write what he had to say. Sometimes he replied himself in writing, sometimes verbally, but always readily and kindly.

SOURCE: Braun von Braunthal, *Süddeutschen Zeitung* (an article written several years after Beethoven's death); quoted Dr. Ludwig Nohl (see above), pp. 301–302.

BEFCHIN, PIERRE (1737–1812). See Plato, archbishop of Moscow.

BELISARIUS (505?–565), Roman general of the Eastern Empire.

Physically ... he was outstandingly gifted, a large man and attractive, though he made himself so affable and easy to approach by any chance acquaintance that he seemed more like a really poor, humble fellow ... In the dangers of war, he mixed courage and caution, boldness with reason, sharpness and care in every encounter with the enemy as occasion demanded. Apart from that he displayed a mind that was confident in trouble and rose above the chaos of events, and in success he was not puffed up or vain at his triumph. No one every saw Belisarius drunk.

SOURCE: Procopius, *History of the Wars*, VII, I; trans. B. K. Workman and included in *They Saw it Happen in Classical Times*, Basil Blackwell, 1964, p. 208.

BELLARMINE, ROBERTO FRANCESCO ROMOLO (1542–1621), Italian cardinal, Archbishop of Capua. Beatified in 1923.

I boldly went to the Jesuit College and Bellarmine then walking in the fields I expected his return at the gate, the students telling me that he would presently come back; which falling out as they said, I followed him into the College (being attired like an Italian and careful not to use any strange gestures; yea, forebearing to view the College or to look upon any man fully lest I should draw his eyes upon me). Thus I came into Bellarmine's chamber, that I might see this man so famous for his learning and so great a champion of the Popes. Who seemed to me not above forty years old [he was in fact 52] being lean of body and something low of stature with a long visage, and a little sharp beard upon the chin of a brown colour, and a countenance not very grave and for his middle age wanting the authority of grey hairs.

IN 1594.

SOURCE: Fynes Moryson, *Itinerary: containing his ten Yeeres Travell through Germany, Denmark, Poland, Italy, etc.* Part I, Book II, pp. 141–142; quoted James Brodrick, S.J., *Robert Bellarmine 1542–1621*, Longmans, Green & Co., Revised edition 1950, Vol. I, pp. 323–324. Moryson was a student of Peterhouse, Cambridge. In 1589, aged twenty-three, he was appointed one of the travelling fellows, and in 1591 he left England.

BERGY, COMTESSE DE (1619–1693); member of the French court, miscellaneous writer and correspondent of Henrietta Maria, Queen of England, Christina of Sweden, etc.

A self-portrait:

My person is neither too large nor too small, but perfectly well proportioned. I have a certain negligent air, which convinces me that I am one of the finest women of my size. My hair is brown and glossy; my complexion clear and smooth; the form of my face oval, and all my features perfectly regular. I have fine eyes, in which there is a certain mixture of colour that is brilliant and sparkling; my nose is of the most pleasing form, my mouth indeed is none of the smallest, but perfectly pleasing as to its colour and shape; and, as to my teeth, they are exquisitely beautiful, and allowed to be the finest in the world. My neck is equally beautiful, and, as to my hands and arms, they are delicately white; all these are accompanied with a lively and delicate air, and my glass persuades me I can see nothing superior to myself . . . I am truly sorry that many of my faults proceed from pride, but none from meanness; and, since I am not able to conquer that pride, which governs the greater part of my actions, I employ it for those purposes which put me into a condition of appearing without shame or confusion to myself.

SOURCE: quoted T. P. Lathy, *Memoirs of the Court of Louis XIV*, London, 1819, Vol. 1, pp. 254–256.

BERLIOZ, HECTOR (1803–1869), French composer.

Although this account is more recent, it incorporates the descriptions given by several contemporaries:

In legendary portraits he appears as a dark southerner with black hair and sparkling eyes. But he was really very fair and had blue eyes, and Joseph d'Ortigue tells us they were deep-set and piercing, though sometimes clouded by melancholy or languor. He had a broad forehead furrowed by wrinkles by the time he was thirty, and a thick mane of hair, or, as E. Legouvé puts it, 'a large umbrella of hair, projecting like a movable awning over the beak of a bird of prey.' His mouth was well cut, with lips compressed and puckered at the corners in a severe fold, and his chin was prominent . . . He was of medium height, rather thin and angular in figure, and when seated he seemed much taller than he really was.

SOURCE: Joseph d'Ortigue, *Le Balcon de l'Opéra*, E. Legouvé, *Soixante ans de souvenirs*, etc.; quoted in Romain Rolland, *Musicians of To-Day*, Kegan Paul, Trench, Trübner & Co. n.d., pp. 8–9.

BERNADETTE OF LOURDES, SAINT (1844–1879)

Everything about Bernadette was simple, one might even say common, at first sight. There was nothing remarkable about her face, when in repose. Her dress was plain and simple with an irreproachable neatness, indicative of self-respect and dignity amid poverty; that is all. Her headdress (a sort of madras with the patterns almost faded out from frequent washing) covered half her forehead and was bound tightly round her hair. Her neck, shoulders, waist, wrapped in folds of a material similar to her headdress, recalled one of those busts roughed out by the sculptor's chisel. Afflicted with some complaint of the respiratory passages, the poor child wore a chest-protector so heavy and ill-fitting that she seemed to breathe with even greater difficulty.

It is true that, when she spoke, her unaffected language and her quiet, earnest tone won one's confidence. It is equally true that, when she expressed some noble sentiment or less commonplace thought, there spread over her features a charm all the more impressive in that one could discover there nothing but the outpouring of a sincere soul.

SOURCE: Monsieur Dutour, Public Prosecutor of Lourdes; quoted Francis Trochu, *Saint Bernadette Soubirous*, trans. John Joyce, S.J., Longmans, Green & Co., 1957, p. 75.

BERNADOTTE, JEAN BAPTISTE (1763–1844). See Charles XIV John, King of Sweden and Norway.

BERRY, MARIE LOUISE ÉLISABETH D'ORLEANS, DUCHESS OF (1695–1719).

In point of fact, she is not pretty, at all, either in face or figure. She is thick set, with long arms, and short hips; she walks badly, and is ungraceful in all her movements; has a discontented face; is marked by small pox; has red eyes—light blue in the iris—and a ruddy complexion, and looks much older than she is. What is perfectly beautiful about her is her throat, her hands and her arms, which are very white and well formed.

SOURCE: Elizabeth-Charlotte of Bavaria, the Princess Palatine, and the Duchess of Berry's grandmother; quoted H. Noel Williams, *A Rose of Savoy*; Methuen & Co., 1909, p. 248.

BISMARCK, OTTO, PRINCE VON (1815–1898), statesman. The inscription he chose for his tomb reads, 'A true German servant of the Emperor William I.'

He was very young . . . not quite seventeen; but in precocity of character . . . he went immeasurably beyond any person I have ever known . . . I have seldom seen a more unprepossessing person . . . though on better acquaintance . . . I began to think him rather well-looking. He had coarse, scrubby hair, of a mixed colour, something between red and whity-brown. His face was peppered all over with freckles, and his eyes were colourless in the centre, and looked as if edged with red tape. An enormous scar, the relic of a recent duel . . . extended from the tip of his nose to the edge of his right ear, and had been sewed up with fourteen stitches . . . he had recently shaved off one of his eyebrows, his face certainly might lay claim to a bizarre and very unique character. His figure was slender, and not yet mature, but already of a tolerable height . . . He wore a chaotic coat, without collar or buttons, and as destitute of colour as of shape; enormous wide trousers, and boots with iron heels and portentous spurs. His shirt collar, unconscious of cravat, was doubled over his shoulders, and his hair hung down about his ears and neck. A faint attempt at moustachios, of an indefinite colour, completed the equipment of his face, and a huge sabre, strapped round his waist, that of his habiliments.

SOURCE: John Lothrop Motley, his fellow student, from a novel published a few years later in which Bismarck appears as Otto von Rabenmark; quoted Emil Ludwig, *Bismarck*, trans. E. and C. Paul, George Allen & Unwin Ltd., 1927, p. 32.

At that time Bismarck was forty-five, slightly bald, with fair hair turning grey; not noticeably corpulent; sallow complexion. Never gay, even when telling amusing anecdotes, a thing he did only occasionally, in particularly congenial company. Total impression one of a dissatisfied man, partly a hypochondriac, partly a man insufficiently reconciled to the quiet life led in these days by the Prussian representative in St. Petersburg. His every utterance revealed that for him action and existence were one and the same thing ... He certainly did not lead a healthy life. He ate only one meal a day, but then, as is well known, he ate and drank very heavily. The fact that he was able to continue this mode of life up to about 1880, that is, until he was over sixty-five, shows how well equipped he was, physically as well as mentally, to sustain exceptional demands. But there is no doubt that the black moods to which Bismarck was so frequently a prey were due as much to physical as to mental strain. I have scarcely ever known anyone so joyless as Bismarck. When he was at the height of his intellectual powers one received the impression that he was always striving towards some goal, and putting behind him all past achievements.

SOURCE: Friedrich von Holstein (1837–1909). *Memoirs, Diaries and Correspondence*, edit. Norman Rich and M. H. Fisher, Cambridge University Press, 1955, Vol. I (Memoirs), pp. 5–6.

He was much taller than I had imagined. I had never seen him except at Madame Tussaud's in London, where there is only a small figure of him—and when I saw this giant in uniform enter the room I was quite taken aback. There was something still more extraordinary about his head. His ears were large, wide open to the hundreds of rumours which came to them from the four corners of the universe. His chin made a strong foundation for the big jaws, which would certainly never loose anything they held until it was in shreds; whilst his eyes, well set, with their projecting eyelids and well-exposed eyebrows, had a far-away look in them, as though they were gazing out beyond the visible horizon.

SOURCE: Henri Stephan de Blowitz, *My Memoirs*, Edward Arnold, 1903, pp. 156–157.

BOERHAAVE, HERMANN (1668–1738), Dutch physician and famous professor of medicine; Peter the Great of Russia (q.v.) was among students from all over Europe who took lessons from him.

Boerhaave was naturally of a robust frame and healthy constitution, early inured to constant exercise, and the inclemencies of weather, whence he acquired a very uncommon strength of body; no man could have a fairer prospect of longevity; but he, who was temperate in every thing except application, sacrificed to literature in all probability a fourth of his days; yet on this account he may truly be said to have died at seventy, older than another at an hundred. His stature was rather tall and his habit corpulent, having always had a great appetite which he indulged at dinner only; . . . It cost him much more to nourish his mind than his body. He was negligent of dress and in his gait and deportment there was an honest and somewhat awkward simplicity, but yet accompanied, which is very rarely seen, with a distinguishable dignity. He had a large head, short neck, florid complexion, light brown curled hair (for he did not wear a wig) an open countenance, and resembled Socrates in the flatness of his nose, and his natural urbanity. His eyes were small, but very lively, and piercing . . . A cheerful serenity dwelt in his countenance, agreeing in this respect also with the wise Grecian's, that it never seemed much elated by joy, nor depressed by sorrow, an indication of that tranquillity of mind, which is the agreeable attendant and guard of virtue.

SOURCE: William Burton, *Life of Dr. H. Boerhaave*, second edition, London, 1746, pp. 60–63. Burton enrolled as a student under Boerhaave in 1724 and was his fervent admirer.

BONAPARTE FAMILY

It was my good fortune, during a winter at Rome, to come into contact with several members of this illustrious family, then in exile. I have had the honour of being introduced to Madame Mère (as the mother of the great Napoleon was called); and have often met La Reine Hortense (she was then styled Duch-esse de St. Leu) in her promenades on the Monte Pincio, or the gardens of the various palaces open to the public.

I have also seen at Rome Jérôme Bonaparte, ex-king of Westphalia, with his devoted wife, a daughter of the king of Württemberg . . . Le Roi Jérôme, as he was generally called, was at the time of which I write a very handsome man, bearing a striking resemblance to his brother the Emperor Napoleon. He had the same deep-set eye, the square, massive jaw, the broad, thoughtful brow, the pallid complexion, the delicately-formed white hand, but he was a good deal taller and fairer.

The ex-queen was a true German in appearance, fat, fair, and forty, with that good natured *ménagère* look which is characteristic of the Teutonic race. Under that calm house-wife-like exterior, you would never have supposed her to be the enduring, heroic wife and mother . . .

Madame Mère was the very living image of the statue Canova made of her. Her features were classical, her eyes large and expressive, and her bearing full of imperial dignity and grace. There was no pride in her manner, but you saw the consciousness of greatness—the stately calm as of the reflected light from her son's glory.

Whatever La Reine Hortense might have been in her youth, when I saw her she was no longer handsome; and, to say the honest truth, I must confess that I have my doubts as to her ever having been remarkable for personal attractions. But the charm of her manners and the grace of every movement, were indisputable facts; and I think she has transmitted to her son, Napoleon III, much of that peculiar fascination which has subjugated and gained over to him so many hostile spirits . . .

Louis, the ex-king of Holland, I once saw at Florence, and he struck me as being a heavy and unintellectual-looking man. Joseph, the ex-king of Spain, must, in his youth, have been very handsome; but he had a listless and weak expression of counten-ance, which accorded well with his character.

SOURCE: *Reminiscences of Captain Gronow*, first published 1862–1866; edit. by John Raymond, The Bodley Head, 1964, pp. 207–209.

BONAPARTE, JÉRÔME (1784–1860), brother of Napoleon I. King of Westphalia. See Bonaparte Family.

BONAPARTE, JOSEPH (1768–1844), brother of Napoleon I. King of Naples and Spain. See Bonaparte Family.

BONAPARTE, LOUIS (1778–1846), brother of Napoleon I. King of Holland. See Bonaparte Family.

BONAPARTE, or BUONAPARTE, NAPOLEON (1769–1821). See Napoleon I.

BORGIA, CESARE (1476–1507), Duke of Valentinois and Romagna; he was the son of Pope Alexander VI and himself became Archbishop of Valencia; noted for his military skill, astute diplomacy and suspected crimes.

On the day before yesterday I found Cesare at home in Trastavere. He was on the point of setting out to go hunting, and entirely in secular habit; that is to say dressed in silk and armed. Riding together, we talked a while. I am among his most intimate acquaintances. He is a man of great talent and of an excellent nature; his manners are those of the son of a great prince; above everything, he is joyous and light-hearted. He is very modest, much superior to, and of a much finer appearance than his brother the Duke of Gandia [i.e. Giovanni Borgia] who also is not short of natural gifts. The Archbishop never had any inclination for the priesthood. But his benefice yields him over sixteen thousand ducates.

SOURCE: Gianandrea Boccaccio, a letter of March, 1493; quoted Rafael Sabatini, *The Life of Cesare Borgia*, Stanley Paul, first published 1912, tenth edition 1926, p. 69.

BORGIA, LUCREZIA (1480–1519), daughter of Rodrigo Borgia, later Pope Alexander VI, Duchess of Ferrara; notorious for her involvement in numerous scandals.

She is of medium height and slender figure. Her face is somewhat long. She has a good profile, golden hair, light eyes. Her mouth is rather large with dazzling teeth. Her throat is smooth and white and charmingly rounded and her whole being radiates gaiety and laughter.

AGED 20, IN HER SECOND WIDOWHOOD.

SOURCE: Nicolo Cagnolo; quoted Joan Haslip, *Lucrezia Borgia*, Cassell & Co., 1953, p. 173.

BOUDIN AND ST. GERMAIN, two French assassins in the early nineteenth century.

St. Germain was a man of about five feet eight inches high, with strongly developed muscles, an enormous head, and very small eyes, half closed, like those of an owl; his face, deeply marked with the small pox, was extremely plain; and yet, from the quickness and vivacity of his expression, he was by many persons considered pleasing. In describing his features, a strong resemblance would suggest itself to those of the hyena and wolf, particularly if the attention were directed to the immensely wide jaws, furnished with large projecting fangs; his very organisation partook of the animal instinct common to beasts of prey; he was passionately fond of hunting; the sight of blood exhilarated him; his other passions were gaming, women, and good eating and drinking. As he had acquired the air and manners of good society, he expressed himself when he chose with ease and fluency, and was almost always fashionably and elegantly dressed; he might be styled a 'well-bred thief'. When his interest required it, no person could better assume the pleasant mildness of an amiable man; at other times he was abrupt and brutal. His comrade Boudin was diminutive in stature, scarcely reaching five feet two inches; thin, with a livid complexion; his eyes dark and piercing, and deeply sunk in his head. The habit of wielding the carving-knife, and of cutting up meat had rendered him ferocious. He was bow-legged; a deformity I have observed amongst several systematic assassins, as well as amongst many other individuals distinguished by their crimes.

SOURCE: Vidocq, *Memoirs*, English edition, London, 1829, Vol. II, pp. 185–186. Vidocq was principal agent of the French police until 1827.

BOURIGNON, ANTOINETTE (1616–1680), Flemish Quietist who gained many followers in Holland, France, and especially Scotland; her doctrines were denounced by the Presbyterian general assemblies of 1701, 1709 and 1710, and equally by the Roman Catholic Church.

She was of the middle stature, neat and slim, of a symmetrical countenance, a dark complexion, a clear forehead, an un-wrinkled brow: a frank look from eyes of a bluish tint and of such excellent sight that she never used glasses: rather a large mouth, full lips and slightly prominent teeth: her hair blanched with age: illness had wasted her cheeks and deepened the setting round her eyes: her aspect, address and mien were sweet, natural, and attractive: her pace was deliberate and when she walked she held her head a trifle high. At upwards of sixty years of age, she looked scarcely more than forty. All her senses except the palate were singularly acute; her spirits were lively and sustained, never sad, always equable.

SOURCE: Pierre Poiret, her disciple and editor; the three earliest editions of her works, of 1679–1684, 1686, and 1717, all contain the continuation of her autobiography by Poiret, *Sa Vie Continuée, reprise depuis sa naissance, jusqu'à sa mort, par Pierre Poiret*; quoted Alex. R. Macewen, *Antoinette Bourignon, Quietist*, Hodder & Stoughton, 1910, pp. 24–25.

BRAHE, TYCHO (1546–1601), Danish astronomer.

[After a duel fought as a result of a mathematical argument. In the fight a portion of the astronomer's nose was cut off, though it does not seem to be certain whether it was the bridge or the tip.] As Tycho was not used to going around without a nose, and did not like to, he went to the expense of purchasing a new one. He was not satisfied, as some others might have been, to put on a wax one, but, being a nobleman of wealth, ordered a nose made of gold and silver so soberly painted and adjusted that it seemed of a natural appearance.

SOURCE: Peter Gassendi's life of Brahe, published in 1654 (Latin); Gassendi gives full details of the quarrel with another nobleman, Manderup Parsbjerg, and states that the subsequent fight took place in complete darkness; quoted John Allyne Gade, *The Life and Times of Tycho Brahe*, Princeton University Press, 1947, p. 35.

Another contemporary, Willem Jansson Blaer, who spent two years with Brahe at Hveen, told Gassendi that Tycho commonly carried a small box in his pocket, filled with salve or glue, which he applied when the nose became wobbly.

BRIAND, ARISTIDE (1862–1932), French socialist statesman; one of the authors of the Locarno Pact.

'What a beautiful man!' exclaimed a German lady-journalist peeking over my shoulder. My drawing, however, showed a fragile Frenchman on wobbly legs, stooped under the weight of a shaggy head, looking like a poet who had just received twelve rejection slips on an empty stomach. His transparent paper nose, eyes cold as blue-point oysters, mustache drooping over a crooked mouth that opened right oblique—all these I had been drawing piece-meal, but together they made up more than their sum; they made up Briand . . .

SOURCE: Emery Kelen, *Peace in Their Time*, Victor Gollancz, 1964, pp. 153–154.

BUFFON, GEORGES LOUIS LECLERC, COMTE DE (1707–1788), French naturalist and writer.

We first saw the wild animals—a lion, very beautiful and majestic, reminded me of M. de Buffon; the face of that great writer in reality resembled that of a lion.

D

SOURCE: *Memoirs of the Countess de Genlis . . . Written by Herself*, London, 1826, Vol. VIII, pp. 86–87.

BULGARIANS IN 1620.

The manner of these poor Bulgarians as far as I could learn, is the men, generally labourers, clothed in white cloth, the women for the most part in russet. The virgins go in their hair, which hangeth down behind handsomely plaited, adding thereunto other hair to increase its length, also upon their heads and about their neck they have a great many *shasis* [*shahi* = a small silver coin of Persia] and other pieces of silver and brass, which, by making little holes in them, they sew and weave together; also in their ears great ear-rings of silver, whereof some weigh at least four ounces the pair. They go in their smock-sleeves which are very wide and wrought, although not very fine, and barefooted. The married women differ in this. They wear a linen cloth plaited which hangeth down behind over the tress of their hair. At our passage through any village they would stand ready with hot cakes . . . also milk sweet and sour, fresh cheese, butter, eggs, etc., being brought to us by the youngest and prettiest wenches among them; and if we lodge near any of these villages, after they had brought us of their provisions, then would they gather together young women and children and holding hand in hand in a round, they would dance and sing very merrily, although with no great melody.

SOURCE: Peter Mundy, *Travels in Europe and Asia 1608–1667*, Vol. I, Hakluyt Society, 1907, pp. 76–78.

BUONARROTI, MICHELANGELO (1475–1564). See Michelangelo.

CAGLIOSTRO, ALLESSANDRO, COUNT (1743–1795), Italian alchemist and impostor; seller of love-philtres and elixirs of youth; condemned to death as a heretic, but eventually died in prison.

Cagliostro seemed moulded for the express purpose of playing

Signor Tulipano at the Italian Theatre; he was of a medium height, rather stout, with an olive complexion, a very short neck, round face, two large eyes on a level with the cheeks, and a broad turned-up nose . . . His hair was dressed in a way new to France, being divided into several small tresses that united behind the head, and were twisted up into what was then called a club.

He wore on that day an iron-grey coat of French make, with gold lace, a scarlet waistcoat trimmed with broad Spanish lace, red breeches, his sword looped to the skirt of his coat, and a laced hat with a white feather, the latter a decoration still required of mountebanks, tooth-drawers, and other medical practitioners who proclaimed and retailed their drugs in the open air. Cagliostro set off this costume by lace ruffles, several valuable rings, and shoe-buckles, which were, it is true, of antique design, but bright enough to be taken for real diamonds . . . I could only look at him furtively, and did not yet know what to think. The face, the attire, and the whole man made an impression on me that I could not prevent. I listened to the talk. He spoke some sort of medley, half French half Italian, and made many quotations which might be Arabic, but which he did not trouble himself to translate. He alone spoke, and had time to run over twenty subjects, for he only allowed them to be discussed as far as he liked. He never failed continually to ask if he were understood, and the company bowed all round to assure him that he was.

SOURCE: edit. Charlotte M. Yonge, *Life and Adventures of Count Beugnot*, London, 1871, Vol. I, pp. 51–53. Beugnot was a minister under Napoleon.

CALVIN, JOHN (1509–1564), Swiss divine and reformer.

He lived 54 years, 10 months, 17 days, the half of which he spent in the ministry. He was of moderate stature, of a pale and dark complexion, with eyes that sparkled to the moment of his death, and bespoke his great intellect. In dress he was neither over careful nor mean, but such as became his singular modesty. In diet he was temperate, being equally averse to sordidness and luxury. He was most sparing in the quantities of his food, and for many years took only one meal a-day, on account of the weakness of his stomach. He took little sleep, and had such an astonishing memory, that any person whom he had once seen he instantly recognised at the distance of years, and when, in the course of dictating, he happened to be interrupted for several hours, as often happened, as soon as he returned he commenced at once to dictate where he had left off. Whatever he required to know for the performance of his duty, though involved in a multiplicity of other affairs, he never forgot. On whatever subject he was consulted, his judgment was so clear and correct, that he often seemed almost to prophesy; nor do I recollect of any person having been led into error in consequence of following his advice. He despised mere eloquence, and was sparing in the use of words, but he was by no means a careless writer.

SOURCE: Theodore Beza's life of Calvin, first published in 1564, a few weeks after Calvin's death. Beza worked with Calvin for sixteen years and editions of his *Life* are to be found in many places, including Henry Beveridge's translation of *Tracts and Treatises on the Reformation of the Church, by John Calvin*, new edition, Oliver & Boyd, 1958, Vol. I, pp. cxxv–cxxvi.

CAMOENS (CAMOES), LUIS DE (1524–1580) Portugal's renowned epic poet and one of the greatest lyric poets of sixteenth-century Europe; especially famed for his 'Lusiads'.

He was of a middle stature; his face full, and his countenance a little lowering; his nose long, raised in the middle, and large at the end. He was much disfigured by the loss of his right eye. Whilst young, his hair was so yellow, as to resemble saffron. Although his appearance was not perhaps prepossessing, his manners and conversation were pleasing and cheerful, as may be inferred from his motes and glosas. He was afterwards a prey to melancholy; was never married, and left no child.

SOURCE: Manoel Severim de Faria, *Discursos varios e politicos*, 1624; quoted John Adamson, *Memoirs of the Life and Writings of Luis de Camoens*, London, 1820, Vol. I, pp. 210–211.

CANROBERT, FRANÇOIS CERTAIN (1809–1895), French marshal; commander-in-chief of French forces in the Crimea.

A large dinner party, but not many invitations. General Canrobert, only just returned from the trenches . . . was the principal addition. He sat next to me, and I was delighted with him, such an honest good man, so sincere and friendly, and *so* fond of the English, very enthusiastic, talking with much gesticulation. He is short, and wears his hair, which is black, rather long behind, has a red face and rolling eyes, moustaches and no whiskers, and carries his head rather high.

SOURCE: Queen Victoria, *Leaves from a Journal*, André Deutsch, 1961, p. 82.

CARLOTA, JOAQUINA DE BORBON (1775–1830), Queen of Portugal, daughter of Charles IV of Spain; her husband the prince of Brazil was regent of Portugal for his mother, the insane Maria I, before himself becoming King.

The Princess of Brazil was hardly five feet high, measured along the longest straight line in her body. I use that curious expression because a fall from her horse had shortened her hip to such an extent that she limped grotesquely, and that one of her shoulders, no less thrown out of the straight, had taken an entirely different direction to that taken by the other. As a result of all this, the bust of the unfortunate Princess was, like the rest of her body, a mystery of Nature when it amuses her to go all wrong. I have heard it said by those who have had the privilege of seeing it unveiled that the rest too was a riot of malformation.

The head which this body supported might, as is often the way with hunchbacks, have compensated the general deformity by being beautiful; but Nature had decided to finish her handiwork as she had begun, and on this misshapen body rested the most grotesquely ugly head that the world can ever have seen.

The eyes were small and squinting, and looked out with a vicious or mocking air. Her nose, because of much hunting and libertine and vagabond life, was nearly always as red and swollen as that of a Switzer; her mouth, quite the oddest part of this repulsive face, was furnished with several rows of black, green and yellow teeth, set askew like a pipe of Pan or a fringe of curtain! Her skin, besides being rough and tanned, was, for good measure of ugliness, covered with pimples which were nearly always suppurating, and was hideous in the extreme to look at; her hands, which were black and ungainly, were set at the end of bony and utterly shapeless arms. Her feet subtracted nothing from this charming ensemble. Her hair was half-fuzzy and black, or, more accurately, brown, and of a kind which brush and comb and pommade combined can never make seem human or deprive it of its horselike quality.

SOURCE: Madame Junot, the future Duchess of Abrantès; quoted Jacques Chastenet (trans. J. F. Huntingdon, *Godoy*) The Batchworth Press, 1953, pp. 105–106.

CASANOVA DE SEINGALT, GIOVANNI JACOPO (1725–1798), Italian adventurer, secret service agent and author.

... a frank face, and the head held high, well-attired ... He is a man of forty years at most [47, in fact] of high stature, of good and vigorous aspect, very brown of skin, with a vivacious eye. He wears a short and chestnut-coloured wig. From what I am told he is of a bold and disdainful character, but, especially, he is full of the gift of the gab and, as such, witty and learned.

SOURCE: G. M. Bandierra, Venetian agent; included in A. Baschet, *Les Archives de Venise*, Paris, 1870, p. 141, and quoted J. Rives Childs, *Casanova*, George Allen & Unwin, 1961, p. 265.

CATHERINE I (1683–1727), daughter of a Lithuanian peasant, she began life as a servant. She became the mistress and then the second wife of Peter the Great of Russia, in 1711. In 1722 Catherine was proclaimed Peter's successor, and was crowned in 1724; she ruled at his death as Catherine I.

The Tsarina was short and stout, very tawny, and her figure was altogether destitute of gracefulness. Its appearance sufficiently betrayed her low origin. To have judged by her attire, one would have taken her for a German stage-actress. Her robe had been purchased off an old-clothes broker; it was made in the antique fashion, and heavily laden with silver and grease. The front of her stays was adorned with jewels, singularly placed; they represented a double eagle, badly set, the wings of which were of small stones. She wore a dozen orders and as many portraits of saints and relics, fastened to the facing of her gown: so that when she walked, the jumbling of all these orders and portraits one against the other, made a tinkling noise like a mule in harness ... The tsarina, who spoke very bad German, and did not well understand what was spoken to her by the Queen, beckoned to her fool, and conversed with her in Russian.

SOURCE: Margravine of Bareithe, *Memoirs*, English edition, 1828, Vol. I, p. 34. The Margravine was the sister of Frederick the Great of Prussia (q.v.).

CATHERINE II (1729–1796), Empress of Russia, known as "the Great"; wife of Peter III.

Finally, after much suffering [aged 7, after being in bed three weeks with a violent cough and fever], I was well enough to get up and it was discovered, as they started to put on my clothes, that I had in the meantime assumed the shape of the letter Z: my right shoulder was much higher than my left, the back-bone running in a zig-zag and the left side falling in. [She was put in a special corset and was straight again by the age of ten.]

... I began to grow taller and the extreme ugliness with which I was afflicted was beginning to disappear. [1739] ... Princess Gagarine used often to tell me ... that I was improving in looks from day to day. It was the right time for it, too, for I was then 18 years of age ... I was tall and had a magnificent figure, but I could have allowed myself a little more weight, as I was rather thin. I did not like using powder, and my hair was a soft brown, very thick and well planted on the forehead.

The fashion for leaving one's hair unpowdered was, however, beginning to wane, and that winter I used it now and then . . .

Once at a public masquerade, having heard that everyone was ordering new and most beautiful clothes, and despairing of surpassing the other women, I remember I decided to put on a bodice of rough white cloth (I had then a very slim waist) and a skirt of the same on a very small hoop; my hair was smoothly dressed in front, behind I had it curled; it was long and thick then and very beautiful and I had it tied with a white ribbon in the shape of a fox's tail; on my head I wore a single rose with a rosebud and leaves, that looked remarkably real and I had another rose in my corsage. I had a ruff of white gauze round the neck, cuffs, and a little apron of the same material, and that is how I went to the ball.

As I entered I saw at once that I was the target of all eyes. I crossed the gallery without stopping and passed into the next apartments. There I met the Empress who said: 'Good God, what simplicity, what, not even a mouche!' I began to laugh and replied that I did not wish to add to the weight of my dress. She pulled out of her pocket a box of mouches, chose a small one and applied it to my face.

As I left her I went quickly into the gallery and showed all my friends the mouche. I did the same to the Empress's favourites, and as I was very gay, that night I danced more than usual. I do not remember ever getting as many compliments from everyone as on that night. They told me I was beautiful as the dawn and very striking. To tell the truth, I never believed myself to be very beautiful. I had charm and that, I think, was my strength.

IN 1750.

SOURCE: *The Memoirs of Catherine the Great*, edit. D. Maroger, trans. Moura Budberg, Hamish Hamilton, 1955, pp. 29, 33, 133, 190–191.

The Grand Duchess is romantic, ardent, passionate. Her eyes are brilliant, their look fascinating and glassy—the expression of a wild beast. Her forehead is lofty, and, if I am not mistaken, a long and terrifying future is written on it. She is prepossessing and affable, but when she comes close to me I instinctively recoil, for she frightens me.

SOURCE: The Chevalier d'Eon; ibid., p. 13.

CATHERINE DE MEDICI (1519–1589), Queen of France.

I have seen her twice on horseback, but not sufficiently well to give a complete judgment about her. She seems to me rather large for her age, fairly good looking without the help of any cosmetic, a blonde with a rather stout face. But she appears very young and I do not believe that she can be called or considered a woman for a year and a half longer. It is said that she has good feelings and a very acute and adroit mind for her age.

IN 1530.

SOURCE: A latter from the ambassador of the Duke of Milan, in Baschet, von Reumont, *Le Jeunesse de Catherine de Médicis*, Paris, 1866, pp. 282, 283.

The modesty of Her Majesty the Queen is very praiseworthy. She is a young woman of thirty-five years but not very pretty. She has the big eyes and the thick lips of the Medici, and resembles very much her great uncle, Pope Leo. She loves the King her husband as much as can be imagined. She dresses rather severely and modestly. She is a good Catholic and very religious and when the King is in camp she dresses in black and in mourning and has her court do the same and exhorts every one to make the most devoted prayers, praying the Lord God for the happiness and the prosperity of the absent King.

SOURCE: The Venetian Ambassador, in Alberi, edit., *Relazioni degli Ambasciatori Veneti al Senato*, Firenze, 1839, I, 2, p. 286. The above descriptions are included in Paul van Dyke, *Catherine de Médicis*, John Murray, 1923, Vol. I, pp. 19, 61.

CAVOUR, CAMILLO BENSO, COUNT OF (1810–1861), Italian statesman.

Now in his thirty-seventh year and somewhat below middle height, Cavour at this time had still a fresh, almost rosy complexion which later became dark and sallow. The dominating feature of his face was his eyes, blue in colour, so bright and vivacious and full of changing expression that it was difficult to determine their permanent character. His habit of body was full but robust, without as yet showing the tendency to extreme stoutness which afterwards became apparent. His facial angle, his extraordinarily full forehead and his peculiar way of fixing objects he wished to study, indicated him at the first glance as one called to high destinies. His neck was short and thick, set between two massive shoulders already somewhat bent from the habit of contemplation. His legs were short and stout in proportion to his body. His carriage was instinctively aristocratic, without however any suggestion of vulgar pride. In speech quick and incisive, with a keen sense of humour, he was a most polite and attentive listener no matter to whom he was speaking, a quality he retained even after he became famous, and which often saved him from impetuous or too hasty speech.

SOURCE: Guiseppe Torelli; quoted A. J. Whyte, *The Early Life and Letters of Cavour 1810–1848*, Oxford University Press, 1925, pp. 344, 345.

The basis of Cavour's character was inexhaustible joyousness, evinced by the agreeable turn which he gave to conversation, by his pleasant smile, by his ready and hearty laugh, by the intonation of his voice, by a certain original way of putting things, by the facility with which he accommodated himself to other people and to every circumstance, by the quickness of his movements and gestures, by his manner, now become historical, of rubbing his hands. 'Cavour is rubbing his hands', used to be said at Turin, 'things are going on well.'

SOURCE: William de la Rive, *Reminiscences of the Life and Character of Count Cavour*, trans. Edward Romilly, London, 1862, pp. 107, 108.

CEPEDA, TERESA DE (1515-1582.) See Teresa of Avila, Saint.

CERVANTES, SAAVEDRA, MIGUEL DE (1547-1616), Spanish
novelist, playwright and poet; creator of Don Quixote.

This man you see here with the aquiline countenance, the
chestnut hair, the smooth, untroubled brow, the bright eyes,
the hooked yet well proportioned nose, the silvery beard that
less than a score of years ago was golden, the big mustache,
the small mouth, the teeth that are scarcely worth mentioning
(there are but half a dozen of them altogether, in bad condition
and very badly placed, no two of them corresponding to another
pair), the body of medium height, neither tall nor short, the
high complexion that is fair rather than dark, the slightly
stooping shoulders, and the somewhat heavy build—this, I may
tell you, is the author of *La Galatea* and *Don Quixote de la Mancha*;
he it was who composed the *Journey to Parnassus*, in imitation of
Cesare Caporali of Perusa, as well as other works that are
straying about in these parts—without the owner's name,
likely as not.

He is commonly called Miguel de Cervantes Saavedra. He
was a soldier for many years and a captive for five and a half,
an experience that taught him patience in adversity. In the
naval battle of Lepanto he lost his left hand as the result of a
harquebus shot, a wound which, however unsightly it may
appear, he looks upon as beautiful, for the reason that it was
received on the most memorable and sublime occasion that
past ages have known or those to come may hope to know;
for he was fighting beneath the victorious banner of the son of
that thunderbolt of war, Charles V of blessed memory.

AGED 66.

SOURCE: Cervantes, prologue to *Novelas Exemplares*, trans. Putnam, as *Three Exemplary Novels*, Cassell & Co., 1952, pp. 3-4.

CEZANNE, PAUL (1839-1906), French post-impressionist painter.

When I first saw him I thought he looked like a cut-throat
with large red eyeballs standing out from his head in a most

ferocious manner, a rather fierce-looking pointed beard, quite grey, and an excited way of talking that positively made the dishes rattle.

SOURCE: Mary Cassatt; quoted Laurence Hanson, *Mountain of Victory*, Secker & Warburg, 1960, p. 174.

CHARLEMAGNE (742?–814), King of the Franks and Lombards, and on Christmas Day, 800, crowned Western Emperor; at the height of his power he ruled all the Christian lands of Western Europe except the British Isles, Southern Italy and Sicily.

Charles was large and strong, and of lofty stature, though not disproportionally tall (his height is well known to have been seven times the length of his foot); the upper part of his head was round, his eyes very large and animated, nose a little long, hair fair, and face laughing and merry. Thus his appearance was always stately and dignified, whether he was standing or sitting; although his neck was thick and somewhat short, and his belly rather prominent; but the symmetry of the rest of his body concealed these defects. His gait was firm, his whole carriage manly, and his voice clear, but not so strong as his size led one to expect . . . He used to wear the national, that is to say, the Frank dress—next his skin a linen shirt and linen breeches, and above these a tunic fringed with silk; while hose fastened by bands covered his lower limbs, and shoes his feet, and he protected his shoulders and chest in Winter by a close fitting coat of otter or marten skins. Over all he flung a blue cloak, and he always had a sword girt about him, usually one with a gold or silver hilt and belt; he sometimes carried a jewelled sword, but only on great feast days, or at the reception of ambassadors from foreign nations. He despised foreign costumes, however handsome . . . On great feast days he made use of embroidered clothes and shoes bedecked with precious stones, his cloak was fastened by a golden buckle, and he appeared crowned by a diadem of gold and gems, but on other days his dress varied little from the common dress of the people.

SOURCE: Einhard, *The Life of Charlemagne*, trans. Samuel Epes
Turner, Ann Arbor Paperbacks, 1960, pp. 50–52. Einhard, a
member of Charlemagne's court, wrote his history between 817
and 836. His *Life of Charlemagne* draws both on his personal knowledge and extensive use of the chronicles known as the *annales
royales*.

CHARLES V (1500–1558), Roman Emperor from 1519; King of
Spain; abdicated 1555.

Upon this short pause I followed Adrian [Charles' Groom
of the Chamber], and found the Emperor at a bare table,
without a carpet or any thing else upon it, saving his cloak,
his brush, his spectacles, and his picktooth. At my coming in I
offered to stand at the side of his Majesty which was next to
the door, but, it being on his left hand, he willed me to go
almost round about the table, that I might stand on his right
side, perhaps for that he heareth better on th' one side than
on the other; but, as I took it, he did it to h[onour] the King
my master. Here, after the delivery of the King's Highness'
letters, [which] his Majesty received very gently, putting his
hand to his bonnet and uncovering the upper part of his head,
I did efforce myself with as good countenance as I could ...
He did not suffer me to go on, but, on the least pause that I
could make, he did utter unto me in gentle words that he took
the King his good brother's letters in very thankful part;
* * saying as well as he could (for he was newly rid of his gout
and fever, and therefore his nether lip was in two places broken
out, and he was forced to keep a green leaf within his mouth at
his tongue's end, —a remedy, as I took it, against such his
dryness as in his talk did increase upon him)—saying, therefore,
as well as he could, he neither had nor could forget the King's
Majesty's father's love at sundry times showed unto him ...
yet hath he a face unwont to disclose any hid affection of his
heart, as any face that ever I met with in all my life; for where
all white colours (which, in changing themselves, are wont in
others to bring a man certain word how his errand is liked or
misliked) have no place in his countenance, his eyes only do

betray as much as can be picked out of him. He maketh me oft think of Solomon's saying, 'Heaven is high; the earth is deep; a King's heart is unsearchable.' There is in him almost nothing that speaks beside his tongue; and that at this time, by reason of his leaf and soreness of his lip, and his accustomed softness in speaking, did but so-so utter things to be well understand without great care to be given to his words; and yet he did so use his eyes, so move his head, and order his countenance, as I might well perceive his great desire was that I should think all a good deal better meant than he could speak it.

SOURCE: Sir Richard Morysine, the English ambassador at the Emperor's court, edit. Lord Hardwicke, *State Papers*, Vol. I, p. 32, quoted P. F. Tytler, *England Under the Reigns of Edward VI and Mary*, London, 1839, Vol. II, pp. 134–137.

A white full, pock-marked face, with a beard, and head polled, grey and auburn cut off short, with a plain black cap.

SOURCE: a curious and badly written document, from which the above is a modernized extract, at the College of Heralds, called *'Description of the faces and visages of moste of the Princes of Christendome in the time of K.H.8 . . . '*, 1552.

CHARLES VI (1685–1740), Roman Emperor.

The present emperor is of a middling stature and a majestic. His penetration and judgment, his equity and regard to merit, with many other virtues, render him one of the best sovereigns that *Europe* has enjoyed for many years past. He speaks and writes *Latin, Italian, Spanish,* and *French*: he loves the sciences and is well versed in the mathematics, especially that part which relates to civil and military architecture. His skill in music is such, that he not only plays on several instruments, but is also a perfect master of the rules of composition. He affects no great show in dress, and has a professed aversion to all affectation of *French* modes; and particularly large open sleeves. On solemnities, he generally appears in a black *Spanish* habit, with small cuffs of purple, embroidered with silver; his shoe ribbons are also embroidered, and he wears a red feather in his hat. The emperor's hunting dress is a brown surtout and a black bag wig; but at other times he generally wears a brown peruke. He's very happy in his marriage, and his behaviour to the empress is very fond; for he generally addresses her in the most endearing terms. But she never fails to give him the title of, your majesty.

IN 1730.

SOURCE: J. G. Keysler, *Travels through Germany, Bohemia, Hungary, Switzerland, Italy and Lorraine*, second edition, London, 1756, Vol. IV, pp. 28–29.

CHARLES II (1661–1700), King of Spain; he became increasingly infirm and mentally deranged.

I must tell you, then, that his complexion is delicate and fair; he has a broad forehead; his eyes are fine and have a great deal of sweetness in them; his face is very long and narrow; his lips, like those of the House of Austria, are very thick, and his mouth is wide; his nose is very much hawked; his chin is sharp and turns up; he has a great head of hair, and fair, lank, and put behind his ears; his stature is pretty high, straight and slender; his legs are small and almost all of a thickness ... He is not of vindictive spirit, he is sober, liberal and pious; his inclinations are virtuous; he is of an even temper, and of easy access.

SOURCE: Madame D'Aulnoy, *Travels into Spain 1691*, edit. R. Foulché-Delbosc, Geo. Routledge & Sons, 1930, pp. 248–249.

CHARLES III (1716–1788), King of Spain.

His dress seldom varies from a large hat, grey Segovia frock, a buff waistcoat, a small dagger, black breeches, and worsted stockings; his pockets are always stuffed with knives, gloves and shooting tackle. On gala days, a fine suit is hung upon his shoulders, but as he has an eye to the afternoon sport, and is a great economist of his time, the black breeches are worn to all

coats. I believe there are but three days in the whole year that
he spends without going out a-shooting, and these are noted
with the blackest mark in the calendar. Were they to occur
often his health would be in danger, and an accident that was
to confine him to the house would infallibly bring on a fit of
illness. No storm, heat, or cold, can keep him at home, and when
he hears a wolf distance is counted for nothing.

SOURCE: contemporary description by an English visitor; quoted
   Sir Charles Petrie, *The Spanish Royal House*, Geoffrey Bles, 1958,
   pp. 87–88.

CHARLES XII (1682–1718), King of Sweden; reigned from the age of fifteen.

No physiognomy appears to me so strange and so incomprehensible as that of King Charles. There is that about it, I
know not what, that commands our respect and I had almost
said affrights us. Yet he is in every way so unaffected and sits
so thoughtful, that I cannot so describe it. He sits hunched
and strides out lumpishly when he walks ... No one under-
stands his humours ... and all say that they cannot discern
from his face or behaviour what his thoughts may be or whether
he be in spirits or no, so unchanging is his mien ... As his
countenance is unchanging, so his clothes must ever be of the
same fashion, strong and loose fitting ... His coat is always
buttoned up and he wears boots constantly; he has worn them
ever since he left Sweden and he possesses no shoes. He has a
pair of great gloves of elkskin and a sword belt of the same sort,
somewhat large, and he wears a sword that is bigger than any
carried in the army. I have seen him stand with the chape
of the scabbard in the ground, resting his left elbow on the hilt.
When sitting and standing he stoops somewhat, but when
mounted there is none looks so bravely ... When all are
fatigued he is as fresh as ever.

SOURCE: Description by Anders Alstrin, a Swedish student,
   Uppsala, 1706; quoted in Frans G. Bengtsson, *Life of Charles XII*,
   Macmillan, 1960, p. 230.

CHARLES XIV JOHN (1763–1844), King of Sweden and Norway; started life as a soldier of fortune (Jean Baptiste Bernadotte); he became Marshall of France and was crowned King of Sweden and Norway in 1818.

I have never seen so remarkable a countenance as that of Bernadotte. An aquiline nose of most extraordinary dimensions, eyes full of fire, a penetrating look, with a complexion darker than a Spaniard, and hair so black that the portrait painters can find no tint dark enough to give it the right hue; it forms a vast dusky protuberance round his head, and he takes great pains, I understand, to have it arranged in proper form.

IN 1812.

SOURCE: Sir Hudston Lowe, *Journal*; quoted Sir Dunbar Plunket Barton, *Bernadotte, Prince and King, 1810–1844*, John Murray, 1925, p. 52.

His [Bernadotte's] conversation was refined, but was seasoned with a Gascon accent of the most pronounced kind. He was at this date forty–nine years of age. He was tall and striking in appearance. His eagle-like countenance recalled the great Condé. His abundant black hair harmonised with his dark Béarnais complexion. His cavalry uniform was, perhaps, a little too theatrical, but his reputation for *sang-froid* on the field of battle made one forget that slight defect. It would be impossible to meet a man more fascinating in his manners and conversation. He captivated me completely, and if I had been attached to his service I would have been sincerely devoted to him. Some people say that, in order to win people, he employs Gascon promises which he does not always keep. I saw no trace of duplicity or hypocrisy, but rather of a genuinely kind and generous heart.

IN 1813.

SOURCE: Count de Rochechouart, *Souvenirs*; quoted Barton (see above), p. 98.

The Prince of Sweden received us, mounted on a big white horse. He wore a pelisse of violet velvet braided with gold, with white plumes and a panache of Swedish colours. He held

E

in his hand a baton draped in violet velvet ornamented with gold. He looked superb, with shot and shell falling round him, encircled by dead and wounded, encouraging by his presence a brigade of English artillery.

IN 1813.

SOURCE: Count de Rochechouart, *Souvenirs*; quoted Barton (see above), p. 105.

I was placed by the side of the marshal, who looked astonishingly like all the portraits of the great Condé. His fine appearance, the nobleness of his manners, and his politeness, aided this glorious resemblance, which he completed in other respects by his great and warlike qualities. I believe I have already stated that on leaving the table I said in a low tone to M. de Cabre, that the marshal had the manners of a king. I did not think at the time that I was uttering a prophecy. He afterwards returned to Paris as crown Prince of Sweden. I went to pay my respects to him, and found him just as polished and obliging in manners as before his extraordinary rise. In short, he thought sufficiently well of himself personally (and he had a good right to do so) not to fancy it necessary to change any of his external habits.

SOURCE: *Memoirs of the Countess de Genlis . . . Written by Herself*, London, 1825, Vol. V, pp. 172–173.

CHARLES, PRINCE OF SAXONY (born c. 1752), brother to King Frederick Augustus I.

I have the honour to know him, and to see him frequently. Scarron himself must have been handsome, compared to Prince Charles of Saxony, whose face, hands, body, legs, and feet, are all more or less distorted. Incapable of walking, standing or mounting a horse, on account of his numerous infirmities, he is wheeled about from one apartment to another. Under such an accumulation of corporeal ailments, he is nevertheless cheerful, conversible, and almost gay. One should be tempted to suppose by his conversation and deportment, that he is not unhappy. From necessity, not less than from inclination, he has cultivated his mind, the only part of his formation which admits of improvement. It is singular that he was not born in a state of deformity, but gradually became so at the age of eleven or twelve, previous to which time his limbs were apparently well made: he is now about six-and twenty. Such a person seems to be incapacitated by his infirmities for marriage. Yet, as the Elector [later King Frederick Augustus I] has no children, and the succession would by his death devolve on Prince Charles, the Electress Dowager his mother wishes to procure him a bride. For the honour of human nature and of wedlock, it is to be hoped that the project will never be carried into execution.

IN 1778.

SOURCE: N. W. Wraxall, *Memoirs of the Courts of Berlin, Dresden, Warsaw, and Vienna*, London, 1799, Vol. II, pp. 189–190.

CHARLES THE BOLD (1433–1477), Duke of Burgundy; also known as 'the Rash'; succeeded his father in 1467.

His stature was small and nervous, his complexion pale, hair dark chestnut, eyes black and brilliant, his presence majestic but stern. He was high-spirited, magnanimous, courageous, intrepid, and impetuous. Capable of action, he lacked nothing but prudence to attain success.

SOURCE: the Strasburg chronicler Trausch; quoted Ruth Putnam, *Charles the Bold*, G. P. Putnam's Sons, 1908, p. 340.

Since the son is as mortal as the father [Philip the Good, q.v.] I would straightaway depict and describe him for all time, present and future; I will speak of him in the past tense, which will serve for always. This Duke Charles was a prince who was not as tall as his father; but he was stout, well-made and well-formed; strong in his arms and in his back; he stooped a little and was rather plump around the shoulders; he had good legs, large thighs, a long hand and a handsome foot; he had neither too much flesh nor too little bone; but his body was light and nimble, most apt for strength and work; he was

rounder of countenance than his father, and he had skin of a
light brown colour; his eyes were bright and laughing, and as
clear as an angel's, so that when he was musing, his eyes seemed
to contain his father alive within them; he had his father's full
and crimson lips; his nose was rather long and his beard
brown; his complexion was fresh and light brown, he had a
handsome brow and thick, bushy hair, and a white, well-
sculptured neck; as he walked he looked towards the ground;
he was not so straight backed as his father, but was a handsome
and well favoured prince. He was fluent in speech; sometimes
at the beginning of his argument he was awkward in expressing
it, but once launched he was most eloquent. His voice was clear
and pleasing, except in singing, though he had some skill at
this; he was wise and measured in his speech, and even more
elegant and cogent in argument than was his father; he spoke
profoundly and with good sense, and he continued at length
when need arose; he was zealous in his pleading and ardent of
expression; he was obstinate in his opinions, but wise and just;
in council he was penetrating, subtle and most intelligent.
He listened to the arguments of other men, praising these when
they were good; and sometimes his own arguments concluded
the whole discussion. He was most skilful in business, and was
even more active and diligent than befitted such a prince;
morning and night he was in council, ever considering some
great business, whether of finance or of war, or of some provis-
ion for the public good.

SOURCE: Georges Chastellain, *Oeuvres*, Vol. VII, edit. Baron
Kervyn de Lettenhove, Brussels, 1865, pp. 228–229.

CHEKHOV, ANTON PAVLOVICH (1860–1904), Russian playwright and short-story writer.

It was possible to call him handsome. A good figure; pleasantly
waving chestnut-brown hair, thrown backward; a small
beard and moustaches. He held himself modestly but without
visible timidity; his gestures were restrained. His voice was a
low bass with a deep metallic quality; his diction was pure

Russian, with a shade of pure Great Russian idiom; his into-
nations were flexible, even passing into a kind of sing-song,
without, however, the slightest sentimentality and certainly
without a shadow of artifice.

In the course of an hour it was possible to note two other
marked characteristics. There was some sort of inner equilibrium, the calm of independence. There was not even the suspicion of that smile which never leaves the faces of two *vis-à-vis*,
meeting on some mutually pleasing theme. You are aware of
that strained amiable smile, expressing: 'Ah! how pleasant it is
for me to chat with you', or, 'We have, of course, one and the
same taste with you!'

But his smile—this was his second characteristic—was unique.
It appeared all at once, quickly, and as quickly vanished.
It was broad, frank, full-faced, and always brief. It was as if
the man had quite sudddenly decided that the matter wasn't
worth smiling about further.

SOURCE: Vladimir Nemirovitch-Dantchenko, *My Life in the Russian
Theatre*, trans. John Cournos, Geoffrey Bles, 1937, pp. 9–10.

CHOPIN, FRÉDÉRICK FRANÇOIS (1809–1849), Polish pianist
and composer.

Chopin is healthy and strong; he turns the head of all the
ladies, and the men are jealous of him. He is now the *mode*,
and the fashionable world will soon be wearing gloves *à la*
Chopin.

AGED 24.

SOURCE: a letter from his fellow-student Anton Orlowski;
quoted Percy M. Young, *More Music Makers*, Dennis Dobson,
1955, p. 51.

CHRISTIAN IV (1577–1648), King of Denmark and Norway.

King Christiern or Christian the fourth then living, was yet
under age, being the seventh king of the Oldenburg family,

and in general the hundred and seventh king of the Danes, who was born in the year 1577, and when his father died was not fully eleven years old . . . [At Roschild] he came attended with ten coaches, and a courtier sat by the King's side in his own coach, which was drawn with three horses . . . He was of fair complexion and big set, and about some fifteen years of age, and they said he could speak the Dutch, French and Italian tongues, and was delighted with shooting in a musket, with music and with reading of histories, and spent two hours in the morning and as many after dinner at his books, and passed the rest of the day in diverse exercises . . . When he vouchsafed to salute any man, he gave them his hand, not to kiss but to take in his hand, neither do any use to kneel to him except they answer before him accused of capital crimes, but the courtiers stood bareheaded to him in great distance.

SOURCE: Charles Hughes (ed.), *Shakespeare's Europe (Unpublished chapters of Fynes Moryson's Itinerary)*, Sherratt & Hughes, 1903, pp. 174–175. For a note on Moryson, see under Bellarmine, Roberto.

CHRISTINA (1626–1689), Queen of Sweden: daughter of the great Gustavus Adolphus, she acceded to the throne at the age of six; abdicated 1654.

As soon as he [i.e. Bulstrode Whitelocke, the author] came within the room he put off his hat, and then the Queen put off her cap, after the fashion of men, and came two or three steps forward upon the foot-carpet. This, and her being covered and rising from her seat, caused Whitelocke to know her to be the Queen, which otherwise had not been easy to be discerned, her habit being of plain grey stuff; her petticoat reached to the ground, over that a jacket such as men wear, of the same stuff, reaching to her knees; on her left side, tied with crimson ribbon, she wore the jewel of the Order of Amaranta; her cuffs ruffled *à la mode*; no gorget or band, but a black scarf about her neck, tied before with a black ribbon, as soldiers and mariners sometimes use to wear; her hair was braided, and hung loose upon her head; she wore a black velvet cap lined with sables, and turned up after the fashion of the country, which she used to put off and on as men do their hats.

Her countenance was sprightly, but somewhat pale; she had much of majesty in her demeanour, and though her person were of the smaller size, yet her mien and carriage was very noble.

AGED 27.

SOURCE: Ambassador Bulstrode Whitelocke, *A Journal of the Swedish Embassy in the years 1653 and 1654*, edit. Henry Reeve, Longman, Brown, Green & Longmans, 1855, Vol. 1, pp. 231–232.

Queen Christina was of more than middling stature. She had a broad and serene brow, well-shaped eyes, a gentle and lively expression, an aquiline nose, and a rather pretty mouth. Her complexion, which was rather sallow, and her uneven shoulders somewhat spoilt the harmony of her figure. Her toilette was very neglected; a quarter of an hour, as a rule, was enough for her to complete it. A comb and a ribbon made up her whole coiffure, supporting her unruly hair. She never wore any jewellery; a ring was her only ornament. She never wore a veil or mask when she went out riding. She was one of the boldest riders, and on such occasions wore only a felt hat and a small dolman, such as Spanish ladies wear. The whole outfit was not worth more than five ducats. Her favourite dress at Court was a grey costume with tassels of gold and black ribbon; her shoes were flat like those of a man. She also wore, in the masculine style, long sleeves, which were covered in ink-stains.

As it is, one portrait cannot represent in full Christina's physiognomy: she changed in appearance as often as the weather. Her face altered according to her variable moods, and could not be recognised from one moment to the next. It was, as a rule, rather pensive and very frequently and quickly its expression changed. It was said, however, that her countenance always preserved its soft lineaments.

SOURCE: Queen Christina, *Memoirs*, trans. in Alfred Neumann, *The Life of Christina of Sweden*, Hutchinson & Co., 1934, p. 154.

CHRISTINE OF DENMARK (1521–1590), Duchess of Milan and Lorraine.

She is, I am informed, of the age of sixteen years, very high in stature for that age—higher, in fact, than the Regent [i.e. Mary of Hungary]—and a goodly personage of competent beauty, of favour excellent, soft of speech, and very gentle in countenance. She weareth mourning apparel, after the manner of Italy—the common saying here is that she is both widow and maid. She resembleth much one Mistress Skelton [cousin to Anne Boleyn, and a great favourite of King Henry VIII] that sometime waited in Court upon Queen Anne. She useth most to speak French, albeit it is reported that she can speak both Italian and High German . . . If it were God's pleasure and the King's, I would that there were some good alliance made betwixt His Highness and the Emperor, and there is none in these parts of personage, beauty and birth, like unto the Duchess of Milan. She is not so pure white as was the late Queen, whose soul God pardon, but she hath a singular good countenance, and when she chanceth to smile there appeareth two pits in her cheeks and one in her chin, the which becometh her right excellently well.

SOURCE: John Hutton, English Ambassador at the Court of the Regent of the Netherlands, Mary of Hungary; a letter of 9th December, 1537, to Thomas Cromwell, in answer to his enquiries as to Christina's suitability as a prospective bride for Henry VIII, and a postscript written later the same day to Cromwell's secretary, Thomas Wriothesley; quoted Julia Cartwright, *Christina of Denmark*, John Murray, 1913, p. 149.

CHRISTLIEB, THEODOR (1833–1889), for twenty-one years occupied the chair of Pastoral Theology at the University of Bonn.

Varied indeed were the talents which had been bestowed on Christlieb. A full, rich musical voice that in speaking and singing delighted his hearers; a poetical vein that enabled him to clothe his deep thoughts in befitting language; a fine, well-developed physique, features so regular that a sculptor's hand might have chiselled them, and lighted up with a flashing eye; eloquence of an unusual order.

SOURCE: trans. T. L. Kingsbury and Samuel Garratt, *Theodor Christlieb, a Memoir by his Widow*, Hodder & Stoughton, 1892, pp. 22–23.

To hear him preach was something never to be forgotten. During the singing of a hymn, a robust form with firm step, but pale and earnest face, was seen to enter the pulpit. His whole appearance was that of a man having a great message to deliver. The very lip seemed to quiver with suppressed excitement. His eyes were lit up as with the light of another world.

SOURCE: Rev. C. H. Irwin of Bray, Ireland, who studied under Christlieb; quoted Kingsbury and Garratt (see above), p. 5.

CLEMENCEAU, GEORGES (1841–1929), Prime Minister of France; called 'The Tiger'.

The figure and bearing of Clemenceau are universally familiar. At the Council of Four he wore a square-tailed coat of very good thick black broad cloth, and on his hands, which were never uncovered, grey suede gloves; his boots were of thick black leather, very good, but of a country style, and sometimes fastened in front curiously, by a buckle instead of laces. His seat in the room in the President's house . . . was on a square brocaded chair in the middle of the semi-circle facing the fire-place . . . He spoke seldom . . . he closed his eyes often and sat back in his chair, with an impassive face of parchment, his grey gloved hands clasped in front of him . . . But speech and passion were not lacking when they were wanted, and the sudden outburst of words, often followed by a fit of deep coughing from the chest, produced their impression rather by force and surprise than by persuasion . . .

My last and most vivid impression is . . . of . . . the President and the Prime Minister as the centre of a surging mob and a babel of sound . . . and Clemenceau, silent and aloof on the outskirts—for nothing which touched the security of France was forward—throned, in his grey gloves, on the brocade chair, dry in soul and empty of hope, very old and tired, but surveying the scene with a cynical and almost impish air . . .

SOURCE: J. M. Keynes, *The Economic Consequences of the Peace*, Macmillan, 1920, pp. 26–29; included in *They Saw it Happen*, *1897–1940*, Basil Blackwell, 1960, pp. 299–300.

The truth is that Clemenceau embodied and expressed France. As much as any single human being, miraculously magnified, can ever be a nation, he was France. Fancy paints nations in symbolic animals—the British Lion, the American Eagle, the Russian double-headed ditto, the Gallic Cock. But the old Tiger, with his quaint, stylish cap, his white moustache and burning eye, would have made a truer mascot for France than any barnyard fowl.

SOURCE: Winston S. Churchill, *Great Contemporaries*, Thornton Butterworth, 1939, p. 302.

COEUR, JACQUES (c. 1395–1456), Merchant Prince, Royal Minister, and leader of a papal expedition against the Turks.

I was a servitor of Jacques Coeur for eighteen months or thereabouts, and was such at the moment of his arrest. With regard to the tonsure, I have been present several times, each time to hold the candle, when Jacques Coeur was being shaved. On my oath I swear that I have no recollection whether the barber or barbers whom I have seen shave him, tonsured him or not . . .

With regard to his habit, I have seen him in the past wear one without a collar, the sleeves of the doublet being striped with red against a black background. During his visit to Normandy, I have seen him wear a hat covered with velvet with large silk folds on top; long pointed laced shoes. I have also seen him wear generally a short robe, reaching half-way to the knees, gathered at the shoulders and open at the sleeves, red or green-and-gray shoes, and robes of all colours, several of them being without a collar, in the style that gentlemen of the court are wont to attire themselves.

SOURCE: André Vidal, watchman at the Toulouse mint, testifying at the trial of Jacques Coeur, when the question at issue was as to Coeur's being tonsured and apparelled as a *clerc*. (The charges against Coeur included poisoning and extortion.) Quoted in translation in Albert Boardman Kerr, *Jacques Coeur, Merchant Prince of the Middle Ages*, Charles Scribner's Sons, 1927, pp. 130–131.

COLBERT, JEAN BAPTISTE (1619–1683), French statesman.

He was of a middle stature, rather lean than fat; his hair was black, and so thin, that he was obliged to begin very soon to make use of a cap. His mien was low and dejected; he had a gloomy air, and stern aspect. He spoke little, and would never return a present answer, till he had first received a particular account in writing of what was proposed to him. He managed business with unwearied application, and a surprising exactness: the clearness of his judgment enabled him to expedite all sorts of affairs speedily and without confusion. He was of a slow conception but spoke judiciously of everything after he had fully comprehended it . . . He was crafty and subtle; his outward behaviour was modest, accompanied with a great deal of seeming plainness and simplicity . . . He slept little and was sober. Though he was naturally sour and morose, he knew how to act the lover in the company of those ladies who had touched his heart, but he always treated them in public with his accustomed gravity, that he might not be thought capable of suffering himself to be governed by the fair sex.

SOURCE: Gatien de Courtilz de Sandras, *The Life of John Baptist Colbert*, English edition, 1695, pp. 1–3.

COLUMBUS, CHRISTOPHER (c. 1446 or 1451–1506), Genoese mariner; constituted by Ferdinand and Isabella of Spain, Admiral, Viceroy and Governor General of all islands and continents discovered in the Western Ocean.

The Admiral was a well built man of more than average stature, the face long, the cheeks somewhat high, his body neither fat nor lean. He had an aquiline nose and light coloured eyes; his complexion too was light and tending to bright red. In youth his hair was blond, but when he reached the age of thirty it all turned white. In eating and drinking, and in the adornment of his person, he was very moderate and modest. He was affable in conversation with strangers and very pleasant to the members of his household, though with a certain gravity.

SOURCE: Ferdinand Columbus [son of Christopher], *The Life of Christopher Columbus*, trans. Benjamin Keen, Folio Society, 1960, p. 34.

COMNENA, MARIA (died 1439), wife of John Palaeologus, Greek Emperor of Constantinople.

At length she appeared. A bench was brought forth and placed near her horse, which was superb, and had a magnificent saddle. When she had mounted the bench, one of the old men took the long mantle she wore, passed to the opposite side of the horse, and held it in his hand extended as high as he could; during this she put her foot in the stirrup, and bestrode the horse like a man. When she was in her seat, the old man cast the mantle over her shoulders; after which one of those long hats with a point, so common in Greece, was given to her; at one of the ends it was ornamented with three golden plumes, and was very becoming. I was so near that I was ordered to fall back, and consequently had a full view of her. She wore in her ears broad and flat earrings, set with precious stones, especially rubies. She looked young and fair and handsomer than when in church. In one word, I should not have had a fault to find with her, had she not been painted, and assuredly she had no need of it.

IN 1433.

SOURCE: Chevalier Bertrandon de le Brocquière, *Memoirs*; quoted Chedomil Mijatovich, *Constantine, Last Emperor of the Greeks*, Sampson Low, Marston & Co., 1892, p. 53.

CONDÉ, LOUIS II DE BOURBON, PRINCE OF (1621–1686), one of the foremost military leaders of the age, and commonly known as 'the Great'.

His eyes were very blue and full of vivacity; his nose was aquiline, his mouth was disagreeable from being very large and his teeth too prominent; but in his countenance generally there was something great and haughty, somewhat resembling an eagle. He was not very tall; but his figure was perfectly well proportioned. He danced well, had an agreeable expression, a noble air, and a fine head.

SOURCE: Madame de Motteville, *Memoirs*, 1723 edition, Vol. III, p. 526; quoted in *Marshal Turenne* (introduced by Francis Lloyd), Longmans, Green & Co., 1907, p. 65.

CONDULMARIO, GABRIEL. See Eugenius IV, Pope (1431–1447).

CONSTANTINE (1868–1923), King of the Hellenes, 1913 to 1922.

King Constantine, from first appearance, is as kings should be: tall, well-built, magnetic, and full of charm. He wore a simple uniform, and though we had been told that his health was impaired he looked in good condition, and no older than thirty-five—though he is forty-nine . . . [His eyes, blue as] the bluebells of his garden, clear and honest-looking as those of his youngest child, encouraged me to go on. Now and then he would smile, and the most attractive thing about this very attractive man is his smile. It has a childlike appeal which few women can resist. Only when one's eyes travel to his protruding ears and to the curious shape of the top of his head is one dissatisfied. These are disturbing details which do not fit in with the rest of the well-built man. Fortunately what dominates is his magnificent figure, his eyes and his smile. My husband told the Crown Prince the next day that all during the interview he was thinking what a splendid guard for the Harvard Eleven was wasted to make a king.

SOURCE: Demetra Vaka, *Constantine, King and Traitor*, The Bodley
Head, 1918, pp. 46, 48.

CORDAY D'ARMONT, MARIE ANNE CHARLOTTE (1768–1793), French patriot; assassinator of Marat.

She was very tall and very beautiful. Her figure was robust
but it was noble, her complexion of a dazzling whiteness and
of the most wonderful freshness. The tissue of her skin was very
fine—you could see the circulation of her blood. She blushed
easily and then she became truly ravishing. Her eyes were deep-
set and lovely, but their expression was veiled. Her chin was
too long and there was something obstinate about it, but her
appearance was full of charm and distinction and had an expression of surpassing purity and frankness. The sound of her
voice was indescribably low and sweet. Her hair was light
chestnut. She did not always have the best posture. Her head
often seemed to droop a little.

SOURCE: quoted Stanley Loomis, *Paris in the Terror*, Jonathan
Cape, 1964, p. 39.

She looked with an expression of indescribable sweetness at the
ebb and flow of the multitude and when the populace, mad
with excitement, or a group of furies disguised as women
hailed her with strident cries, a glance from her beautiful
eyes was often sufficient to reduce them to silence. It was by her
smile alone that she revealed to the outside world what she was
feeling. As she approached the scaffold she seemed to be coming
to the end of an exhausting voyage. She was alone. Unaided
she climbed the steps of the bloodstained platform preserving
to the last the pink and white cheeks of a contented young girl.
It was only when her neck was bared before the people that a
deeper hue rushed to her virginal cheeks. Her noble head, her
bare shoulders and the quiet looks which she cast around
her, deeply impressed those who were there to see. Already
half transfigured, she looked like an angel of light ... A solemn
silence reigned. The fatal blade came down and cut off that
most beautiful of all heads.

SOURCE: Klause, a German onlooker; quoted Georges Pernoud and Sabine Flaissier, *The French Revolution*, trans. Richard Graves, Secker & Warburg, 1961, p. 229.

CÓRDOBA, GONZALO FERNÁNDEZ DE (1453–1515), Spanish general and statesman, known as the 'Great Captain' and 'Prince of the Caballeros'.

He was unrivalled in his person, so graceful and gallant; in his manners so truly regal; in his intelligence so acute and so quick; in his conversation, now easy, now animated, always eloquent. Everything in him was in harmony, fully integrated. He was of great strength and of the utmost dexterity in all military exercises. He was forever practising himself in horsemanship and jousting. He handled arms in the Spanish manner and was also adept at tossing them in the adroit Moorish fashion.

AS A YOUNG LIEUTENANT, AGED 26.

SOURCE: a contemporary writer; quoted Mary Purcell, *The Great Captain*, Alvin Redman, 1963, p. 56.

The Great Captain was of lordly bearing. In the carrying out of momentous and laudable enterprises he was of indomitable spirit. His mind was clear and serene, his glance always alert. Whether on foot or mounted he personified the authority he represented. Though small as a child, in manhood he was not so. In hard battles he was terrible, with a voice full of fury, and mighty strength and vigour. But in peacetime he lived a quiet family life and went about with easy modest gait. In conversation he spoke clearly but not loudly. Baldness did not prevent him from doffing his bonnet when speaking to others.

Neither lack of sleep nor hunger affected him when on his fighting campaigns, and when need required he took upon himself the hardest tasks and greatest risks. Although not a man for jesting, being always very much in earnest, in times of danger he would crack jokes with his men to cheer them and raise their spirits. He used to say that kind words from a captain won him the love of his soldiers. He was as competent in perfecting many affairs as he was diligent in bringing one to a successful end. Ability and diligence were so united in him that he not only defeated his foes by his great courage and vigorous efforts but surpassed them by his intelligence and wisdom.

SOURCE: Hernan Peréz de Pulgar, Cordoba's friend and fellow Captain; quoted Mary Purcell (see above), p. 159.

COROT, JEAN-BAPTISTE CAMILLE (1796–1875), French landscape painter.

Corot is of short but Herculean build; his chest and shoulders are solid as an iron chest; his large and powerful hands could throw the ordinary strong man out of the window. Attacked once, when with Marilhat, by a band of peasants of the Midi, he knocked down the most energetic of them with a single blow, and afterwards, gentle again and sorry, he said, 'It is astonishing; I did not know I was so strong.' He is very full blooded, and his face of a high colour. This, with the *bourgeois* cut of his clothes and the plebian shape of his shoes, gives him, at first sight, a look which disappears in a conversation that is nearly always full of point, of wit and matter.

IN ABOUT 1850.

SOURCE: Théophile Silvestre, *Histoire des Artistes Vivants*; quoted Everard Meynell, *Corot and his Friends*, Methuen & Co., 1908, pp. 207–208.

Walking the galleries of the Champs-Elysées, with the strong step of a countryman, big, thick-set, robust in his ample *redingote* of blue; his colour animated; newly shaved, in a collar of stout linen, tied round with a stock of black satin; his eye clear and lively, his lip heavy, good natured, humorous; his hat rather on the back of his head, showing a forehead framed in white hair, the aged master seemed to be promised many days and years of life; he recalled the glorious old age of Titian.

IN 1873.

SOURCE: Ernest Chesneau; quoted ibid., pp. 285–286.

CORTES, HERNANDO (1485–1547), the Spanish conqueror of Mexico.

He began to adorn himself and be more careful of his appearance than before, and he wore a plume of feathers with a medal, and a gold chain, and a velvet cloak trimmed with knots of gold, in fact he looked like a gallant and courageous Captain . . . he was affable in his manner and a good talker.

SOURCE: Bernal Diaz del Castillo, *Discovery and Conquest of Mexico*, trans. A. P. Maudslay, George Routledge & Sons Ltd., 1928, pp. 76–77.

He was of a good height and body and well-proportioned and of strong limbs and the colour of his face was somewhat ashy and not very merry and had his face been longer he would have been handsomer and his eyes had a somewhat loving glance yet grave withal; his beard was dark and sparse and short and the hair, which in those days was worn [long], the same as the beard, and his chest was high and his back of a good state and he was lean and of little belly and somewhat bow-legged and his legs and thighs well set and he was a good horseman and skilful with all weapons on foot or on horseback and knew very well how to handle them, and above all a heart and a courage . . . In everything, in his presence as well as his talk and conversation, in his table and his dress, in everything he showed signs of being a great lord. The clothes he wore depended on the time and purpose and he cared nothing for silks and damask, but they were very plain and very clean, nor did he wear heavy gold chains but just a thin chain of gold of simple pattern and a trinket with the image of our Lady the Virgin Saint Mary with her precious son in her arms and with a legend in Latin on our Lady's side and on the other side of the trinket the Lord St. John Baptist with another legend; and he also wore on his finger a very rich ring with a diamond, and in his cap, which in those days was worn of velvet, he wore a medal the figure of which I forget.

SOURCE: Bernal Diaz, c. 1519; quoted Salvador de Madariaga, *Hernán Cortes, Conqueror of Mexico*, Hollis & Carter, second edition, 1954, p. 103. The passage comes from the later part of Diaz's

F

history and is not included in most standard English editions, which deal only with the conquest of Mexico (e.g. Maudslay, see above). Salvador de Madariaga's source is the Mexican edition, *Historia verdadera de la conquista de la Nueva España, por Bernal Diaz del Castillo, uno de sus Conquistadores. Unica Edición Lecha ségun el Códice Autógrafo.* La publica Genaro Garcia, Mexico, 1904, ch. cciv, Vol. II, pp. 439–444.

COSTA, GIOVANNI (1826–1903), Italian painter, specialised in landscapes.

He [i.e. Frederick, Lord Leighton] came into the *Caffè* with a tall dark Roman [i.e. Costa] whose gleaming eyes, big hooked nose, and curly black hair, struck me in a moment as a presence of remarkable personality . . . I was taken up to Costa, who, with a kind of graceful bluntness, shook hands, and we began to speak in French—my Italian was not then fluent, and Costa's French was very Roman; however, we made one another's acquaintance, and talked for some time.

SOURCE: Olivia Rossetti Agresti, *Giovanni Costa, His Life, Work, and Times.* Grant Richards, 1904, p. 129.

COUTO, DIOGO DO (1542–1616), Portuguese historian.

Diogo do Couto was of medium height, of a cheerful and imposing presence, with keen eyes and a sallow complexion, and nose somewhat aquiline. He was very industrious, as the multitude of his writings testifies; he was a man of wise counsel, and as such was frequently consulted by the Viceroys in matters of the greatest importance. He was not greedy of gain, which for a man who lived so many years in India is little short of a miracle, and he was thus richer in parts and in desert than in worldly goods, although he always possessed sufficient means to maintain himself honourably.

SOURCE: Manuel Severim de Faria. *Vida de Diogo do Couto*, in Couto's *Decadas IV*, 1, p. xix, reproduced from the *Discorsos Varios Politicos*, 1624; quoted Aubrey F. G. Bell, *Diogo do Couto*, Oxford University Press, 1924, pp. 37–38.

CYRANO DE BERGERAC, SAVINIEN (1620–1655), French romance writer and dramatist.

Let us now sketch the portrait of my hero, that is, his physical portrait . . . His head appeared almost devoid of hairs; you could have counted them ten yards away. His eyes were lost under his eyebrows; his nose, wide and hooked, was like that of these yellow and green chatterboxes [i.e. parrots] which are imported from America. His legs had quarrelled with his flesh and looked like spindles . . . His stomach was a copy of the Aesopian paunch. It is not true that our hero was unclean; but it is true that his shoes were much in love with Madame Mud: they scarcely left each other for a moment.

SOURCE: Dassoucy, friend of Cyrano de Bergerac, *Combat de Bergerac avec le Singe de Brioché*; included in M. Edouard Fouriuer, *Variétées Historique et Littéraires*, Paris, 1855, Vol. I, p. 280.

My great friend, I am sick.
I have hollow beaten eyes,
An earthy and sullen complexion,
Knees thin and pointed.
Those who see me from the roadside,
Yellower than old cod,
Waddling like a foundered lover,
Reckon that it is the pox
Which makes me reel as though I'm at sea
And become drunken without having drunk.

    :   :   :   :   :

A little loft is my Louvre;
My cloak covers me day and night.
I am given one sheet in three months;
My only curtain is the wall
With a bundle of straw
On a mattress of wood.

Alas! before my illness
I was as cool as a mackerel;
My face was plump

And I was supple as a hangman.
Now my cough whittles me away . . .

:   :   :   :   :

I am no longer one of the fair-haired,
Since my head is moulting;
My long hair can no more be seen there
Than on a pumpkin.

IN 1645.

SOURCE: A poem by Cyrano de Bergerac himself, entitled *La Maladie*; quoted Henriette Magy, *Le Véritable Cyrano de Bergerac*, Le Rouge et le Noir, 1927, pp. 40–41.

DALBOQUERQUE, AFONSO (1453–1515). See Albuquerque, Affonso de.

DANTON, GEORGES JACQUES (1759–1794), one of the leaders of the French Revolution; sent to the guillotine in 1794.

The only member of the Government I saw whose brutality revolted me was Danton. There was something inexpressibly savage and ferocious in his looks, and in his stentorian voice. His coarse shaggy hair gave him the appearance of a wild beast. To add to the fierceness of his repulsive countenance, he was deeply marked with the small-pox, and his eyes were unusually small, and sparkling in surrounding darkness, like the famous carbuncle. David, who looked upon him as a demi-God, attempted several times to delineate this horrid countenance, but in vain; exclaiming: 'It would be easier to paint the eruption of a volcano, than the characteristics of this great man.'

SOURCE: J. G. Millingen, *Recollections of Republican France*, 1848; quoted Thompson, *English Witnesses of the French Revolution*, Blackwell, 1938, p. 255. J. G. Millingen's *Recollections* are composed of memories of France between 1790 and 1792, when his father held a position at the Paris mint and he himself was only eight to ten years of age.

D'AREZZO, LIONARDO (d. 1443), Italian writer.

Messer Lionardo was grave in seeming, small in person and of middle height. He wore a cloak of red camlet which came almost to the ground with lined sleeves turned back, and over the cloak he wore a red mantle open on one side and reaching the ground. On his head was a red hood arranged after the fashion. His manners were gentle and pleasing and he had many good stories to tell about Germany, whither he went to attend the Council. He was sparing in words and he looked with especial favour upon those whose worth he knew. He was of choleric nature; at times he would become angry and then quickly let his anger cool.

SOURCE: Vespasiano da Bisticci, *The Vespasiano Memoirs*, trans. William George and Emily Waters, George Routledge & Sons, 1926, p. 367. Vespasiano da Bisticci (1421–1498) was a bookseller whose shop in Florence became a meeting place for many eminent persons.

DEBUSSY, CLAUDE ACHILLE (1862–1918), French composer.

[At a meeting of the 'Music Club', in 1909.] The great composer, an inordinately shy man, was planted in a chair in the exact centre of the platform facing the audience. He was clearly utterly nonplussed and could only attempt to solve his problems by rising and making a stiff little bow whenever he recognized his own name amid Kalisch's guttural mumblings. [Alfred Kalisch, President of the Club, was critic of *The Star*] ... Never shall I forget the impression made on me by that thick-set, clumsy figure, the huge greenish, almost Moorish face beneath the dense thicket of black hair, and the obscure dreaming eyes that seemed to be peering through me at some object behind my back. As he lumbered vaguely forward, extending a cushioned hand, he looked like some Triton arisen from 'the glaucous caverns of Old Ocean'. 'A mythological survival!' I said to myself.

SOURCE: Sir Arnold Bax's memoirs; quoted Edward Lockspeiser, *Debussy, His Life and Mind*, Cassel, 1965, Vol. II, p. 123.

I was shocked not so much by his emaciated, wasted appearance as by his absent-mindedness and his lassitude. His complexion was of the colour of melted wax or of ashes. There was nothing feverish in his eyes, they seemed to reflect the shadows of some dark pool. In his gloomy smile there was not even bitterness, it merely spoke of the weariness of suffering and anguish ... His rather large hand, roundish, supple and plump, an episcopal hand, weighed down his arm, his arm dragged down his shoulder, and his head, the seat of his unique but cruel life, hung down from his body. Speaking about him, a few people made a show of confidence and pretended that he was in better health than they imagined he would be. Meanwhile, having sat down, he allowed his eyes, under their flickering lids, slowly to roam over the audience, like one who wishes to see but is careful to remain unseen himself. Furtive glances were stolen at people or objects he was hardly able to perceive. He was overcome by confusion, as an artist often is who both loathes and is almost ashamed of suffering. It was even said that by concealing his disease he allowed it to develop. [In 1917, shortly before his death.]

SOURCE: André Suarès; quoted Lockspeiser (see above), pp. 202–203.

DE RETZ, CARDINAL (1614–1679). See Retz, Jean François Paul de Gondi, Cardinal de.

DE RUYTER, MICHAEL ADRIANZOON (1607–1676), Dutch naval officer.

He was of less than medium height, a quality which he had in common with several great heroes; well-made in figure, agile, robust, and as if born for work. He had a wide forehead, a ruddy complexion, somewhat high in colour. In his piercing eyes his vivacious spirit could be seen shining. They were brown, as was the hair of his head and arms before age whitened it. He had a bushy, curled-up moustache, in the fashion of sailors of former times. His physiognomy was remarkable in that it had an air of severity mingled with gentleness, which inspired at the same time both respect and love. He was naturally healthy, but in his youth he had once been accidentally poisoned through eating bad fish; this resulted in a slight trembling in all his limbs, which lasted to the end of his life. In addition when he was advanced in years he was afflicted by gravel which sometimes caused him great pain. His natural strength and life-long habits allowed him to bear the strain and exhaustion of life at sea with extraordinary vigour, so much so that in the prime of his life he would laugh at sailors who changed when their clothes got wet. In all his life he was not once seen to allow himself to be swayed by pleasure, or to look after his own interests, to the extent of neglecting his duty to the smallest degree. Sober in eating and drinking, hating drunkenness and drunkards, he loved delicate food much less than the coarse fare provided at sea; so that when the grandees of Spain wished to feast him they caused to be served some dishes of this latter type along with their own fine food, because he could not eat any fresh meat except in his own country, and everywhere else he had to have it salted . . . He spoke eloquently and expressed himself happily; he knew how to support his opinions by the force of his reasoning and was never at a loss when he had to speak to men of higher status than himself, be they princes or kings. He understood several languages, not through learning them at school, but solely through travelling round in the course of his work, and by the long periods he had stayed in foreign lands.

SOURCE: Gerard Brandt, who knew De Ruyter personally and also talked with many of his friends; his life of the Admiral was translated into French as *La Vie du L'Amiral de Ruiter*, in 1698. The description of De Ruyter is from p. 698. Other contemporary accounts, including that of Cosimo de Medici, are unanimous in noting his high colour and somewhat coarse appearance. (See P. Blok, *The Life of Admiral de Ruyter*, trans. G. J. Renier, Ernest Benn Ltd., 1933, pp. 293–296.)

DE VIGNY, ALFRED (1797–1863). See Vigny, Alfred de.

DI SER UGOLINO, FILIPPO (d. 1454), Italian statesman.

He was small in stature with a handsome sagacious face. He wore a long purple mantle with armholes on each side. He was of a lively humour and cheerful, and it was considered a miracle that he should remain insensible to the charms of the ladies. He never married. He led a religious and God-fearing life, simple and temperate in his diet, with one old woman as housekeeper and one manservant.

SOURCE: Vespasiano da Bisticci, *The Vespasiano Memoirs*, trans. William George and Emily Waters, George Routledge & Sons, 1926, p. 320. For a note on Vespasiano da Bisticci, see under D'Arezzo, Lionardo.

DOLET, ÉTIENNE (1509–1546), French scholar and printer; an opponent of Erasmus (q.v.).

I who when at Lyons both saw the man (or rather the mindless thing in human form) and talked with him, know him to be a worthless beast. He somewhere calls himself a young man, but he is nearer to his fortieth than to his thirty-eighth year. He is bald to the middle of his senseless head. He wore a short Spanish jacket, coarse and much worn, scarcely covering his buttocks. His countenance is of such a funereal and black pallor, and has such a wretched air, that you would fancy an avenging fury had fastened on his breast and was dragging him to the punishment of the wheel.

SOURCE: A letter from Joannes Angelus Odonus, an Italian supporter of Erasmus, to Gilbert Cousin, Erasmus' secretary; quoted Richard Copley Christie, *Étienne Dolet*, Macmillan & Co., 1899, p. 225.

DOMINIC, SAINT (1170–1221), Spanish founder of the Dominican order of Preaching Friars.

He was of middle height, his countenance beautiful with little colouring, his hair and beard very fair, and his eyes strikingly fine. A certain radiance shone from his forehead and from under his eyelashes attracting love and respect. His hands were long and beautiful, and his voice strong, noble and sonorous. He never became bald, and always retained his perfect tonsure, though the white hairs of age had begun to appear.

SOURCE: Sister Cecilia, a description dictated in her old age to Sister Angelica, in Mamachi, *Annals*, Appendix, p. 263; quoted Bede Jarrett, *The Life of Saint Dominic*, (*1170–1221*), Burns Oates & Washbourne Ltd., 1924, p. 145.

I have never seen a man so humble or one who despised the glory of the world and all that belongs to it. He despised himself greatly, and reckoned himself as nought. He passed whole nights without sleep, sighing and weeping for the sins of others. I have never heard or known of his having any other bed than the church, if a church was within reach; but if there was no church near he lay on a bench or on the ground or the planks of the bed which had been prepared for him, after carefully removing first all the bedding.

SOURCE: The Abbot of St. Paul of Narbonne, who had preached with Dominic in Languedoc, and who was a witness at the Process of Canonisation. His testimony is included in Bollandus, *Acta Sanctorum*, August 4th, 1867 edition, p. 639, and is quoted Bede Jarret (see above), p. 146.

DORÉ, PAUL GUSTAVE (1832–1883), French artist.

Picture to yourself a face of squarish oval shape surmounted by masses of dark brown hair, and perfectly smooth, save for one questioning wrinkle just above the right eyebrow; a firm, broad, intelligent forehead, full at the temples and but thinly covered with an almost transparent clothing of flesh, not hiding but indicating the powerful mental mechanism of a perfectly constructed instrument. On looking at this prominent feature of Doré's countenance one felt that, although rich in those outward signs which phrenologists call intellectual, there was much more in it than mere intellectuality. It told a tale of exhaustless reserve of power, and an everflowing fount of invention and genius which he would never succeed in draining dry . . . Doré's eyes were a greyish blue, dark, soft, yet fathomless. Their prevailing expression, while proud, was one of anxiety and half-trouble, half-interrogation. Ever and anon a momentary resentful light sparkled in them as when he first saw strangers in his studio. But that look soon vanished from his features, and the true, straight-forward gaze, about which his friends were enthusiastic as constituting his greatest beauty, was revealed in all its vaunted honesty.

But I have nearly finished my portrait without having as yet spoken of his mouth, which, shaded by a slight moustache, was too small for a man's face. It was well formed, but closed so tightly that the lips had borrowed their humour from his eyes and forehead. Pride and self-consciousness was there signalized to an extreme degree, especially in that of the upper-lip. The rest of the face was soft and mobile. Yet the salient expression stamped on his forehead and brows gave one plainly to understand that those lines were no caprice of form, but an index to his real character, which was bound to repeat itself in his every lineament. This feature seemed to reiterate the expression of the others, which appeared to say, 'Whatever the world think of me, I know what I have in myself and am able to do' . . . I noticed that he was of medium stature, perhaps not even so tall. His build was compact and elegant, although slightly inclined to embonpoint; His hands were shapely, delicate, and full of character; his feet small but heavily shod in English fashion. The elasticity, elegance and vivacity of his slightest movement denoted him as one of Nature's spoiled children, endowed with perpetual youth.

SOURCE: Blanche Roosevelt, *Life of Gustave Doré*, Sampson Low & Co., 1885, pp. 396–399.

D'ORSAY, ALFRED GUILLAUME GABRIEL, COUNT (1801–1852); 'the Dandy of Dandies', his ancestry was a mixture of French, German, Italian, and Flemish. Despite his foppish exterior

he was a good marksman, fencer and horseman, and also painted
and sculpted well.

. . . Carlyle in his grey plaid suit and his tub-chair, looking
blandly at the Prince of Dandies, and the Prince of Dandies on
an opposite chair, all respondent as a diamond beetle, looking
blandly at him. D'Orsay is a really handsome man, after one
has heard him speak, and found that he has wit and sense;
but at first sight his beauty is of that rather disgusting sort
which seems to be, like genius, 'of no sex'. And this impression is
greatly helped by the fantastical finery of his dress: sky-blue
satin cravat, yards of gold chain, white French gloves, light
drab great-coat lined with velvet of the same colour, invisible
inexpressibles skin-coloured and fitting like a glove . . . but his
manners are manly and unaffected, and he convinces one,
shortly, that in the face of all probability he is a devilish clever
fellow.

IN 1839.

SOURCE: a letter of Mrs. Jane Welsh Carlyle to her mother;
    quoted Willard Connely, *Count D'Orsay*, Cassell & Co., 1952, pp.
    295–296.

He was tall, and with a good figure and carriage, and had
fine hazel eyes; but he had one great defect which made me
wonder he was so much admired. His teeth had gaps between
them, which caused his smile to degenerate into something
approaching a sneer; and his hands, large and white and apparently soft, had not the physiognomy which pleases the critical
student of hands . . . I thought his conversation commonplace;
but perhaps, though he spoke English fluently enough, his
vocabulary was somewhat limited. He struck me as being
mannish rather than manly, and yet with a touch of effeminacy
quite different from that woman-like tenderness which adds to
the excellence of a man.

IN 1846.

SOURCE: Camilla Toulmin; quoted ibid., p. 443.

I believe, and I like to think, that had Count d'Orsay fallen into good hands, he might have been a great many things that he was not. Unfortunate circumstances, which entangled him as with a web from his early youth, dragged him downwards and led him step by step to his ruin . . . But he was a grand creature in spite of all this; beautiful as the Apollo Belvedere in his outward form, full of health, life, spirits, wit, and gaiety, radiant and joyous, the admired of all admirers— such was D'Orsay when I first knew him . . . His smile was bright and genial, his manner full of charm, his conversation original and amusing, and his artistic taste undeniable. It might have been objected that this taste was somewhat too gaudy; but the brilliant tints with which he liked to surround himself suited his style of beauty, his dress and manner. When I used to see him driving in his tilbury some thirty years ago, I fancied that he looked like some gorgeous dragon-fly skimming through the air; and though all was dazzling and showy, yet there was a kind of harmony which precluded any idea or accusation of bad taste. All his imitators fell between the Scylla and Charybdis of tigerism and Charlatanism; but he escaped these quicksands, though, perhaps, somewhat narrowly, and in spite of a gaudy and almost eccentric style of dress . . .

He was rather above six feet in height, and when I first knew him, he might have served as a model for statuary. His neck was long, his shoulders broad, and his waist narrow, and though he was, perhaps, somewhat underlimbed, nothing could surpass the beauty of his feet and ankles. His dark chestnut hair hung naturally in long waving curls; his forehead was high and wide, his features regular, and his complexion glowed with radiant health. His eyes were large and of a light hazel colour, he had full lips and very white teeth, but a little apart; which sometimes gave to the generally amiable expression of his countenance a rather cruel and sneering look, such as one sees in the heads of some of the old Roman emperors.

SOURCE: *Reminiscences and Recollections of Captain Gronow*: first published 1862–1866; abridged edit. by John Raymond, Bodley Head, 1964, pp. 196–199.

DOSTOEVSKY, THEODORE (FYODOR) MIKHAYLOVICH
(1821–1881), Russian author.

Dostoevsky seemed strange to me [at their first meeting in 1866]. At the first glance he looks rather old, but presently one can see that he is not more than thirty-seven. He is of middle height, erect. His face is worn, sickly. Bright brown, even slightly reddish hair, well greased and strangely smoothed. His eyes fail to match. One is an ordinary brown eye, the pupil of the other is very much dilated, and the iris cannot be seen. This dissimilarity gives his face a mysterious expression. Dostoevsky's face appeared very familiar to me, probably because I had seen his portraits before. He was dressed in a rather old blue jacket, but his shirt was snow white. To tell the truth, at first sight I did not at all take to him.

SOURCE: Madame Dostoevsky, *Dostoevsky Portrayed by his Wife*, trans. S. S. Koteliansky, George Routledge & Sons, 1926, pp. 8–9. Anna Grigorievna, Dostoevsky's secretary, became his second wife in 1867. She adds in a footnote that Dostoevsky fell down when in an epileptic fit and stumbled on a sharp object, injuring his right eye. Professor Yunge, who treated him, prescribed atropine, owing to which the pupil of his eye dilated.

DREBBEL, CORNELIUS (1572–1634), Dutch physician and philosopher.

The famous philosopher Drebbel I have seen only in the street, where he exchanged a few words with me in passing. He is staying in the country, some distance from London. This man is like those things of which Machiavelli speaks, which, in the popular opinion, appear greater at a distance than at close range ... I shall visit him at home and talk with him intimately, if possible. I do not recall ever having seen a physiognomy more extraordinary than his, *and something remarkable, I do not know what, emanates from the ragged man, and not even his thick cloak makes him ridiculous, as it would a lesser person.*

SOURCE: Letters from Peter Paul Rubens to Peiresc, August, 1629; in Ruth Sandars Magurn, edit., *The Letters of Peter Paul Rubens*, Harvard University Press, 1955, p. 323.

DU BARRY, MARIE JEANNE BÉCU, COUNTESS (1746–1793), Mistress of Louis XV.

I had frequently seen the Comtesse du Barry, but only from a distance so that I had never been able to study her famous beauty in detail. She was reclining carelessly on a large fauteuil and wore a dress of some white material with garlands of roses which even as I write this, fifteen years later, I can still see very vividly. She was one of the prettiest women at the Court where there were so many, and assuredly the most fascinating because of the perfections of her whole person. Her hair, which she often left unpowdered, was fair and of a most beautiful colour in such a profusion that she seemed at a loss to know what to do with it. Her blue eyes had a kind and open expression and she always fixed them closely upon those to whom she spoke, seeming to follow in their faces the effect of her words. She had a tiny nose, a very small mouth and a skin of dazzling whiteness. She quickly bewitched everyone and in the delight I had in gazing at her I very nearly forgot my petition. I was then about twenty-five years old. [Madame du Barry was also aged 25 at the time.]

SOURCE: Belleval, *Souvenirs d'un chevau-léger*; quoted Stanley Loomis, *Du Barry*, Jonathan Cape, 1960, pp. 65–66.

DUBOIS, GUILLAUME (1656–1723), Abbé, later Cardinal; French Foreign Minister; negotiated treaty of the Triple Alliance.

The Abbé Dubois was a little, pitiful, wizened, herring-gutted man, in a flaxen-wig, with a weazel's face, brightened by some intellect . . . Avarice, debauchery, ambition, were his gods; perfidy, flattery, foot-licking his means of action . . . The most impudent deceit had become natural to him, and was concealed under an air that was simple, upright, sincere, often bashful. He would have spoken with grace and forcibly, if, fearful of saying more than he wished, he had not accustomed himself to a fictitious hesitation, a stuttering which disfigured his speech, and which, redoubled when important things were in question, became insupportable and sometimes unintelligible.

SOURCE: *Memoirs of the Duke of Saint-Simon*, trans. Bayle St. John, Allen & Unwin, 1913, Vol. II, pp. 327–328.

DU GUESCLIN, BERTRAND (1320?–1380), French commander in the Hundred Years' War and Constable of France.

Reynaud du Guesclin was the infant's father
By a very gentle and beautiful lady;
But the child of whom I speak and of whom I am going to tell you,
Was, I believe, uglier than any other between Rennes and Dinant.
He was flat-nosed and swarthy, ill-formed and squat.

SOURCE: Cuvelier, *Chronique de Bertrand du Guesclin*. Paris, 1839, Vol. I, p. 5. Cuvelier's metrical chronicle was written in approximately 1387.

DÜRER, ALBRECHT (1471–1528), German painter, draughtsman and engraver.

Nature gave our Albrecht a form remarkable for proportion and height and well suited to the beautiful spirit which it held within; so that in his case she was not unmindful of the harmony which Hippocrates loves to dwell upon, whereby she assigns a grotesque body to a grotesquely-spirited ape, while she enshrines the noble soul in a befitting temple. He had a graceful hand, brilliant eyes, a nose well formed . . . the neck a little long, chest full, stomach flat, hips well-knit, and legs straight. As to his fingers, you would have said that you never saw anything more graceful. Such, moreover, was the sweetness and charm of his language that listeners were always sorry when he had finished speaking.

SOURCE: Camerarius, a friend of Dürer, in the Preface to his Latin translation of Dürer's *Four Books of Human Proportion*; quoted Mrs. Charles Heaton, *The History of the Life of Albrecht Dürer of Nürnberg*, Macmillan & Co., 1870, p. 51.

ELIZABETH (1709–1762), Empress of Russia from 1741.

The Empress Elizabeth had keen natural intelligence, was of a gay disposition, and indulged in excessive pleasures. I think she was kind at heart; she had great highmindedness and much vanity; she wanted to shine and was fond of admiration. I believe that the beauty of her body and her natural laziness did much damage to her character. Her beauty ought to have preserved her from the envy and sense of competition which she felt towards all women, unless they were ugly, but the effect was quite the opposite. Her extreme preoccupation was that her beauty should not be dimmed by any other's.

SOURCE: Catherine the Great, *Memoirs*, trans. Moura Budberg, Hamish Hamilton, 1955, p. 372.

[At a ball in 1744 where all the women dressed as men.] The only woman who looked really well and completely a man was the Empress herself. As she was tall and powerful, male attire suited her. She had the handsomest leg I have ever seen on any man and her feet were admirably proportioned. She dressed to perfection and everything she did had the same special grace, whether she dressed as a man or as a woman one felt inclined to look at her and turn away with respect because nothing could replace her.

SOURCE: ibid., p. 185.

ELIZABETH, PRINCESS (1618–1680), eldest daughter of Frederick V, Elector Palatine, the 'Winter King' and his wife, Elizabeth, daughter of James I of England; the princess became Abbess of Herford.

My sister [the writer is Sophia, a younger sister], who was called Madame Elizabeth, had black hair, a dazzling complexion, brown sparkling eyes, a well-shaped forehead, beautiful cherry lips, and a sharp aquiline nose, which was rather apt to turn red. She loved study, but all her philosophy could not save her from vexation when her nose was red. At such times she hid herself from the world. I remember that my sister,

Princess Louise, who was not so sensitive, asked her on one such unlucky occasion to come upstairs to the Queen, as it was the usual hour for visiting her. Princess Elizabeth said, 'Would you have me go with this nose?' The other replied, 'Will you wait till you get another?'

AGED 24.

SOURCE: Sophia, Electress of Hanover, 1630–1680, *Memoirs*, trans. H. Forester, Bentley & Sons, 1888, p. 14.

ELIZABETH ALEXIEIEVNA (1779–1826), Empress of Russia, wife of Alexander I; before her marriage she was known as Louise, Princess of Baden.

The Grand Duchess Elizabeth had grown in height and loveliness, and attracted universal attention. Her angelic face, her slight and elegant figure, and her graceful movements were a constant surprise, and when she came into the Empress's rooms, all eyes were turned upon her . . . One evening when I arrived at the Grand Duchess's, she came in by one of the doors of her boudoir as I entered through the other, and as soon as she saw me, flew towards me. I confess that, for a moment, I took her for an apparition of goodness. Her hair was down and she was wearing a white dress called a *chemise à la grecque*: she had a little gold chain round her neck, and her sleeves were turned up (she had just been playing the harp). I stopped short and exclaimed: 'Heavens! madame, how well you look!' to prevent myself saying: 'My God, how beautiful you are!'

SOURCE: trans. G. M. Fox-Davies, *Memoirs of Countess Golovine, 1766–1821*, London, David Nutt, 1910, pp. 52, 70.

ELIZABETH FARNESE, QUEEN OF PHILIP V OF SPAIN (1692–1766).

She is of medium height and has a good figure; the face long, rather than oval, much marked with small-pox; there are even some scars, but all this is not disagreeably prominent. Her head

G

is nobly set on her shoulders; she has blue eyes, which, without being large, are as sparkling as can be; she can say everything with them. The mouth is rather large, beautified by admirable teeth, which are often disclosed by the pleasantest of smiles. Her voice is charming. Her conversation with everyone is gracious, and is said to be prompted from the heart ... Lombard heart and Florentine head; her will is extremely strong.

SOURCE: letter from the Prince of Monaco to the Marquis de Torcy, describing the new queen-to-be as she passed through his dominions on the way to Madrid; quoted Sir Charles Petrie, *The Spanish Royal House*, Geoffrey Bles, 1958, p. 48.

ELIZABETH OF HESSE (1864–1918), a grand-daughter of Queen Victoria; became Grand Duchess Serge of Russia; killed in the Russian Revolution.

Aunt Ella on these occasions [Court ceremonies] was so fairy-like an apparition that I would like to dip my pen in colour, so as to be able to make her live again, if only for a moment, because eyes that have never beheld her will never be able to conceive what she was. With that divine smile curving her perfect lips, with a blush on her cheeks, only comparable to almond-blossoms, and an almost bashful look in her long-shaped, sky-blue eyes ... Her gown, heavily embroidered in silver, is a colour which is neither blue nor green, the colour of glaciers or of aquamarine; her *kakoshnik* of emeralds and dia-monds is truly a halo for her angelic face, and the gorgeous jewels, covering arms and throat, have, when she wears them, the aspect of gifts, piously offered to some beloved saint.

SOURCE: Queen Marie of Roumania, *Memoirs*; quoted Meriel Buchanan, *Queen Victoria's Relations*, Cassell & Co. Ltd., 1954, p. 97.

I cannot now say definitely what year it was, but I remember being taken to see some *tableaux vivants* in the Palace at Darm-stadt, and seeing the Grand Duchess Serge taking the part of her ancestress St. Elizabeth, who was a daughter of the King of Hungary, and was married to a Landgraf of Thuringia, in Hesse-Marburg...

The tall, slender figure of the Grand Duchess Serge, dressed in a long blue velvet robe, with a silver veil covering her lovely head, a little secret smile on her lips, and her deep blue eyes full of a mystic radiance as she held out her basket full of deep-red roses, had remained in my mind like the picture of a saint in some old cathedral window.

SOURCE: Meriel Buchanan (see above), pp. 97–98. Another contemporary called the Grand Duchess 'the most beautiful creature of God I have ever seen'.

ENGELS, FRIEDERICH (1820–1895), German Socialist, the friend and collaborator of Karl Marx [q.v.]

Engel's face I knew from a photograph, but he was thinner than the picture showed him to be. He is a tall, bony man with sharp-cut features, long, sandy whiskers, ruddy complexion and little blue eyes. His manner of moving and speaking is quick, determined and convinces the observer that the man knows exactly what he wants and what will be the consequences of his words and actions. In conversation with him one learns something new with every sentence he utters.

SOURCE: Theodor Cuno; quoted *Reminiscences of Marx and Engels*, Foreign Languages Publishing House, Moscow, 1959, p. 209.

Engels is now seventy years old. But he bears his three score and ten years with great ease. He is vigorous in body and soul. He carries his six foot odd so lightly that one would not think he is so tall. He wears a beard that grows curiously to one side and is beginning to turn grey. His hair, on the contrary, is brown without a streak of grey; at least a careful inspection was not able to detect any grey hairs. Even as far as his hair is concerned he is younger than most of us. And although Engels looks young, he is even younger than he looks. He is really the youngest man I know. As far as I can remember he has not grown any older in the last twenty hard years.

SOURCE: Eleanor Marx-Aveling; quoted ibid., p. 187.

ERASMUS, DESIDERIUS (1465?–1536), Dutch scholar and humanist; friend of Sir Thomas More.

In body he was thick-set and neat, but because he was of delicate complexion he was easily affected even by very small changes of circumstance, such as food, wine, or the weather . . . The skin of his body and face was pale, and his hair was light blonde when he was a young man. His eyes were bluish-grey, his voice dry, his language clear and beautiful. His dress was respectable and sober as befits the emperor of Counsellors, Theologians, and Priests.

SOURCE: Beatus Rhenanus, *Ep. Car. Coes*; quoted Robert Blackley Drummond, *Erasmus, His Life and Character*, Smith Elder & Co., 1873, Vol. I, pp. 31–32.

EUGENE OF SAVOY, PRINCE (FRANÇOIS EUGENE DE SAVOIE-CARIGNAN) (1663–1736), Austrian general; co-operated with Marlborough in the victories of Blenheim, Oudenarde and Malplaquet.

He was never good-looking or distinguished in appearance. It is true that his eyes are not ugly, but his nose ruins his face; he has two large teeth which are visible all the time. He is always dirty and has lanky hair which he never curls.

DESCRIPTION OF HIM AS A BOY.

SOURCE: *Correspondence Complète de Madame, Duchesse d'Orleans*, edit. G. Brunet, 1886; quoted Nicholas Henderson, *Eugen of Savoy*, Weidenfeld & Nicolson, 1964, p. 9.

Small and ugly in appearance, with an upturned nose, extended nostrils, and an upper lip so narrow as at present to prevent him ever shutting his mouth.

SOURCE: Duchesse d'Orleans (see above), II, p. 22; quoted
Henderson, pp. 9–10.

I was at Prince Eugene's Levée at Leicester House. He is not
so little as I have heard him represented to be, of a swarthy
complexion, and something very brisk about the eyes.

SOURCE: H. Isham Longden, *The Diaries of . . . Sir Justinian
Isham, 1703–1736*, Transactions of Royal Historical Society,
1907, I, p. 198; quoted Henderson, p. 195.

I have waited for his arrival in Holland, before I would let my
Correspondents know, that I have not been so uncurious a
Spectator, as not to have seen Prince Eugene. It would be very
difficult . . . to answer every expectation of those who have
writ to me on that head; nor is it possible for me to find words
to let one know what an artful glance there is in his countenance
who surprised Cremona; how daring he appears who forced the
trenches of Turin; but, in general, can say that he who
beholds him will easily expect from him anything that is to be
imagined or executed by the wit or force of man. The Prince is
of that stature which makes a man most easily become all parts
of exercise; has height to be graceful on occasions of state and
ceremony, and no less adapted for agility and dispatch. His
aspect is erect and composed; his eye lively and thoughtful,
yet rather vigilant than sparkling; his action and address the
most easy . . . imaginable; and his behaviour in an assembly
peculiarly graceful, in a certain art of mixing insensibly with
the rest, and becoming one of the company, instead of receiving
the courtship of it. The shape of his person and composure of
his limbs are remarkably exact and beautiful. There is in his
look something sublime, which does not seem to arise from his
quality or character, but the innate disposition of his mind.
It is apparent that he suffers the presence of much company,
instead of taking a delight in it; and he appeared in public,
while with us, rather to return good-will, or satisfy a curiosity,
more than to gratify any taste he himself had of being popular.
As his thoughts are never tumultuous in danger, they are as
little discomposed on occasions of pomp and magnificence . . .

Thus, were you to see Prince Eugene, and were told he was a

private gentleman, you would say he is a man of modesty and merit. Should you be told that was Prince Eugene, he would be diminished no otherwise than that part of your distant admiration would turn into familiar good-will.

SOURCE: Joseph Addison, *The Spectator*, March 1712; quoted Abel Boyer, *Quadriennium Annae Postremum: or the Political State of Great Britain* . . . second edition, 1718, Vol. III, pp. 173–174.

EUGÉNIE, EMPRESS (1826–1920), wife of Napoleon III, Emperor of the French; her full name was Marie-Eugénie-Ignace-Augustine de Montijo.

The Empress wore a wreath of pink chrysanthemums, and a grey silk dress trimmed with lace, underneath which there were little pink bows, and pink bows trimmed round the body; a necklace and brooch of emeralds and diamonds, no earrings, and beautiful bracelets. The profile and the line of the throat and shoulders are very beautiful. The expression charming and gentle, quite beautiful. The pictures of Winterhalter are very like her. The hair light brown, the face very pale, the mouth and teeth lovely. She does not bear standing well.

SOURCE: Queen Victoria, *Leaves from a Journal*, André Deutsch, 1960, p. 32.

In the conservatory to which Lord Ribblesdale and I were taken by Count Primoli, I thought once more that I must be the victim of a hallucination. My reason told me that I should see an old lady of eighty-nine, the ghost of the former Empress. But this ghost confronting me was not hers. It was the shadow of my mother-in-law! I could not believe two people could look so much alike! There she sat in a rattan armchair, having not yet taken off her hat after her daily drive in the park. The hat was of black straw, the very shape I knew so well, draped in the very same way. On her shoulders a travelling cape of black wool, lined with a certain gray and white Scotch plaid worn only for mourning: wearing the same gloves, the same shoes, using the same cane with a handle like a crow's beak, I saw before me not the Empress Eugénie but the Princess Valentine come to life. This impression was so strong that I stood there for a long moment without speaking, and my friends must have thought me suffering from an attack of sudden shyness— natural enough, after all, in a young woman, unknown and from a foreign country, in the presence of a sovereign made famous by so much beauty, such unexpected glory and such an abyss of misfortune.

SOURCE: Princess Marie Bibesca, *Royal Portraits*, D. Appleton & Co., 1928, p. 187.

EUGENIUS IV (c. 1383–1447), Pope; born Gabriel Condulmaro, he became Pope on the death of Martin V in 1431.

Pope Eugenius . . . was tall, very handsome to look at, thin and serious in appearance, and he inspired reverence to such a degree that none could look him in the face because of his aspect of authority. He embodied in a marvellous way the papal dignity. While he was in Florence he did not show himself or leave his residence, S. Maria Novella, except at Easter and for the solemn feasts, and such was the impression of veneration he produced that few who beheld him could restrain their tears . . . I remember that several times the Pope was with the cardinals on a dais near the gate leading into the cloister of S. Maria Novella, and that not only the square in front but all the streets giving on to it were packed, and such was the awe of the people who were there, that they stood open eyed at the sight of him and none spoke, but all had their eyes fixed on him . . . it seemed that those people beheld not only the vicar of Christ, but the divinity of Christ Himself. His Holiness stood there with very great devotion and all the Cardinals, who surrounded him, all of them men of great worth, did the same. Of a truth, at that time he seemed to be indeed the embodiment of what he represented.

SOURCE: Vespasiano da Bisticci, *Virorum illustrium C III . . . vitae*, *in Spicilegium Romanum*, Tom. I, A. Mai (Rome), 1839, pp, 18–19; quoted Joseph Gill, S.J., *Eugenius IV, Pope of Christian Union*, Burns & Oates, 1961; p. 120. For a note on Vespasiano da Bisticci see under D'Arezzo, Lionardo.

EYQUEM (EYGHEM), PIERRE DE (d. 1568). Noted in his day for his Latin verses, he is now remembered as the father of Michel de Montaigne, the essayist (q.v.)

For his demeanour, it was of a gentle gravity, humble and very modest. And he took marvellous thought for the decency and comeliness of his person and his clothes whether he was on foot or on horseback. In his speech he kept such scrupulous good faith as to be excessive; his conscience and his religion were generally, in truth, nearer to superstition than to the other extreme. As a man he was little of figure, full of energy, of upright and well-proportioned stature. His face was pleasant, rather brown. And he was exquisitely skilful in every noble exercise . . . I have seen him, when he was sixty, making mock of *our* agility—now throwing himself, just as he was, in his furred robe, upon the back of a horse, now going round the table on his thumb. And he hardly ever went to his room without bounding over two or three steps at a time.

SOURCE: Michel de Montaigne, *Essais*, iii, 8: 'De l'Art de conférer'; quoted Edith Sichel, *Michel de Montaigne*, Constable & Co., 1911, p. 5.

FEODOR I (1557–1598). See Theodore I.

FERDINAND I (1751–1825), King of the Two Sicilies from 1816.

He must be five feet seven inches, and therefore a good inch taller than me, very thin, gaunt and raw-boned . . . his knees always bent and his back very supple, since at every step he bends and sways his whole body. The part below his waist is so limp and feeble that it does not seem to belong to the upper part, which is much stronger. He has muscular arms and wrists, and his coarse brown hands are very dirty since he never wears gloves when he rides or hunts. His head is relatively small, surmounted by a forest of coffee coloured hair, which he never powders, a nose which begins in his forehead and gradually swells in a straight line as far as his mouth, which is very large with a jutting lower lip, filled with fairly good but irregular teeth. The rest of his features, his low brow, pig's eyes, flat cheeks and long neck, are not remarkable.

Although an ugly Prince, he is not absolutely repulsive: his skin is fairly smooth and firm, of a yellowish pallor; he is clean except for his hands; and at least he does not stink. So far he shows no trace of a beard. But he is very oddly dressed: his hair smoothed back behind the head and gathered in a net; he wears a large white collar, cuffs of embroidered muslin, and sometimes lace, a grey coat of mixed cloth which we call pepper and salt in Vienna, a waistcoat of yellow leather with a little gold braid and copper buttons across his chest, lined with green satin, of which he also wears a sleeveless doublet over his shirt, large yellow deerskin breeches with designs round the button-holes, grey silk stockings and heavy leather shoes with copper buckles; and he never wears a hat, sword or hunting knife indoors, not even when he dines in public, or goes to church or the theatre ... But his hunting garb is even more peculiar. He wears a large hat let down on every side, a shaggy grey coat with pockets hanging half-way down his legs, an old leather waistcoat, breeches of the same, a large pouch containing his bags of small shot and a hunting-knife like a bayonet, heavy grey stockings of beaver and wool, which not being suspended fall in thick folds over his shoes, a long and heavy Spanish gun on his shoulder, a powder horn dangling beside it with a knitted green game-bag, and various whistles attached to his button holes. Thus attired he goes hunting every morning.

IN 1769.

SOURCE: the Emperor Joseph II's account of his visit to Ferdinand's court; quoted in translation in Harold Acton, *The Bourbons of Naples* (*1734–1825*); Methuen & Co., Ltd., 1956, pp.
138–139.

FLAUBERT, GUSTAVE (1821–1880), French novelist.

Gustave Flaubert was born at Rouen on the 12th December 1821; he was therefore twenty-one years old when I first knew him, and he was as handsome as a god. Those who only knew him in his later years, when he had grown heavy, bald and grey-headed, with drooping eyelids and a coarse complexion, cannot possibly form any idea of his appearance when we were about to be united in indissoluble friendship. With his fair skin and delicate colouring, his soft, flowing hair, his broad-shouldered, tall figure, full beard of pale gold, large eyes grey as the sea, shaded by black eyebrows, his voice like the sound of a trumpet, his violent gestures and resounding laughter, he was like one of those young Gallic chieftains who resisted the advance of Roman legions . . . Gustave was a giant, come of a Norman and Champenois stock, and he prided himself upon the possession of a drop of Iriquois blood, transmitted through an ancestor who had lived in Canada . . . As he sat on the benches occupied by the students his dress made him remarkable. Even as early as eight o'clock in the morning he always wore a black suit, with white gloves and cravat. Only long experience of Paris life and our persistent ridicule finally cured him of this practice, which made him look like a groomsman at a wedding.

SOURCE: Maxime du Camp, *Literary Recollections*, Remington & Co. Ltd., 1893, Vol. I, pp. 154–155.

FLEURY, ANDRÉ HERCULE DE (1653–1743), the last of the great French cardinal-ministers of the *ancien régime*.

. . . at court . . . he behaved himself with so much ease, disinterestedness, and affability, that he daily gained new friends without provoking the envy or jealousy of any. In his person he was graceful and agreeable rather than handsome or well made; he had something in his countenance that seem'd to bespeak condescension and good nature, tho' in process of time there wanted not some who fancied they could discern, under the smile that generally appeared in his face, a great degree of vanity and self conceit; but this perhaps might be the pure effect of imagination. His learning was suited to his function, and he never discovered more of it than became a gentleman. He always affected a superior degree of piety in his actions and discourses, which however, admitted of some doubts, considering the liberties of his youth.

SOURCE: *Memoirs of the Life and Administration of the Late Andrew Hercules de Fleury, by an Impartial Hand*, London, 1743, p. 5.

FLORENTINE PAINTERS, YOUNG (c. 1550).

Under the pretence of living like philosophers, they lived like swine and brute beasts; they never washed their hands, nor their faces or hair or beards; they did not sweep their houses and never made their beds save once every two months; they laid their tables with the cartoons for their pictures, and they drank only from the bottle or the jug; and this miserable existence of theirs, living, as the saying goes, from hand to mouth, was held by them to be the finest life in the world.

SOURCE: Vasari's *Lives of the Painters*; quoted Rudolf and Margot Wittkower, *Born Under Saturn*, Weidenfeld & Nicolson, 1963, p. 71.

[The leader of this group of young artists was Jacone (d. 1553), a pupil of Andrea del Sarto.]

FOCH, FERDINAND (1851–1929), French marshal.

His whole bearing was martial, and he gave the impression of being a man of relentless energy and determination. In conversation he often employed gestures to emphasise his words; two blows in the air with his fists, followed by two kicks, used to show the fate which he reserved for his enemies. In any conversation of importance he began by saying: '*De quoi s'agit-il?*' and he had a way of sweeping away any difficulties metaphorically with his hands; in explaining his own views he used to say: '*Ah si. Ah si*', in a firm and persuasive manner; or, if he disagreed: '*Ah non. Ah non*', in a very decided way. He also had a way of putting both hands on the shoulders of the man with whom he was taking, especially if he were taller than himself, in a manner that was both appealing and convincing.

His voice was deep and he spoke in short, quick sentences, sometimes using rather colloquial language which at times made it difficult for a foreigner to understand him, but he used to add: *'Vous comprenez bien?'* and repeated his remarks if he felt he had not been understood.

He always thought a great deal before answering, but, when once his mind was made up, he seldom or never changed his opinion, unless a new point of view persuaded him.

SOURCE: Colonel C. J. C. Grant, *Army Quarterly*, January 1921;
    quoted Sir George Aston, *The Biography of the late Marshal Foch*,
    Hutchinson & Co., 1929, p. 129.

He is of medium height, neither tall nor short, and strongly built without any superfluous weight, seeming to be alert as well as powerful; his forehead is broad and well shaped, his nose straight and clean-cut; a grey moustache hides the lips which hold his perpetual cigar (a pipe was substituted during office work in later years). His eyes are his most striking feature; their look is at one moment abstracted, as if his thoughts are far away, and the next extraordinarily keen, darting suddenly from under somewhat heavy lids. His utterance is crisp and at times rather abrupt; his voice is that of one used to command. He gives the impression of being frank, loyal, and clear-sighted; if I had to choose a motto for the General I think this would suit him as well as another: 'clear vision'.

SOURCE: Récouly, *Foch, His Character and Leadership*, p. 16;
    quoted Sir George Aston (see above), pp. 132–133. It is interesting
    to note that a British officer who later became a great admirer of
    Foch's had described him before the Great War as 'a little man
    in elastic-sided boots and impossible clothes, with a rather con-
    temptuous and almost hostile attitude.'

FOUCHÉ, JOSEPH, DUKE OF OTRANTO (1759–1820),
French Minister of Police.

After him [Talleyrand] came Fouché, a little spare, shallow, shrewd-looking man, who seems to unite all parties in one common feeling—horror of his character, and the policy of not betraying it. He is, I conclude, the worst and most useful man the King could have found in his whole dominions.

SOURCE: Harriet, Countess of Granville, *Letters, 1810–1845*; quoted John Fisher, *Eighteen Fifteen, an End and a Beginning*, Cassell, 1963, p. 199.

FRANCIS OF ASSISI (GIOVANNI FRANCESCO BERNADONE), SAINT (c. 1182–1226).

This our most blessed Father, from the time of his conversion until the end of his life, treated his body with great austerity, although he was by nature slender and delicate, and had lived luxuriously in the world . . . He would only wear an old tunic, well patched inside and seldom would he wear one of new cloth, preferring that which another friar had worn for some time. Sometimes he would obtain part of his habit from one friar and the other part from another. On account of his many infirmities, and chill of the stomach and spleen, they would line his habit with pieces of new cloth. This manner of poverty in his clothing he observed until the year of his departing to God, when by reason of dropsy and his other ailments the friars made for him several tunics, so that he might have a change both day and night.

SOURCE: Brother Leo of Assisi (ascribed to), *The Mirror of Perfection*; trans. Constance, Countess de la Warr, Burns & Oates Ltd., 1902, pp. 41, 48. Brother Leo was one of St. Francis's first and best loved followers.

FRANKS, THE (A.D. 470). An eye witness account of a Frankish prince and his retinue seen by a traveller on a visit to Lyons.

The appearance of the Kinglets and confederates who accompanied him inspired terror even in peace-time. Their feet were covered entirely, up to their ankles, in boots of bristly hide. Their knees, their legs, and their calves were without any covering. Besides this, they wore high, tight, and many-coloured garments which hardly reached down to their bare thighs;

their sleeves only covered their upper arms; their cloaks were green, embroidered with red. Their swords hung from their shoulders on baldricks, and round their waists they wore a belt of fur adorned with bosses ... In their right hands they held barbed lances and throwing-axes, and in their left shields, on which the light shone, white on the circuit and red on the boss, displaying both opulence and craftsmanship.

SOURCE: Sidinius Apollinaris, *Letters*, Book iv, no. xx; quoted R. H. C. Davis, *A History of Medieval Europe*, Longmans, 1957, pp. 108–109.

FRANZ JOSEF I (1830–1916), Emperor of Austria.

Immediately after the young Emperor stepped out of the church and attended by all the clergy in their purple robes and his magnificent suite, they then received the benediction of the Patriarch, every one being on their knees as well as himself. It was a beautiful & impressive sight ... The troops then defiled before him and he stood out touching his hat to every officer that saluted him as he passed. Radetzky stood beside him all the time, and his magnificent Jaegers wearing scarlet dresses & Polish hats with white cloaks lined with fur and embroidered in gold thrown over their shoulders.

The Emperor is very like his portrait, a tall fair young man of 20, a very handsome figure, tall and straight, walks remarkably well & has very neat feet. His face is pleasant and from the way he moved about and spoke to people he appeared to have very easy and affable manners.

SOURCE: Mary Luytens (edit.), *Effie in Venice—Unpublished Letters of Mrs. John Ruskin, 1849–52*, John Murray, 1965, pp. 188–189.

FREDERICK I BARBAROSSA (1123–1190), Holy Roman Emperor from 1155.

Now divine, august Frederick is ... in character and appearance such a man that he deserves to be studied even by those not in close touch with him ... His person is well proportioned.

He is shorter than very tall men, but taller and more noble than men of medium height. His hair is golden, curling a little above his forehead. His ears are scarcely covered by the hair above them, as the barber (out of respect for the empire) keeps the hair on his head and cheeks short by constantly cutting it. His eyes are sharp and piercing, his nose well formed, his beard reddish, his lips delicate and not distended by too long a mouth. His whole face is bright and cheerful. His teeth are even and snow white in colour. The skin of his throat and neck (which is rather plump but not fat) is milk white and often suffused with the ruddy glow of youth; modesty rather than anger causes him to blush frequently. His shoulders are rather broad, and he is strongly built. His thighs, supported by stout calves, are proper and sturdy.

His gait is firm and steady, his voice clear, and his entire bearing manly. Because of his figure, he has an air of dignity and authority, standing or sitting. His health is very good, except that sometimes he is subject to a day's fever. He is a lover of warfare, but only that peace may be secured thereby. He is quick of hand, very wise in counsel, merciful to suppliants, kind to those taken under his protection.

SOURCE: Otto of Friesling (and his continuator, Rahewin), *The Deeds of Frederick Barbarossa*, trans. and edit. Charles C. Mierow, Columbia University Press, 1953, pp. 331–332. Although Rahewin, the author of this passage from Book IV of the *Deeds*, was a contemporary of Frederick and must have had ample opportunity to observe him, there is little original in his description. Much of it is drawn directly from Apollinarius Sidonius' description of Theodoric II of the Visigoths (453–466). For details see Mierow's footnotes.

FREDERICK II (1194–1250), Holy Roman Emperor from 1221, and King of Sicily (from 1198)—he was formally crowned King at the age of three and a half.

The stature . . . of the king is neither small, nor taller than one would expect of his age. But the Universal Author of Nature has given him robust limbs and a strong body, with which his vigorous spirit can achieve whatever he undertakes. He is never idle, but passes the whole day in some occupation or other, and so that his vigour may increase with practice, he fortifies his agile body with every kind of exercise and practice of arms ... To this is added a regal majesty and majestic features and mien, to which are united a kindly and gracious air, a serene brow, brilliant eyes, and expressive face, a burning spirit and a ready wit. Nevertheless his actions are sometimes odd and vulgar, though this is not due to nature but to contact with rough company ... He is intolerant of admonitions, and judges himself capable of acting according to his own free will, and considers it shameful for himself to be subject to a guardian and to be considered a boy ... he has virtue in advance of his age, and though not adult he is well versed in knowledge and has the gift of wisdom, which usually comes with the passage of years.

AGED 13.

SOURCE: A contemporary letter of uncertain authorship, written in 1208 when Frederick still had poor prospects. He was a dependant of the Pope, and no more than the titular head of a state; quoted Georgina Masson, *Frederick II of Hohenstaufen, a life*; Secker & Warburg, 1957, p. 36–37.

FREDERICK II (1712–1786), King of Prussia, called 'the Great'; reigned from 1740.

Frederick the Second is the oldest reigning Sovereign in Europe, and has nearly completed his sixty-sixth year. His constitution, naturally sound, if not vigorous, retains its force; and his body is accustomed to, as well as still capable of great fatigue. The gout and infirmities almost inseparably attendant on his period of life, have indeed enfeebled his legs; but, once on horseback, and seated in the saddle, he is equal to prodigious efforts, sustained for a very considerable length of time. He is of middle size, inclined to thin, and he stoops in walking or in riding. His face, though now become wrinkled, more perhaps by fatigue and agitations, than from the progress of age, or the effects of disease, is one of the most animated and interesting ever beheld. There is in it a fire and an intelligence, which widely distinguishes him from common men. Every line and every feature may be studied, and have their meaning. His eye is uncommonly clear and brilliant, though he is so short-sighted, as usually to have recourse to a glass, even when on horseback. He has a bold and finely-formed, but not an aquiline nose. Of his hair, time has only spared some few thin and scattered locks about the crown of his head. In order to supply the want, he wears false curls and a long queue.

Nothing can be so simple as his dress, and it never varies. It is indeed scarcely exempt from the imputation of meanness, and by no means always entitled to the praise of cleanliness. His coat is a plain uniform of common blue cloth, without ornament or embroidery of any kind. On his breast appears the star of the Prussian Order of the 'Black Eagle'; but he very rarely wears the riband, or other insignia. He is always booted, as becomes a soldier; and those who see him constantly, have scarcely ever beheld his legs. Round his middle is tied his sash. Charles the Twelfth of Sweden might have worn Frederic's sword, without departing from the characteristic simplicity of his dress. It is a military one, perfectly unornamented, with a plain silver hilt, to which hangs a sword-knot. His hat is of a monstrous size, surmounted with a white panache or plume. Either economy, or carelessness, or both, induce him to wear his clothes as long as decency will permit; indeed, sometimes, rather longer. He is accustomed to order his breeches to be mended, and his coat to be pierced under the arms. It was an unusual mark of attention to the Great Duke of Russia, when he was here last year, that the King made up a new uniform suit and hat, in honour of so illustrious a guest. To complete the negligence of his appearance, he takes a great deal of snuff, and lets no small portion of it slip through his thumb and fingers upon his clothes. It must be owned that this custom gives him sometimes almost a disgusting air. Yet across so much neglect and contempt of external forms, I think one may easily, without any aid of imagination, perceive the hero, the philosopher, and the King.

H

SOURCE: N. W. Wraxall, *Memoirs of the Courts of Berlin, Dresden, Warsaw, and Vienna.* London, 1799, Vol. I, pp. 108–110.

FREDERICK AUGUSTUS I (1750–1827), King of Saxony (formerly the Elector Frederick Augustus III).

The reigning Elector, Frederick Augustus, is in the prime of his age, not having yet completed his twenty-eighth year. Of a middle size, inclining rather to short than tall, his limbs are neither active or muscular, though he possesses sound health and a strong constitution. Over his whole figure there is diffused something easier perceived than described, altogether destitute of grace, and deficient in dignity. Nor are his manners calculated to compensate for the want of personal accomplishments. In his address he is shy, distant, and reserved. Coldness and inanimation characterise his behaviour, pervade his conversation, and accompany all his actions. He displays none of the gracious and communicative disposition which almost equally characterise in different ways, his three contemporaries, Frederick the Second, Stanislaus, and the present Emperor.

IN 1778.

SOURCE: N. W. Wraxall, *Memoirs of the Courts of Berlin, Dresden, Warsaw, and Vienna,* London, 1799, Vol. II, pp. 181–182.

FRENCH HOUSEWIFE, FOURTEENTH CENTURY

[An invaluable picture of the medieval housewife is given in *Le Ménagier de Paris,* written 1392–1394 by a prosperous Parisian citizen of over 60 to his wife of 15, an orphan girl from the provinces who, though of gentler birth than himself, was less experienced in the ways of the world and who sought his guidance.]

Have a care that you be honestly clad, without new devices and without too much or too little frippery. And before you leave your chamber and house, take care that the collar of your shift, and of your *blanchet, cotte* and *surcotte,* do not hang out one over the other, as happens with certain drunken, foolish or witless women, who have no care for their honour, nor for the honesty of their estate or of their husbands, and who walk with roving eyes and head horribly reared up like a lion, their hair straggling out of their wimples, and the collars of their shifts and *cottes* crumpled the one upon the other, and who walk mannishly and bear themselves uncouthly before folk without shame ...

When you go to town or to church go suitably accompanied by honourable women according to your estate, and flee suspicious company, never allowing any ill-famed woman to be seen in your presence. And as you go bear you head upright and your eyelids low and without fluttering, and look straight in front of you about four rods ahead, without looking round at any man or woman to the right or to the left, not looking up, nor glancing from place to place, nor stopping to speak to anyone in the road ...

Know that it does not displease, but rather pleases me that you should have roses to grow and violets to care for and that you should make chaplets and dance and sing.

SOURCE: *Le Ménagier de Paris, Tracté de Morale et d'Economic Domestique, composé vers 1393 par un Bourgeois Parisien* ... Paris, 1846; quoted Eileen Power, *Medieval People*, Methuen & Co., 1924 (tenth edition, 1963), pp. 102–103.

FRÖBEL (or FROEBEL), FRIEDRICH (1782–1852), German educationist; founder of the kindergarten system.

Unprepossessing in appearance, but making even hostile observers forget all outward circumstances when the inner man was revealed—equally ready to play with children—to instruct the inquirer—to discuss with the learned—defending his system with the simplicity of genius, as proudly confident in the power of his theories as he was humble in his personal pretensions.

SOURCE: Recollections of Friedrich Frobel by B. von Marenholtz Bülow, included in Emily Shirreff, *A Short Sketch of the Life of Friedrich Frobel*, new edition, Chapman & Hall, 1887, p. 112.

...a tall thin man with long grey hair, leading a troup of village children of from three to eight years old, mostly bare-footed, and but scantily clothed, marching in time, two and two, up a neighbouring hill, where he set them down to a game with an appropriate song. The loving unselfishness and patience with which he conducted this, and the whole bearing of the man while he made the children play several games under his guidance had something in them so touching that tears stood in my eyes and in those of my companion; and I said to the latter, 'This man may be called an old fool by those around him, but perchance he is one of those whom their contemporaries despise, or cast stones at, and to whom future generations erect monuments.'

SOURCE: ibid., pp. 112–113.

GALILEO GALILEI (1564–1642), Italian astronomer and ex-perimental philosopher.

Signor Galileo was jovial and merry, especially in his old age, well-built, and of medium height, having a naturally sanguine temperament, phlegmatic and quite strong, weakened how-ever by cares and troubles, both of soul and body, which often caused him to lapse into a state of listlessness. He developed many illnesses and hypochondriacal symptoms, and was often a prey to serious and dangerous illness, chiefly caused by the continual discomfort of his star-gazing vigils, to which he very often devoted whole nights. For more than forty-eight years, perhaps to the end of his life, he suffered the most acute pain, which at different times harshly tormented him, affecting different parts of his body.

SOURCE: Vincenzo Viviani, *Racconto Istorico della vita di Gaelileo*, printed in Antonio Favaro, edit., *Edizione Nazionale Delle Opere di Galileo*, 1890–1910, Bol. XIX, p. 624.

Signor Galileo was a serious looking man, rather tall, strong limbed and squarely built, with bright eyes, fair complexion and reddish hair.

SOURCE: Niccolo Gherardini, *Vita di Galileo*, printed in Antonio Favaro, edit., *Edizione Nazionale* . . . (see above), Vol. XIX, p. 646.

Both the above descriptions are included in J. J. Fahie, *Memorials of Galileo Galilei, 1564–1642,* Courier Press, 1929, p. 1.

GALLUS CAESAR (325/6–354), half-brother of Julian the Apostate (q.v.); crowned 'Caesar' under the Emperor Constantius, but later executed for misgovernment.

He was a man of splendid stature and great beauty of person and figure, with soft hair of a golden colour, his newly sprouting beard covering his cheeks with a tender down, and in spite of his youth his countenance showed dignity and authority. He differed as much from the temperate habits of his brother Julian, as the sons of Vespasian, Domitian and Titus differed from each other.

SOURCE: Ammianus Marcellinus, in *The Roman History of Ammianus Marcellinus*, trans. C. D. Yonge, Henry G. Bohn, 1862, p. 43.

GARIBALDI, GUISEPPE (1807–1882), Italian patriot and guerrilla leader of the *Risorgimento*.

A man . . . of barely five feet seven or eight, broad shouldered and deep chested, with . . . the complexion of a healthy Englishman, beard and hair of chestnut brown, bordering on reddish blonde, cut short and slightly grizzled. He had the bearing of a real gentleman. He used little of the gestures of a Southerner and it was only when we were talking of the sympathy of the English people for Italy that his calmness, which is almost British, left him.

AGED 52.

SOURCE: *The Times*, July 26th, 1859 (A report from Como); quoted in John Parris, *The Lion of Caprera*, Arthur Barker Ltd., 1962, p. 168.

GAUGIN (EUGENE HENRI), PAUL (1848–1903), French post-impressionist painter.

The authors of this description talked with Gaugin's daughter, etc.

He was not handsome in any recognised form, but gave an immediate impression of solidity and power. He was a heavy-faced young man with dark hair grown long over a bull neck. His high, well-set cheekbones, long firm chin and the suggestion of heavy jowls conveyed forcefulness. He wore a red-brown moustache. His complexion, like his manner, was heavy and coarse. He had a generous mouth, large and full in the lower lip, tending to a supercilious curve in the upper. When he smiled, which was not often, the supercilious expression changed to one of irony—but gentle irony. He had a pleasant smile.

The least satisfactory part of his face was the narrow forehead, but neither Mette nor any other woman wasted more than a moment on it—the eye went instinctively to the two features, his nose and his eyes, which made the rest appear almost ordinary.

His nose, a great beak broken at the bridge, jutted from the long space between the brow and mouth with the arrogance of a pirate chief; it was positively rakish, it could with difficulty be reconciled with the Bourse, the bank, the black clothes. And his eyes! Almost covered by heavy lids, they seemed at first small and dull; then one would catch a gleam of blue green and realise that they missed nothing. He made no effort to raise the lids, glancing lazily from under them. But there were moments . . . when the iris was exposed, the dullness disappeared and the glance became a bold stare, difficult to meet.

He talked, as he walked, slowly, deliberately. He raised his voice, as he raised his lids, rarely. He had no need of emphasis.

SOURCE: Lawrence and Elizabeth Hanson, *The Noble Savage*, Chatto and Windus, 1954, p. 16.

GAVARNI, PAUL (1804–1866), became the most popular graphic artist in Paris; his real name was Guillaume Sulpice Chevalier.

I was horribly fatigued, even unwell, and dragged myself over to this last corner so as to have seen everything before going home to bed. —By chance the door was unencumbered, an open space between two crowds. —So on I went, peering through my lorgnette, and as I crossed the threshold I found myself face to face, nose to nose, with a person who was also peering through his lorgnette—and could not understand, at first, why, since the door was a wide one, this unknown fellow (in morning dress) was walking straight into me. —We looked at each other, —his was a disagreeable expression; the man's face was pale and sweating, he had a beard that I thought tousled and too long, —and there was something horrible, yet sad in the whole cast of his countenance. —I remembered! this was the dreadful face that was printed in one of the numbers of the *Illustrated London News* last January; —and then at last, waking up completely, I realised that it was *I*. —Drowsiness was leading me into a mirror, my back turned to the group of woman I had been going to see.

SOURCE: Letter of Paul Gavarni to Louis Leroy, London, 1848; quoted Richard Friedenthal, *Letters of the Great Artists, from Blake to Pollock*, Thames & Hudson, 1963, pp. 60–61.

GODOY, MANUEL DE (1767–1851), became the lover of Queen Maria Luisa of Spain and virtual dictator of Spain from 1792 to 1808.

A big, strong, coarse man, with a bright red complexion and a heavy, sleepy, sensual look.

AGED 36.

SOURCE: Lady Lolland; quoted Jacques Chastenet, trans. J. F. Huntingdon, *Godoy*, The Batchworth Press, 1953, p. 24.

Don Manuel Godoy, who owed the start of his career to his physical attractions, was tall, strongly-made without corpulence, broad-shouldered, slightly bent and very clear complexioned. The whiteness of his skin showed up the rosiness of his cheeks, a rosiness said by many of his enemies to be artificial but which was in fact certainly natural. He wore a Captain-General's uniform and held in his hand his baton and his plumed hat. His face was gentle but expressionless; his remarks were precise but unsparkling, though an occasional joke from him was sure to raise smiles whose spontaneity was not above reproach. The reception over, the crowd melted away, cursing as it did so the very man to whom, a minute earlier, it had bent in supplication.

SOURCE: Alcana Galiana, *Memorias de un Anciano*; quoted Jacques Chastenet (see above), p. 70.

GODUNOV, BORIS FEDOROVICH (1551/2–1605), Tsar of Russia; he first acquired power during the reign of his brother-in-law, Theodore (q.v.) and himself became the next Tsar in 1598.

He is of comely person, well-favoured, affable, easy and apt to evil counsel, but dangerous in that to the giver; of good capacity, about forty-five years of age, affected much to necromancy, not learned, but of sudden apprehension, and a natural good orator to deliver his mind with an audible voice; subtle very precipitate, revengeful, not given much to luxury, temperate of diet, heroical in outward show.

SOURCE: Sir Jerome Horsey, *Travels*; edit. E. A. Bond, in *Russia at the Close of the Sixteenth Century*, Hakluyt Society, 1856, p. 258. (Spelling modernised.) Horsey was in Russia from 1575 to 1591, first as an agent of the Russia Company, and then as an envoy from the English Court.

GOETHE, JOHANN WOLFGANG VON (1749–1832), German poet and dramatist.

While I was reading, a young man, booted and spurred, in a short green shooting jacket thrown open, had come in and mingled with my audience. I had scarcely remarked his entrance. He sat down opposite to me, and listened very attentively. I scarcely knew what there was about him that struck me particularly, except a pair of brilliant black Italian eyes.

SOURCE: Johann Gleim, musician and song-writer, born 1719; quoted Falk, von Müller, etc., *Characteristics of Goethe pourtrayed from Familiar Personal Intercourse*, trans. Sarah Austin, London, Effingham Wilson, 1833, Vol. II, pp. 25–26.

The very evening of my arrival in Frankfurt I had an interview with Herr Goethe, the author of *Götz* . . . He is a slender young man of about my height. His colour is pale; his nose big and aquiline; he has a longish face and medium black eyes and black hair. (We meet every day.) His expression is serious, even melancholy, although comic and laughing and satiric moods gleam through. He is very eloquent and produces a very stream of witty notions.

IN 1773.

SOURCE: Letters from G. F. E. Schönborn to H. W. Gerstenberg (two Danish diplomats and scholars); quoted Ludwig Lewisohn, *Goethe: the Story of a Man*, Bodley Head, London, 1949, Vol. I, pp. 87–88.

At last I can tell you something about Goethe. My first look at him was rather destructive of all I had heard about his charm and personal beauty. He is of middle height, holds himself stiffly, and walks stiffly too. He looks reserved, but his eye is very expressive and animated, and one waits eagerly for his kindling glances. Though he looks stern enough, there is something very kind and sweet about his expression.

SOURCE: Friedrich Schiller, in a letter to his friend Körner; quoted Emil Ludwig, *Goethe, The History of a Man*, (trans. Ethel Colburn Mayne), G. P. Putnam's Sons, 1928, Vol. II, p. 4.

He is tall of stature and gives an impression of slimness, because one can see that he has lost *embonpoint*. The colour of his face is dark, almost like night. A certain hardness in his features, which are very alive, almost prevents one recognising any longer the beauty there used to be in his face and still is in his look. Only his eye remains, as of old, a hidden beam of light which shines the moment he smiles, and then the rogue in him peeps out unmistakably as well. His manners are not exactly elegant. To me they seem rather shameless and, for this very

reason, to have a quality amounting almost to a lack of pre-
ciosity. When he wants to be merely polite he lapses into a kind
of affectation which does not suit him, because it is artificial;
but I have seen him glow with warmth and heard the seething of
the riches within, and so I recognise the lion by his claws.

SOURCE: Karl Freidrich Reinhard; quoted Richard Friedenthal,
Goethe: His Life and Times, Weidenfeld & Nicolson, 1965, p. 385.

GOGH, VINCENT WILLEM VAN (1853–1890). See Van Gogh,
Vincent Willem.

GOGOL, NIKOLAI VASILEVICH (1809–1852), Russian novelist
and dramatist.

His fair hair, which fell straight from the temples, as is usual
with Cossacks, still preserved its youthful tint [October 1851]
but had thinned noticeably; his smooth, retreating white forehead conveyed, as before, the impression of great intelligence.
His small brown eyes sparkled with gaiety at times—yes, gaiety
and not sarcasm; but mostly they looked tired. Gogol's long,
pointed nose gave his face a sort of cunning, fox-like expression;
his puffy, soft lips under the clipped moustache also produced
an unfavourable impression; in their indelicate contours—so
at least it seemed to me—the dark sides of his character found
expression. When he spoke, they opened unpleasantly, showing
a row of bad teeth. His small chin disappeared in his wide,
black velvet cravat.

SOURCE: Ivan Turgenev, *Literary Reminiscences and Autobiographical Fragments*, trans. David Magarshack, Faber & Faber, 1959,
p. 141.

GONGORA Y ARGOTE, LUIS DE (1561–1627); Spanish poet.
Gongora described himself for the benefit, he says, of certain
young women who wished to see the author of *Hermana Marica*.
A few verses have been selected from this long and rambling
caricature.

They have told me, sisters,
That you are itching
To see the author
of *Hermana Marica*.

So that you need not bestir yourselves,
He himself sends you
By his own hand
His very person.

In the first place
His lordship is
A good-living
Dullard

Who dines at ten
And sups while it is still light,
Who sleeps luxuriously
And drinks elegantly.

Youthful in years,
Old in misfortune,
Open-browed,
Close-mouthed.

He is not tall in stature
But well able
To reach for you the figs
From any fig-tree.

With the usual kind of head,
Well apportioned,
The nape at the back,
The crown on top.

His forehead,
Wide, clean, and clear,
Although with runnels and little channels
Like a town square.

Arched brows
Like cross bows
From getting money from people
Who sign with their foot.
[*i.e. who refuse to hand their money over.*]

His eyes are large,
His sight keen,
Since he can recognise a cock
Amid a hundred hens.

His nose is hooked
So that it might serve well
As a still
In an apothecary's shop.

:   :   :   :

His beard is neither short
Nor over long,
For thus a saving is made
In shirt-collars.

It was once chestnut brown,
But is now reddish black,
Sorrows will turn it
Silver-grey or grizzled.

His back and shoulders
Are such that
He might well be San Blas
Bearing a thousand holy relics.

As for the rest, ladies
That is covered by the cloak—
Part is visions and
Part wonders.

SOURCE: Gongora's poem *Hanme dicho, hermana*, in *Poesias de Don Luis de Gongora y Argote*, Poesias Espanolas 9, Madrid 1789, pp, 123 et seq.; quoted Clara Louisa Penney, *Luis de Gongora y Argote (1561–1627)*, Hisp. Soc. of America, New York, 1926, pp. 15–16.

GONZAGA, VINCENZO I (1562–1612), Duke of Mantua from 1587.

Vincenzo Duke of Mantua (at this time whereof I write) was a young man, having a red beard, a full visage, a cheerful ruddy complexion like the Germans of whom he descends, and of somewhat a low stature, and mourning then for his dead mother, he was apparelled in black *Freesado*.

IN 1594.

SOURCE: Charles Hughes, edit., *Shakespeare's Europe*, (*Unpublished chapters of Fynes Moryson's Itinerary*), Sherrat & Hughes, 1903, p. 117. For a note on Moryson, see under Bellarmine, Robert.

GRIEG, EDVARD (HAGERUP) (1843–1907), Norwegian composer: contributed to the romantic movement and founded the Norwegian national school.

Into the room came a very little, middle-aged man, very thin and with shoulders of unequal height. His hair was brushed back high and he had a thin, almost youthful-looking beard, and side whiskers . . . He had uncannily attractive blue eyes of medium size, irresistibly fascinating, like the gaze of an innocent, noble child.

SOURCE: Petr Ilich Tschaikowsky; quoted John Horton, *Grieg*, Duckworth, 1950, p. 67.

Grieg is a small, swift, busy man, with the eyes of a rhapsode, and in his hair and complexion the indescribable ashen tint that marks a certain type of Norseman.

SOURCE: Corno di Bassetto (George Bernard Shaw), *London Music in 1888–89*, Constable, 1937, p. 80.

GUDUNOFF, BORIS (1551/2–1605). See Godunov, Boris.

GUICIOLI, TERESA, COUNTESS (1800–1873), married in 1818 to a man three times her age, she later fell in love with the poet, Lord Byron; for four years she was his mistress and enjoyed his prolonged constancy.

One night I was at a ball given by the Austrian Ambassador, and was much struck by a lady quite unlike the Italian women who were there, as she had a profusion of auburn hair, which she wore in wavy and massive curls. Her face was handsome, with a brilliant complexion and blue eyes, and full of animation, showing splendid teeth when she laughed, which she was doing heartily at the time I remarked her. When she rose from her chair I saw she was of small stature, although with perfect shoulders, and a bust made for a much taller woman. It is generally the defect in the figures of Italian woman to have legs too short in proportion to their robust frames, thus sacrificing grace to strength. I was told that this was the Countess Guiccioli, of Byronic memory, and that she was very fond of the English, and courted their acquaintance; so I was introduced to her, and was very kindly received. Byron had been dead only five years, and she was then twenty-six. We became great friends, and I found her a charming companion, with a cultivated mind, yet with all the natural *bonhomie* of her race, and fond of fun. She had got over her grief (which I heard was very violent at first) for the loss of her poet, and she liked to talk of him and his eccentricities, but was very proud of her conquest.

SOURCE: Malmesbury, *Memoirs of an Ex-Minister*, Longmans, Green & Co., 1884, Vol. I, pp. 26–27.

GUSTAVUS II ADOLPHUS (1594–1632), King of Sweden from 1611.

Tall and well proportioned, there was a majesty in his aspect that at once inspired awe and affection. His complexion was fair, his cheeks tinged with ruddy colour, his hair and beard of a yellow tint, his forehead broad, his nose aquiline, his eyes of a brilliant blue, sparkling with energy and intelligence. His self possession never forsook him; never did he lose his vigilance, his quick penetration, his promptitude and decision.

SOURCE: Gualdo-Priorato, *Historia delle Guerre 1630–1639*, Venice, 1640; quoted in Carola Oman, *Elizabeth of Bohemia*, Hodder & Stoughton, 1938, pp. 316–317.

He has often told me . . . that he would give all he had to be master of his passions; but that when he begins to be moved, he hath something rises in his brain that makes him forget what he saith or doth . . .

SOURCE: Sir Henry Vane, English envoy, 1632; quoted P. J. Helm, *History of Europe, 1450–1660*, G. Bell & Sons, 1961, p. 274.

GUSTAVUS IV ADOLPHUS (1778–1837), King of Sweden. He first ruled with his uncle as Regent, then took over the reins of government himself in 1796. He was dethroned in 1809 and died in exile.

10th [September, 1822]—Met the ex-King taking his solitary evening walk in the gardens. He is a man of imposing exterior, with a firm upright military port. His dress, in cut and colour, that of an English gentleman; —blue coat, gilt buttons, fastened close round the gorge; light blue pantaloons; well polished *Hessian* boots; and a cane of considerable weight and dimensions. He observed, with an air of suspicion or scrutiny, every individual that passed . . . He is a man of impetuous temperament; and this, fostered by the proud accessories of family history, renders him a little over sensitive on the point of etiquette, and prone to resent anything that appears to infringe upon his prerogative.

SOURCE: William Beattie, *Journal of a Residence in Germany*, London, 1831, Vol. I, pp. 151–152.

HAHNEMANN, SAMUEL (CHRISTIAN FRIEDRICH) (1755–1843), German physician and founder of 'homoeopathy'.

Hahnemann, at that time, was in his sixty-second year. Locks of silver-white clustered round his high and thoughtful brow, from under which his animated eye shone with piercing brilliancy. His whole countenance had a quiet, searching, grand expression; only rarely did a gleam of fine humour play over the deep earnestness which told of the many sorrows and conflicts endured. His carriage was upright, his step firm, his motions as lively as those of a man of thirty. When he went out, his dress was of the simplest; a dark coat, with short small-clothes and stockings. But in his room at home, he preferred the old household, gaily-figured dressing-gown, the yellow stockings, and the black velvet cap. The long pipe was seldom out of his hand, and this smoking was the only infraction he allowed himself to commit upon his severe rules of regimen. His drink was water, milk, or white beer; his food of the most frugal sort. The whole of his domestic economy was as simple as his dress and food.

SOURCE: Ernest von Brunnow, *A Glance at Hahnemann and Homoeopathy*, trans. J. Norton, London, 1845, p. 19.

HEINE, HEINRICH (1797–1856), German lyric poet and journalist.

A small somewhat wiry figure; fair hair touched with white; a high, imposing forehead; an ironic, good-humoured smile constantly playing around his lips; he—Heine—usually puts his hands behind his back and waddles along like a duck. Thinks he's handsome and secretly peeps into the mirror. He speaks well and likes to hear himself talk; whenever he makes a quip he laughs out loud, and his features, which normally are not particularly oriental, assume a wholly Jewish expression and his eyes, at all times small, practically disappear.

SOURCE: Johann Baptist Rousseau, a friend and fellow student; quoted Max Brod, *Heinrich Heine*, trans. Joseph Witriol, Valentine Mitchell, 1956, p. 86.

He was small and slight in stature, blonde and pale. Although there was nothing outstanding about his features individually, their general cast was distinctive, so that one noticed him immediately and did not forget him again easily. His disposition at that time was essentially mild; he had not yet developed the sarcastic sting which was later to prove the thorn in the rose of his poetry. He was himself more sensitive to raillery than disposed to practise it on others. In those days the wholesome feelings he afterwards ridiculed found a harmonious echo in his soul.

SOURCE: Friederike von Hohenhausen; quoted ibid., p. 95.

His figure was indeed somewhat rotund, but he is definitely not fat. His features, with their small sharp eyes, inspire confidence. Both mien and speech proclaim the poet; a profound, true poet; not one who takes a header into the sea on the chance of picking up a few pearls, but one who dwells at the bottom of ocean's depths with fairies and mermaids and has all their wealth in his command.

SOURCE: Hebbel; quoted ibid., p. 277.

HENRY II (1519–1559), King of France; met his death in a tournament, while fighting a Scottish captain, Montgomery.

His Majesty is in his 29th year and although I formerly described him to your Excellencies as a prince of a pale, livid countenance, and so disposed to melancholy that those about him said that they had never known him to laugh heartily, today I must assure you that he has become gay, that he is ruddy in complexion and in perfect health. He has but a scanty beard, but nevertheless he trims it; his eyes are rather large than otherwise, but he keeps them lowered; his face across the jaws and across the brow lacks breadth; his head is on the small side. His body is well proportioned, tall rather than short. In his person he is full of courage, very bold and enterprising.

SOURCE: Report of the Venetian Ambassador; quoted Francis Watson; *The Life and Times of Cathérine de' Medici*, Hutchinson & Co. 1934, pp. 124–125.

I

HENRY THE NAVIGATOR (1394–1460), Portuguese prince, so called because of the encouragement he gave to voyages of discovery. He was the fourth son of King John I.

He was large of frame and brawny, and stout and strong of limb. His naturally fair complexion had by constant toil and exposure become dark. The expression of his face at first sight inspired fear in those who were not accustomed to him, and when he was angry, which rarely happened, his look was very formidable. Stout of heart and keen in intellect, he was extraordinarily ambitious of achieving great deeds. Neither luxury nor avarice ever found a home with him. In the former respect he was so temperate that after his early youth he abstained from wine altogether, while the whole of his life was reputed to have been passed in inviolate chastity . . . His self-discipline was unsurpassed; all his days were spent in hard work, and it would not readily be believed how often he passed the night without sleep, so that by dint of unflagging industry he conquered what seemed to be impossibilities to other men. His wisdom and thoughtfulness, excellent memory, calm bearing, and courteous language, gave great dignity to his address . . . He was universally beloved for he did good to all and injured none. He never failed to show due respect to every person, however humble, without lowering his own dignity. A foul or indecent word was never known to pass his lips.

SOURCE: Gomes Eannes de Azurara, *Chronica do Descobrimento e Conquiste de Guiné*; quoted R. H. Major, *Prince Henry the Navigator*, A. Asher & Co., 1868, pp. 306–307.

HINDENBURG, PAUL VON (1847–1934), German field-marshal and president.

Hindenburg! The name itself is massive. It harmonises with a tall, thick-set personage with beetling brows, strong features, and heavy jowl . . . It is a face you could magnify tenfold, a hundredfold, a thousandfold, and it would gain in dignity, nay, even in majesty . . . slow-thinking, slow-moving, but sure, steady, faithful, warlike yet benignant, larger than the ordinary run of men.

SOURCE: Winston S. Churchill, *Great Contemporaries*, Thornton Butterworth, 1939, p. 111.

HOHENHEIM, THEOPHRASTUS BOMBASTUS VON (c. 1490–1541). See Paracelsus.

HOLSTEIN, FRIEDRICH VON (1837–1909), German statesman; after Bismarck, the most important personality in the political history of the German Empire.

I was a complete stranger to the Great Unknown. On crossing the threshold of this uncanny master of the deepest secrets I felt like the pupil in *Faust*. Like all who approached him, I knew I was in the presence of a man of outstanding gifts. His masterly manner of conducting the conversation and of clothing his thought in striking language commanded respect for his capacities. A powerful will and a warning 'Take care!' seemed written on his face, with its Roman nose and darkly glittering deep-set eyes.

SOURCE: Otto Hammann, Director of Press Department, Foreign Office; quoted G. P. Gooch, *Studies in Modern History*, Longmans, Green & Co., 1932, p. 29.

Holstein, whom Bismarck called 'the man with the hyaena eyes', had almost lost the use of one eye in a shooting accident, and was sometimes known as 'Polyphemus'.

HUGO, VICTOR MARIE (1802–1885), French novelist and poet.

Now Nodier was not one of those persons from whom the author of a book . . . can remain for long concealed. He discovered that the author of *Han d'Islande* was Victor Hugo. But what was Victor Hugo? Some misanthrope like Timon, some cynic like Diogenes, some weeping philosopher like Demosthenes?

He lifted the veil and found—you know whom—that fair, fresh-faced young man, who was just turned twenty, and had the appearance of sixteen. He recoiled in amazement—it was past believing; in the place where he looked to see the sneering features of the old pessimist, he found the smile—young, ingenuous, and full of life—of the rising poet.

SOURCE: *The Memoirs of Alexandre Dumas (Père)*, selected and trans. A. F. Davidson, W. H. Allen & Co., Calcutta, 1891. Vol. II, p. 273.

But Hugo and I have characters diametrically opposite. He is cold, calm, polite, severe, with a long memory for both good and ill; while I am all on the outside—eager, impulsive, sharp of tongue, forgetful of injuries and sometimes of kindnesses.

SOURCE: ibid., p. 295.

The first thing that struck one in Victor Hugo was his truly monumental forehead, which crowned his placid and serious countenance like a marble facade. It did not actually attain the proportions that David d'Angers and other artists afterwards gave it in order to accentuate the genius of the poet; but it was nevertheless of a superhuman beauty and amplitude; there the vastest thoughts could write themselves; there might be placed crowns of gold and laurel, as on the forehead of a god or of a Caesar. It was a symbol of power. The head was framed with light chestnut hair, allowed to grow rather long. No beard, mustache, side-whiskers, or goatee; a face carefully shaven, and with a particular pallor, hollowed-out and illuminated by a pair of reddish-brown eyes, like the pupils of an eagle; a mouth with sinuous lips, the corners turned down, showing firmness of will, and when he smiled, displaying teeth of shining whiteness. He wore a black frock coat, gray trousers, a small turned down collar—a costume most scrupulous and correct. You could not have suspected this perfect gentleman to be the chief of those long-haired, bearded bands, terror of the smooth-faced bourgeois. The image has remained ineffaceable in memory, a precious portrait, handsome, young, smiling, radiating genius and spreading around an aura of glory.

IN 1830.

SOURCE: Théophile Gautier; quoted Lewis F. Mott, *Sainte-Beuve*, D. Appleton and Co., 1925, pp. 32–33.

IBSEN, HENRIK JOHAN (1828–1906), Norwegian poet and dramatist.

I had been about a quarter of an hour in the room, and was standing close to the door, when it opened, and in glided an undersized man with very broad shoulders and a large leonine head, wearing a long, black frock-coat with very broad lapels, on one of which a knot of red ribbon was conspicuous. I knew him at once, but was a little taken aback by his low stature. In spite of all the famous instances to the contrary, one instinctively associates greatness with size. His natural height was even somewhat diminished by a habit of bending forward slightly from the waist, begotten, no doubt, of short-sightedness and the need to peer into things. He moved very slowly and noiselessly, with his hands behind his back—an unobtrusive personality, which would have been insignificant had the head been strictly proportionate to the rest of the frame. But there was nothing insignificant about the high and massive forehead, crowned with a mane of (then) iron grey hair, the small and pale but piercing eyes behind the gold rimmed spectacles, or the thin-shaped mouth, depressed at the corners into a curve indicative of iron will, and set between bushy whiskers of the same dark grey as the hair. The most cursory observer could not but recognise power and character in the head, yet one would scarcely have guessed it to be the power of a poet, the character of a prophet. Misled, perhaps, by the ribbon at the buttonhole, and by an expression of reserve, almost of secretiveness, in the lines of the tight shut mouth, one would rather have supposed oneself face to face, with an eminent statesman or diplomatist.

SOURCE: William Archer 1881; quoted Edmund Gosse, *Ibsen*, Hodder & Stoughton, 1907, p. 235.

IGNATIUS OF LOYOLA, SAINT (1491–1556). See Loyola, Ignatius.

INNOCENT III (LOTARIO DE' CONTI DI SEGNI) (c. 1160–1216), unanimously elected to the Papacy in 1198, though not even a priest.

Pope Innocent III was a man of keen intellect and tenacious memory, learned in theology and in literature, eloquent with tongue and with pen, skilled in singing and psalmody, of medium height and handsome face, of a character midway between niggardliness and prodigality, very generous in alms-giving and hospitality, but in other respects very close unless there was need of spending. He was stern with rebels and the impenitent, but kind to the lowly and the pious, strong and steadfast, high minded and subtle, a defender of the Faith, a foe to heretics, stiff-necked in justice but Christian in mercy, meek in prosperity, patient in adversity; of a nature somewhat quick-tempered, but also quick to forgive.

SOURCE: a contemporary biographer: quoted H. D. Sedgwick, *Italy in the Thirteenth Century*, Constable & Co., 1913, Vol. I, pp. 13–14.

ISABELLA (1830–1904), Queen of Spain, exiled in 1868.

The young Queen herself... is by no means as beautiful as the Infanta, but is much fairer; her figure also is good, and her neck and arms worthy of a sculptor's study; and she seemed already to have sprung to womanhood. She was robed in white satin, waved with flowers of delicate tints, and wore a diadem of silver richly spangled with diamonds...

AGED 13.

SOURCE: Martin Haverty, *Wanderings in Spain in 1843*, T. C. Newby, London, 1844.

At the period she was a stoutly built, very precocious girl with full cheeks, a snub nose, and thick sensuous lips, incredibly ignorant [she had been deliberately ill-educated], but with a great deal of natural shrewdness; in manner somewhat bluff, jovial and outspoken, partaking of her father's malicious jocosity and her mother's frank fascination. She was good hearted, and generous to the point of prodigality, impulsive and impudent beyond belief, even for so young a girl, and this quality she has never lost. With no steadying sense of responsibility whatever, she had yet a high notion of queenly dignity, and a noble carriage, which frequently invested acts of thoughtless levity with an appearance of magnanimous condescension.

SOURCE: Martin A. S. Hume, *Modern Spain, 1788–1898*, T. Fisher Unwin, 1899.

Her face was flabby and round, her eyes without expression, the figure that was supposed to be august seemed like the traditional and picturesque tambourine, inflated by the aerostatic crinoline, the queen grasping the sceptre with a sensuous caress.

IN 1847.

SOURCE: *La Flaca*, a humorous paper.

The queen . . . was still in her carriage dress—a silk gown, I think, with a black lace mantilla. She received us most generously. I was struck by the sweetness of her smile, and the beauty of her expression. Without being handsome, she is certainly a fine looking woman, and though very large for her age, yet being tall and with a very regal port, carried it off well.

1853–1854.

SOURCE: *The Attaché in Madrid, or, Sketches of the Court of Isabella II*, published anonymously, but apparently written by a member of a legation from a minor German Court.

All the above quotations are included in Peter de Polnay, *A Queen of Spain*, Hollis & Carter, 1962, pp. 77–78, 121, 152.

IVAN IV, called 'The Terrible' (1530–1584), Tsar of Muscovy.

. . . there sat a very honourable company of courtiers, to the number of one hundred, all apparelled in cloth of gold, down to their ankles: and being conducted into the chamber of presence, our men began to wonder at the Majesty of the Emperor; his seat was aloft, in a very royal throne, having on his head a Diadem, or Crown of gold, apparelled with a robe of all goldsmith's work, and in his hand he held a sceptre garnished and beset with precious stones: and besides all the notes and appearances of honour, there was a Majesty in his countenance proportionable with the excellency of his estate. On the one side of him stood his chief secretary, and on the other the great Commander of silence, both of them arrayed also in cloth of gold. And there sat the Council of one hundred and fifty in number, all in like sort arrayed and of great state . . .

This so honourable assembly, so great a Majesty of the Emperor, and of the palace, might well have amazed our men and dazzled them out of countenance, but Master Chancellor, nothing dismayed, saluted and did his duty to the Emperor after the manner of England, and delivered unto him the letters of our King, Edward the Sixth.

SOURCE: Richard Hakluyt, *The principal Navigations, Voyages, and Discoveries made by the English Nation*, 1589; quoted Stephen Graham, *Ivan the Terrible*, Ernest Benn, 1932, p. 117.

JEANNETTE, a woman prisoner-of-war, taken by the British at Trafalgar, October 21st, 1805.

Towards the conclusion of the battle the French 80-gun ship *Achille*, after surrendering, caught fire . . . The poor fellows belonging to her, as the only chance of saving their lives, leaped overboard, having first stripped off their clothes, that they might be the better able to swim to any pieces of floating wreck or to the boats of the ships sent by those nearest at hand to their rescue . . . The *Revenge*, to which ship I belonged, received nearly a hundred of the number, some of whom had been picked up by our own boats . . . On the morning after the action I had charge of the deck . . . when another boat load of these poor prisoners of war came alongside, all of whom, with one exception, were in the costume of Adam.

The exception I refer to was apparently a youth, but clothed in an old jacket and trousers, with a dingy handkerchief tied round the head, and exhibiting a face begrimed with smoke and dirt, without shoes, stockings, or shirt, and looking the picture of misery and despair. The appearance of this young person at once attracted my attention and on asking some questions on the subject I was answered that the prisoner was a woman. It was sufficient to know this, and I lost no time in introducing her to my messmates, as a female requiring their compassionate attention . . . I then gave her up my cabin, for by this time the bulk-head had been replaced, and made a collection of all the articles which could be procured to enable her to complete a more suitable wardrobe. One of the lieutenants gave her a piece of sprigged blue muslin, which he had obtained from a Spanish prize, and two new checked shirts were supplied by the purser; these, with a purser's blanket, and my ditty bag, which contained needles, thread, etc., being placed at her disposal, she, in a short time, appeared in a very different, and much more becoming, costume. Being a dress-maker, she had made herself a sort of jacket, after the Flemish fashion, and the purser's shirts she had transformed into an outer petticoat; she had a silk handkerchief tastily tied over her head, and another was thrown round her shoulders; white stockings, and a pair of the chaplain's shoes were on her feet and, altogether, our guest, which we unanimously voted her, appeared a very interesting young woman. Jeannette, which was the only name by which I ever knew her . . . said she was stationed during the action in the passage of the fire-magazine, to assist in handing up the powder, which employment lasted till the surrender of the ship.

SOURCE: a letter written by Captain Moorsom of the *Revenge* to his son; quoted in Edward Fraser, *The Enemy at Trafalgar*, Hodder & Stoughton, 1906, pp. 221–225. Jeannette was the wife of a maintopman on the *Achille*. The only thing to mar the chivalrous hospitality of the British sailors was the fact that she had no idea of the fate of her husband. But there was a perfect story-book ending when, on the fourth day, Jeannette found her husband, hale and hearty, among the rest of the prisoners. They were landed at Gibraltar, with a handsome gift of money from the *Revenge*.

JEANNE D'ARC (JOAN OF ARC) (1412–1431), French heroine of the Hundred Years' War.

I saw her mount, all in white armour but unhelmeted, a small steel sperth [little battle-axe] in her hand. She had a great black horse, which plunged at the door of her house, and would not permit her to mount. 'Lead him to the Cross!' she cried; it stands in the road in front of the church. There he stood as fast as if he were bound with cords, and she mounted and, turning towards the church gate, she said in a sweet womanly voice, 'Ye Priests and churchmen, go in processions and pray to God!' Then 'Forward! forward!' she cried, a gracious page bearing her standard displayed, and she with a little sperth in her hand.

SOURCE: Guy de Laval, in a letter to his mother, June 8th, 1429; quoted Andrew Lang, *The Maid of France*, Longmans Green & Co., 1929, p. 134.

Joan of Arc's standard was white, fringed with silk, with a representation of the world supported by two angels, the portrait of Our Lord, and the words *Jhesus Maria*. This standard, which she carried into battle, Joan said she loved forty times better than her sword, because she wanted to avoid killing anyone, and the standard kept her hands otherwise employed.

A beautiful and well-formed girl . . .

SOURCE: Jean d'Aulon, head of her military household.

. . . of satisfying grace.

SOURCE: Perceval de Boulainvilliers. Both quoted, Johan Huizinga, *Men and Ideas*, trans. J. S. Holmes and Hans van Marle, Eyre & Spottiswoode, 1960, p. 217.

(Contrary to the generally accepted picture of Joan, she was dark-haired. This is stated in a contemporary chronicle and 'is perhaps confirmed by a black hair embedded, apparently intentionally, in the seal of Joan's letter to the town of Riom' (Huizinga).)

JEROME, SAINT (HIERONYMUS, in full EUSEBIUS SO-PHRONIUS HIERONYMUS) (c. 340–420), born at Stridon (modern Stridova) on the borders of Dalmatia; the great Christian scholar of his age.

The few hairs left on my bald head are white, but I still sometimes find myself in my dreams, with a curly mop and in an elegant toga, making an imaginary speech for the defence before the rhetoric master. I wake up overjoyed to be free from this oratorical imposition.

SOURCE: Jerome, *Apology against Rufinius*, I, 30. Jerome refers to the public speaking examinations he had to undergo at the age of about eighteen.

How many times in my days in the desert, in the endless solitude scorched by the pitiless sun, in that horrible habitation of the monks [underground caves near Qinnesrin, a village to the south of Aleppo], have I not dreamed I was back amid the delights of Rome! I sat alone and overwhelmed with melancholy. My unshapely limbs were clothed in a sack. My skin was so dirty that it looked like a negro's. I was forever weeping, forever groaning. And when sleep overcame me in spite of myself, I felt as if my dislocated bones were being broken against the bare ground ... My face was pale with much fasting, but my fancy kept my icy body ablaze with desire, and the flames of lust were crackling in a man who was all but dead ... I remember I went on shouting without stopping all day and all night. I beat my breast endlessly.

ABOUT 375.

SOURCE: Jerome, *Letter XXII*.

Both the above descriptions are included in Jean Steinmann, *Saint Jerome*, trans. Ronald Matthews, Geoffrey Chapman, 1959, pp. 15 and 53–54. Jerome has been described as 'one of the few Fathers to whom the title of Saint appears to have been given in recognition of services rendered to the Church rather than for eminent sanctity'.

JIMÉNEZ DE CISNEROS, FRANCISCO (1436–1517). See Ximenes de Cisneros, Francisco.

JOHN VII PALAEOLOGUS (1390–1448), Greek Emperor of Constantinople from 1425.

During this ceremony the Emperor occupied the place where the Epistle is read by the high altar, in which same place, as I have already said, were all the Greek prelates. All Florence was there to witness this noble function. Opposite to the Pope's seat, on the other side, was a chair covered with a silken cloth on which sat the Emperor, clad in a rich robe of damask brocade and a cap in the Greek fashion, on the top of which was a magnificent jewel. He was a very handsome man with a beard of the Greek cut. Round about his chair were posted the many gentlemen of his retinue, clad in the richest silken robes made in Greek fashion.

AT THE COUNCIL OF FLORENCE IN 1431.

SOURCE: Vespasiano da Bisticci. *The Vespasiano Memoirs*, trans. William George and Emily Waters, George Routledge & Sons, 1926, p. 25. For a note on Vespasiano da Bisticci, see under D'Arezzo, Lionardo.

JOAN OF ARC (1412–1431). See Jeanne d'Arc.

JOHN OF THE CROSS, SAINT (1542–1591), Spanish mystic.

He was a man in body of medium size, of grave and venerable countenance, somewhat swarthy and of good features; his bearing and conversation were peaceful, very spiritual and full of profit for those who listened and talked with him . . . He had a deep knowledge and experience of prayer and contact with God, and to all the questions that were put to him on these points he replied with the deepest wisdom, leaving those who consulted him very satisfied and full of profit. He was fond of recollection and of little speaking; his laughter was rare and very controlled. When as Superior he rebuked, which was often, it was with sweet severity, exhorting with fatherly love and with admirable serenity and gravity.

SOURCE: P. Eliseo de los Mártires, who was with John when he was Rector in Baeza, *Dictámenes del espíritu*, Introd.; quoted Crisógono de Jesús, *The Life of Saint John of the Cross*, trans. Kathleen Pond, Longmans Green & Co. Ltd., 1958, p. 306.

Saint Theresa wrote to King Philip II: 'And this friar [Saint John] so great a servant of God, is so thin from the much he has suffered that I fear for his life.'

JOSEPH II (1741–1790), Emperor of Austria.

Joseph the Second is rather above than below the middle size, and in no degree inclined to corpulency. Though not handsome, he may be accounted agreeable in his person, and when young, he must have been elegant . . . The countess of Pergen, who was a spectatress of his coronation at Frankfort in 1764, has declared to me, that he appeared to her the most majestic and striking object on which she ever looked, when he was invested with the royal robes and Insignia; his thick hair falling down over his back in ringlets. He had then a head of hair such as is ascribed to Apollo by the Poets. So bald is he now become at thirty-eight, that on the crown of his head, scarcely any covering remains; and in order to conceal the defect, he wears a false toupée. His queue is very thin, but it is his own, and not an artificial one, like that of the Great Frederick [i.e. Frederick II of Prussia, q.v.]. The Emperor's countenance is full of meaning and intelligence. I have rarely seen a more speaking physiognomy; and it is impossible to look at him, without conceiving a favourable idea of his understanding. His eye, which is quick, sparkles with animation. The contour of his face is long and thin, his complexion fair, his nose aquiline, his teeth white, even and good. An air of mind, spread over his features, pleases and prejudices in his favour. The formation of his body and legs is by no means without defect, though he is capable of severe exercise, and of sustaining great fatigue. Nor can his state of health be accounted such, as to afford a reasonable prospect of attaining to very advanced age. Besides [an] aneurism in his leg ... he has another extraordinary source of disease; it is an excrescence, of the nature of a wen, on the crown of his head, which naturally increases in size, and may become dangerous in process of time.

SOURCE: N. W. Wraxall, *Memoirs of the Courts of Berlin, Dresden, Warsaw and Vienna*, London, 1799, Volume II, pp. 414–416.

JOSEPH I (1714–1777), King of Portugal from 1750.

The King, though only third in order of descent, was fourth in succession from the Duke of Braganza, denominated John the Fourth, who in 1640 recovered Portugal from the Spanish dominion; and at the time of which I speak, he had passed his fifty-seventh year. He was of good stature, but inclined to corpulency: his features regular, his eye quick and lively, if a habit of holding his mouth somewhat open, had not diminished the expression of intelligence, which his countenance would otherwise have conveyed. In his cheeks he had a high scorbutic humour, attributed commonly to excesses of wine; though it might arise from violent exercise constantly taken under a burning sun. His face, indeed, was nearly as dusky as that of a Moor; and at Fez or Mequinez, habited in the Turkish dress, he might easily have passed for Muley Ismael, the sovereign of Morocco. Never had any Lusitanian peasant coarser or darker hands.

SOURCE: Sir. N. William Wraxall, *Historical Memoirs of My Own Time*, 1815, Vol. I, pp. 10–11.

JOSEPHINE (MARIE ROSE JOSEPHINE TASCHER DE LA PAGERIE) (1763–1814), Empress of the French; first wife of the Emperor Napoleon I.

She has a very good skin, good eyes, good arms, and a surprising taste for music. I gave her a teacher for the guitar while she was at the convent, and she made full use of this and has a very pretty voice ... She is, moreover, very advanced for her years and during the past five or six months has grown to look at least eighteen.

SOURCE: Two letters from her father, M. Tascher.

Her even temper, the gentleness of her disposition, the kindness which animated her looks and was expressed not merely in her language, but in the very tone of her voice; her natural Creole indolence, which showed itself in her attitude as well as in her movements, and which she did not entirely lose when exerting herself to render service—all this gave her a charm which counterbalanced the vivid beauty of her two rivals [Mme. Tallien and Mme. Récamier]. Although she had less brilliance and freshness than the other two, still, thanks to her regular features, her elegant suppleness of figure, and the sweet expression of her countenance, she was beautiful also.

IN 1796.

SOURCE: Amault, *Souvenirs d'un Sexagénaire.*

She was still charming at this epoch [May 1796] ... Her teeth were frightfully bad; but when her mouth was shut she had the appearance, especially at a few paces' distance, of a young and pretty woman.

SOURCE: Duchesse d'Abrantès, *Mémoires*, ii, 51.

Mme. Bonaparte is no longer pretty; she is nearly forty, and quite looks it.

SOURCE: Stanislas Girardin's Journal.

Mme. Bonaparte was announced, and she entered, conducted by M. de Talleyrand. She wore a white muslin dress with short sleeves and a pearl necklace, and her hair was braided simply and confined by a tortoiseshell comb. The murmur of admiration which greeted her entrance must have been exceedingly gratifying to her. I think she never looked more graceful or elegant.

SOURCE: Napoleon's valet, Constant, *Memoirs*, Feb. 21, 1800.

In this fresh and resplendent toilette [a low-cut pink tulle robe, sown with silver stars] her elegant deportment, her charming smile, and the sweetness of her glance produced such an effect that I heard a number of people who were present at the ceremony declare that she eclipsed all the assembly which surrounded her.

SOURCE: Madame de Rémusat.

The above descriptions are all included in Philip W. Sergeant, *The Empress Josephine, Napoleon's Enchantress*, Hutchinson & Co., 1908, 2 vols., pp. 36, 39, 165, 166, 208, 268, 377.

JOUBERT, BARTHÉLEMY CATHERINE (1769–1799), Napoleon I's General.

He was tall and thin, and seemed naturally of a weak constitution; but he had strengthened his frame amidst fatigues, camps and mountain warfare. He was intrepid, vigilant and active.

SOURCE: Napoleon I, *Memoirs*, edit. Somerset de Chair, Faber & Faber, 1948, p. 146.

JULIAN THE APOSTATE (FLAVIUS CLAUDIUS JULIANUS) (c. 331–363), Roman Emperor 361–363; nephew of Constantine the Great, founder of Constantinople; he attempted to reintroduce paganism to this Christian city.

A portrait of him in Athens, where he had been sent to complete his studies, shortly before he became Emperor:

What a curse is the Empire nurturing!... The unsteadiness of his behaviour and the exaggeration of his enthusiasm made me a prophet. It seemed to me no good sign that his neck was not firm; that he was often shrugging his shoulders up and down like a pair of scales; that his glances were shy and wandering; that he rolled his eyes like those of a maniac; and that he did not stand firmly and quietly on his feet. I as little liked his nose,

which breathed of pride and contempt; the laughable dis-
tortions of his face, which witnessed to the same pride; his
inordinate and gusty bursts of laughter; his nods and head-
shakings with no reason for them; his hesitating and convulsive
way of speaking; his sudden and senseless questions, and no
better answers, which often contradicted each other, and made
their appearance without any scientific order.

SOURCE: St. Gregory of Nazianus, *Orat. v.* 23, 24; quoted
Frederick W. Farrer, *Lives of the Fathers*, Adam & Charles Black,
1907, Vol. 1, p. 678.

He was of an unsteady disposition, but this fault he corrected
by an excellent plan, allowing people to set him right when
guilty of indiscretion.

He was a frequent talker, rarely silent . . . As to his personal
appearance, it was this. He was of moderate stature, with soft
hair, as if he had carefully dressed it, with a rough beard ending
in a point, with beautiful brilliant eyes, which displayed the
subtlety of his mind, with handsome eyebrows and a straight
nose, a rather large mouth, with a drooping lower lip, a thick
and stooping neck, large and broad shoulders. From head to
foot he was straight and well proportioned, which made him
strong and a good runner.

SOURCE: Ammianus Marcellinus, a contemporary admirer; in
The Roman History of Ammianus Marcellinus, trans. C. D. Yonge,
Henry G. Bohn, 1862, pp. 386–387.

JULIUS II (GIULIANO DELLA ROVERE) (1443–1513), Pope
from 1503.

Our Pope has nothing of the Pontiff but the dress and the name
. . . The vicar of Christ against a Christian town, a thing till
now unknown. He was old and infirm, and was engaged on a
war he himself had stirred up against Christian princes, yet he
was so fiery and impetuous that nothing went quickly enough
for his taste. He stormed at his captains in a perpetual rage; he
slept so close to the firing-line that two of his cooks were killed,

K

and this in spite of the protests of his cardinals at his scandalous conduct.

SOURCE: Francesco Guicciardini, *Storia d'Italia*, published 1561; quoted in F. Funck-Brentano, *The Renaissance*, Geoffrey Bles, 1936, pp. 225–226.

KAUFFMANN (MARIA ANNA), ANGELICA (1741–1807), Swiss artist and Royal Academician; born at Croire in the Grison and spent much of her life in England; retired to Rome where she died.

She has a peculiar and most womanly dignity which inspires the utmost respect. She is about twenty-seven, by no means a beauty, nevertheless *extremely* attractive. The character of her face belongs to the type Domenichino loved to paint; the features are noble, the expression sweet; it would be impossible to pass such a face without looking at it, and having looked, you must admire, and there are moments when she is absolutely beautiful; thus, when she is seated at her harmonia, singing Pergolesi's *Stabat Mater*, her large expressive eyes are piously raised to Heaven, her inspired look helps the expression of the divine words. At this moment she is a living Saint Cecilia.

IN 1768.

SOURCE: Count Bernsdorff, the Danish Prime Minister; quoted Adeline Hartcup, *Angelica*, William Heinemann Ltd., 1954, p. 59.

KAUNITZ-RIETBURG, WENZEL ANTON, PRINCE VON (1711–1794), Austrian Chancellor and diplomatist.

After dinner the Prince treated us with the cleaning of his gums—one of the most nauseous operations I ever witnessed, and it lasted a prodigious long time, accompanied with all manner of noises. He carries a hundred instruments in his pocket for this purpose—such as glasses of all sorts for seeing before and behind his teeth, a whetting stone for his knife, pincers to hold the steel with, knives and scissors without number, and cottons and lawns for wiping his eyes . . . By-the-bye, he is dressed very oddly; his wig comes down upon his nose, with a couple of small, straggling curls on each side, placed in a very ridiculous manner. He is extremely fond of adulation, and will swallow anything in its shape, and, indeed, lays it upon himself with a very liberal hand.

SOURCE: Henry Swinburne, *The Courts of Europe at the Close of the Last Century*, H. S. Nichols and Co., 1895, Vol. I, pp. 331–432.

KEPLER, JOHANN (1571–1630), German astronomer; originator of Kepler's Laws.

He hath a little black Tent which he can suddenly set up where he will in a Field; and it is convertible (like a windmill) to all quarters at pleasure; capable of not much more than one man, as I conceive, and perhaps at no great ease; exactly close and dark—save at one hole, about an inch and a half in the diameter to which he applies a long perspective Trunk, with the convex glass fitted to the said hole, and the concave taken out at the other end . . .

SOURCE: Sir Henry Wotton, Ambassador to the King of Bohemia; quoted H. W. Turnbull, *The Great Mathematicians*, Methuen & Co., 1929 (fourth edition, 1951). As Carlyle comments in *Frederick the Great* (Book III, Chapter XIV), 'An ingenious person, truly, if ever there was one among Adam's posterity. Just turned fifty, and ill-off for cash. This glimpse of him, in his little black tent with perspective glasses, while the Thirty Years' War blazes out, is welcome as a date.'

I cannot marvel sufficiently that such a mass of solid learning, so many treasures of knowledge about the most profound secrets, can be locked and concealed in such a small body.

SOURCE: a foreign visitor; quoted Max Caspar, *Kepler*, trans. and edit. C. Doris Hellman, Abelard-Schuman, 1959, p. 369.

If you are not more corpulent and of more powerful appearance than I, you will never become a burgomaster.

SOURCE: Kepler, to a stranger who had asked him for a horoscope; quoted ibid.

KOSSUTH, LAJOS (LOUIS) (1802–1894), Hungarian politician and popular leader.

Age—45 years. [Much confusion exists as to the exact date of Kossuth's birth.]
Place of Birth—Jascperin, in Hungary.
Condition—Married.
Religion—Catholic.
Language—German, Hungarian, Latin, Slovac and French.
A Barrister and a Public Writer; of late, President of the Hungarian Committee of Defence.
Size—Middle and Spare.
Face—Round and Full.
Complexion—Brown.
Forehead—High and Open.
Hair—Black.
Eyes—Blue and protruding.
Eyebrows—Large and Black.
Nose—A little flattened.
Mouth—Small and neatly formed.
Teeth—Full in numbers.
Chin—Round.
Black Whiskers and moustachios.
Other distinguishing marks—his hair has a natural curl and begins to get thin on the top of the head; his behaviour is flattering and insinuating; it is not possible to state his dress, but he prefers caps to hats.

SOURCE: *The Hue and Cry*, 1849; quoted *Louis Kossuth, and The Last Revolutions in Hungary and Transylvania*, London, 1850, pp. 18–19.

The day after my arrival, I accompanied General Guyon to an interview with Kossuth. We found the Governor of Hungary residing in apartments scarcely better provided with furniture than our own, which he shared with Count Dembinski, his aide-de-camp, his young and beautiful wife, and another friend. Kossuth received me with his wonted suavity of manner; and at once commenced an animated conversation in English,

which he speaks fluently, and without any perceptible pecu-
liarity of accent . . .

Kossuth had by this time shaved off the handsome beard
by which he is distinguished in the portraits; and misfortune
had given an interesting tinge of melancholy to his striking
countenance, which harmonized with the soft melody of his
voice.

SOURCE: Charles Pridham, *Kossuth and Magyarland, or Personal
Adventures during the War in Hungary*, London, 1851, pp. 157–158.

KUBILAI KHAN (1216–1294), founder of the Mongol dynasty
in China; nominal sovereign of a greater population than had
ever acknowledged one man's supremacy.

Let me tell you next of the personal appearance of the Great
Lord of Lords whose name is Kubilai Khan. He is a man of
good stature, neither short nor tall, but of moderate height.
His limbs are well fleshed out and modelled in due proportion.
His complexion is fair and ruddy like a rose, the eyes black and
handsome, the nose shapely and set squarely in place.

SOURCE: Marco Polo, *Travels*, trans. Ronald Latham, Penguin
Books, 1958, p. 92.

LA FONTAINE, JEAN DE (1621–1695), French poet and author;
well known for his *Fables*.

He was like a plain vase without external adornment, which
contains infinite treasures within. He neglected his personal
appearance, always dressed very simply, his features and expression seemed slightly coarse; but when one looked at him
attentively one read humour in his eye and a certain vivacity
which even age could not extinguish, and this made it evident
that he had more in him than appeared on the surface.

It was true also that with people he did not know or who did not please him, he was grave and dreamy, and even in beginning a conversation with people he liked he was sometimes cold; but directly the conversation began to interest him, and he took part in the argument, he was no longer a dreamer, but a man who spoke much and well, who quoted the ancients and gave fresh charm to them. He was a philosopher, but a gay philosopher—in a word, he was La Fontaine, and La Fontaine as he is in his works.

SOURCE: M*** [probably the Marquis de Sablé] in the preface to La Fontaine's *Posthumous Works*, edit. Ullrich; quoted Frank Hamel, *Jean de la Fontaine*. Stanley Paul & Co., 1911, pp. 359–360.

LALANDE, JOSEPH JÉRÔME LEFRANÇAIS DE (1732–1807), French astronomer.

The elder Lalande, the celebrated Professor of Astronomy, and one of the most extraordinary men of his age, was among the first of the distinguished *savans* with whom it was my good fortune to become acquainted ... Lalande was below the middle size, and exhibited one of the ugliest faces that I have ever seen. He was, however, not a little vain of his person, and extremely fond of narrating the conquests which he had achieved, in his youth, over the hearts of half the Princesses of Europe ... His manners were exceedingly engaging, and his conversation was enlivened by brilliant sallies ...

SOURCE: *Travels of an American*, in *La Belle Assemblée*, March, 1810.

LAUZUN, ANTONIN NOMPAR DE CAUMONT, DUC DE (1632–1723), formerly the Marquis de Puyguilhem; French courtier and soldier; favourite of Louis XIV and lover (possibly husband) of the Duchess of Montpensier, the *Grande Mademoiselle*.

He was little, thin, very well made and proportioned, with the most beautifully shaped leg in the world, even till his extreme old age. He had a blotched face rather like that of a skinned cat, beautiful eyes, and a keen, daring, haughty physiognomy, with a smile which showed depth and falsity . . . those who saw him in his youth declare that he was never better-looking than he has been since his return to Court, and that, besides, he used to have tow-coloured hair, which has been since hidden by a fair wig.

SOURCE: Saint-Simon, *Ecrits inédits*, Vol. vii, p. 308.

He is a little man; nobody can deny that he has the straightest, most elegant and finest figure imaginable. His legs are beautifully shaped; he does everything with grace. He has fair hair—there is not much of it and it is becoming grizzled, it is badly combed, and often greasy; beautiful blue eyes, though they are nearly always bloodshot; a keen expression and graceful air. His smile pleases. The end of the nose is pointed, and red; there is something superior in his physiognomy; he is very careless about his appearance; but when it pleases him to be so, extremely well turned out. Such is the man. As to his moods and his disposition, I defy any one to understand them, to describe or to copy them.

SOURCE: his mistress, the *Grande Mademoiselle*, in Chéruel, *Montpensier Mémoires*, Vol. IV, p. 249.

Both the above quotations are included in Mary F. Sandars, *Lauzun, Courtier and Adventurer*, Hutchinson & Co., 1908, Vol. I, pp. 252–254.

LE BOUTHILLIER DE RANCÉ, ARMAND JEAN (1626–1700). See Rancé, Armand Jean le Bouthillier de.

LEMAÎTRE, FRÉDÉRICK (1800–1876), French actor (his real name was Antoine Louis Prosper Lemaître); He collaborated with Balzac, Hugo and others in several of their works.

He was now just a physical wreck. The striking mask, once so handsome and so often discomposed by the mimicry of every passion, would collapse when he was tired into a sour grimace of fatigue and disgust. The famous Louis-Philippe toupet now crowned a forehead slashed by deep wrinkles. The eyes had not lost their brightness, but they were bloodshot and watery, and half-covered by heavy lids. Under the chin, which still stuck out proudly, there hung an old man's dewlap; and from the mouth, which was turned down at the corners and encumbered with false teeth, the voice emerged only with difficulty, sounding faint and distant.

But as soon as the play got under way and came to some violent situation, Frédérick underwent a transfiguration. He made a sudden effort, an effort of genius, and gave himself up entirely to the pathetic situation expressed by the author in nondescript phrases; he lived and felt his part with all his thoughts, his nerves, his heart. Aged and exhausted by a life of disorder and excess, he regained the strength and agility of youth. He sprang about, filling the stage with his ample, supple gestures and his giant strides. They were real tears that he shed, and the flame of passion burned in his eyes. His face flushed with genuine anger, went pale with real terror, softened with sincere pity. His voice, so faint to begin with, burst forth in cries, groans and sobs. This was truth itself, since it was life, but truth as it should be revealed to the people, that is to say magnified by art, poetic, poignant and grandiose!

ABOUT 1870

SOURCE: François Coppée; quoted Robert Baldick, *The Life and Times of Frédérick Lemaître*, Hamish Hamilton, 1959, pp. 225–226.

LEO XIII (VINCENZO GIOACCHINO PECCI) (1810–1903)
Pope from 1878.

The Pope had a preconceived idea of how he desired his portrait to appear. He squared himself in his seat, uplifted his hand, extending two fingers as in the act of benediction, a conventional smile drawing back his colourless lips. His Holiness sat thus, stiff and motionless, for a moment, then abandoned the attitude as quickly as he had assumed it . . .

It was, however, exactly how I had determined *not* to represent Leo XIII. In painting this remarkable man one must, as it were, paint the mind and soul, which appeared to shine through the frail, almost diaphanous flesh they had subdued. Intellectual, ascetic, with broad, noble forehead (the thin skin showing a tracery of blue veins), with massive features, eyes set deep and close together, of startling brilliancy, in a countenance pallid and composed as that of a corpse, it was thus Leo XIII. appeared to me, a dominant and imposing personality whether, as then, arrayed in simple soltana of white wool and plain calotta (skullcap), or, as I afterwards painted him, in splendid pontifical robes and priceless gems.

Leo XIII. was then seventy-five years of age and at the height of his mental activity. Extraordinarily rapid in all his movements, he spoke incessantly, and so quickly, it was difficult to follow the train of his thought.

SOURCE: H. J. Thaddeus, *Recollections of a Court Painter*, The Bodley Head, 1912, pp. 128, 129.

Leo XIII appeared to me most impressive. His tall, slight, elegant figure, clothed entirely in white, stood out with natural majesty against the simple and solemn framework of his oratory, in which a rather ornate altar was the most conspicuous object ... As soon as the Holy Father was seated, I sat down and the conversation began. The Pope spoke sometimes in French, sometimes in Italian, but always rapidly and in a sonorous voice. He often remained motionless, but at certain moments he would half rise from his chair, in an impetuous way, when he felt anything deeply—and all this added to the impression he made on me ...

During the long hour I spent with him, I noticed that his clear, melancholy eyes were presently fixed with painful intensity on the city of Rome, on the high hills that surround it, on the Quirinal, which faces the Vatican, on that splendid landscape which he could only partially see through the bars which he had voluntarily forged to his prison.

SOURCE: Henri Stephan de Blowitz, *My Memoirs*, Edward Arnold, 1913, pp. 247–248.

LÉON, LUIS PONCE DE (1527–1591), Spanish poet and mystic.

In appearance he was small in stature, well proportioned, with a large well-shaped head covered with rather curly hair which grew thickly on the crown. His brow was broad, his face rounded rather than aquiline . . . ; his complexion was darkish, his eyes green and lively.

So far as his behaviour was concerned he was particularly endowed with the gift of silence; he was the most reserved man there ever was—but at the same time remarkably shrewd in his remarks; extremely moderate and abstemious in eating, drinking and sleeping. Very trustworthy, truthful and reliable —punctilious in keeping his word and fulfilling promises— and not given much to smiling. The gravity of his countenance reflected the firm nobility of his soul; above all there radiated from him a deep humility. He was clean living, chaste and retiring by nature—a pious monk observing the holy laws . . . by nature quick tempered, he was very patient and gentle with all those with whom he had dealings. He was so strict and penitent with himself that most nights he did not go to bed—and the one who had made it up found it next morning exactly as it was (according to Pattre Maestro Fray Luis Moreno de Bohorquez, a credit to his Order, who spent four years in his company).

SOURCE: Francisco Pachecho, *Libro de Descripcion de Verdaderos Retratos de illustres y memorables varones*, Sevilla, 1599; quoted James Fitzmaurice Kelly, *Fray Luis de Leon*, Oxford University Press, 1921, pp. 79, 181–182, 239–240. Pachecho was a painter who may easily in his youth have met Leon and certainly knew many who had seen him.

LEONARDO DA VINCI (1452–1519), Italian painter, sculptor, poet and inventor.

It was the most beautiful face in the world . . .

SOURCE: Paolo Giovvio (a contemporary historian); quoted Antonina Vallentin, *Leonardo da Vinci*, trans. E. W. Dickes, W. H. Allen, 1952, p. 31.

Vasari, who was not a strict contemporary of Leonardo, but who must have known many people who had seen him, records:

In him, to say nothing of the beauty of his person, which yet was such that it has never been sufficiently extolled, there was a grace beyond expression which was rendered manifest without thought or effort in every act and deed ... The radiance of his countenance, which was splendidly beautiful, brought cheerfulness to the heart of the most melancholy, and the power of his word could move the most obstinate to say, 'No', or 'Yes', as he desired; he possessed so great a degree of physical strength that he was capable of restraining the most impetuous violence, and was able to bend one of the iron rings used for the knockers of doors, or a horse-shoe, as if it were lead.

SOURCE: Giorgio Vasari, *Lives of the Most Eminent Painters, Sculptors and Architects*, trans. Mrs. Jonathan Foster, Henry G. Bohn, 1851, Vol. II, pp. 366, 390.

LEOPARDI, GIACOMO (1798–1837), 'Philologist admired even outside Italy, most sublime Philosopher and Poet', according to the inscription on his tomb.

My face, when I was a little boy, had a slightly wistful and serious look which, being without any affectation of melancholy, gave it charm, as I see from a portrait of me at that time. This expression, with simple, natural, unaffected manner, made me much-loved by the ladies who knew me at that age.

SOURCE: Leopardi's description of himself as a boy; quoted Iris Origo, *Leopardi, a Biography*, Oxford University Press, 1935, p. 25.

LESZCINSKA, MARIE CATHERINE-SOPHIE FÉLICITÉ (1703–1768). See Marie Leszcinska.

LE TELLIER, MICHEL (1643–1719), Jesuit; confessor to Louis XIV.

The Père Tellier, in fact, was chosen as successor of Père La Chaise, and a terrible successor he made. Harsh, exact, laborious, enemy of all dissipation, of all amusement, of all society, incapable of associating even with his colleagues, he demanded no leniency for himself and accorded none to others. His brain and his health were of iron; his conduct was so also; his nature was savage and cruel . . . His exterior kept faith with his interior. He would have been terrible to meet in a dark lane. His physiognomy was cloudy, false, terrible; his eyes were burning, evil, extremely squinting; his aspect struck all with dismay.

SOURCE: *Memoirs of the Duke of Saint-Simon*, trans. Bayle St. John, Allen & Unwin, 1913, Vol. II, pp. 78–79.

LINNAEUS, CAROLUS (CARL VON LINNÉ) (1707–1778), Swedish botanist.

Carl von Linné was of small stature, and as he had a slight stoop, he appeared even smaller than he really was. He was otherwise powerfully built, but lean, and when I knew him his advancing age had already furrowed his brow with wrinkles. His face was ingenious, nearly always gay . . . His eyes were the most beautiful I have ever seen. They were anything but large, it is true, but they had a lustre and a penetrating quality that I have never seen in anyone else.

SOURCE: J. C. Fabricius; quoted Knut Hagberg, *Carl Linnaeus*, trans. Alan Blair, Jonathan Cape, 1952, pp. 241–242.

I went . . . into a bookshop and found there a man somewhat up in years, not very tall, with dusty shoes and hose, a very unshaven chin, and an old green coat on which a decoration was hanging. I was not a little amazed when I was told that this was the renowned Linnaeus.

SOURCE: quoted ibid., p. 242.

LISZT, FRANZ (1811–1886), Hungarian pianist and composer.

Liszt entered the hall on the arm of Count Vielgorsky . . . He wore a white cravat, and over it the Order of the Golden Spur

given him by Pius IX. He was further adorned by various
other orders suspended by chains from the lapels of his dress-
coat. But that which struck the Russians most was the great
mane of fair hair reaching almost to his shoulders. Outside the
priesthood, no Russian would have ventured on such a style
of hairdressing. Such dishevelment had been sternly discoun-
tenanced since the time of Peter the Great.

My friend Serov was not favourably impressed at first sight.
Liszt was very thin, stooped a great deal, and though I had
read much about his famous Florentine profile and his likeness
to Dante, I did not find his face beautiful. I was not pleased
with his mania for dressing himself with Orders, and afterwards
I was as little prepossessed by his somewhat affected demeanour
to those who came in contact with him. There were three
thousand people in the audience, Glinka among them. Liszt
mounted the platform, and pulling his doeskin gloves from his
shapely white hands, tossed them carelessly on the floor.
Then, after acknowledging the thunderous applause, such as
had not been heard in Russia for over a century, he seated
himself at the piano.

IN 1842.

SOURCE: Stassov, the critic, writing at the age of twenty, trans-
    lated from his memoirs by Mrs. Rosa Newmarch; quoted
    Sacheverell Sitwell, *Liszt*, Cassel & Co., 1955 edition, p. 105.

Liszt is the most interesting and striking-looking man imaginable. Tall and slight, with deepset eyes, shaggy eyebrows, and
long iron-grey hair, which he wears parted in the middle.
His mouth turns up at the corners, which gives him a most
crafty and Mephistophelian expression when he smiles, and his
whole appearance and manner have a sort of Jesuitical elegance
and ease. His hands are very narrow, with long and slender
fingers that look as if they had twice as many joints as other
people's! They are so flexible and supple that it makes you
nervous to look at them. Anything like the polish of his manner
I never saw. When he got up to leave the box, for instance,
after his adieu to the ladies, he laid his hand upon his heart

and made his final bow—not with affectation, or in mere gallantry, but with a quiet courtliness which made you feel that no other way of bowing to a lady was right or proper. It was most characteristic.

But the most extraordinary thing about Liszt is his wonderful variety of expression and play of feature. One moment his face will look dreamy, shadowy, tragic. The next he will be insinuating, amiable, ironic, sardonic; but always the same captivating grace of manner. He is a perfect study. I cannot imagine how he must look when he is playing. He is all spirit, but half the time, at least, a mocking spirit, I should say. All Weimar adores him, and people say that women will go perfectly crazy over him. When he walks out he bows to everybody just like a King!

SOURCE: Amy Fay, *Music Study in Germany*; quoted Sacheverell Sitwell (see above), p. 267.

He is tall and very thin, his face very small and pale, his forehead remarkably high and beautiful; he wears his perfectly lank hair so long that it spreads over his shoulders, which looks very odd, for when he gets a bit excited and gesticulates, it falls right over his face and one sees nothing of his nose. He is very negligent in his attire, his coat looks as if it had just been thrown on, he wears no cravat, only a narrow white collar. This curious figure is in perpetual motion: now he stamps with his feet, now waves his arms in the air, now he does this, now that.

SOURCE: Charles Hallé; quoted Harold C. Schonberg, *The Great Pianists*, Victor Gollancz, 1964, p. 156.

Precisely at eleven o'clock a silver head of hair and a well-known countenance above a cassock-girt figure moved majestically down the room, and received with Caesar-like condescension the applause of the surrounding crowd. After having remained long enough to allow all the opera glasses a sufficient survey of his fine head, Liszt . . . began an extempore fantasia.

SOURCE: a correspondent of *The Musical Record*, 1875; quoted ibid., p. 152.

LOUIS VI (1081–1137), 'the Fat', King of France; also known as 'the Wideawake' and 'the Bruiser'.

Already our lord King Louis, somewhat weighed down by his vast corpulence and by the continual fatigue caused him by his labours, was beginning to lose his powers as is the common lot of humanity, or at least his physical powers, not those of his mind, for, should anything occur, wherever it might be in the whole extent of his kingdom, that was against the interests of the royal majesty, he would not at any price allow the deed to go unrevenged. Although over sixty, he showed such knowledge and such ability that if it hadn't been for the perpetual hindrance of his fat-laden body he would have triumphed over all his enemies and would have crushed them. From this stemmed the complaints and groans to which he often abandoned himself with those closest to him: 'Alas!' he would say, 'What a miserable lot is ours. We are rarely, or rather never, permitted to unite experience with power. If I had had knowledge when I was young, or if at least I had power now that I am old, I would very easily have subjugated many kingdoms.'

However, all weakened as he was by his obesity, absolutely rigid on his bed, he resisted the King of England, the Count Thibaut, and all his enemies, in such a way that all who saw him or heard tell of his brilliant deeds, loudly praised the nobility of his heart and deplored the weakness of his body. Tormented by his sufferings and lame in one leg, he yet battled on.

SOURCE: Suger, *Vie de Louis VI le Gros*, edit. Henri Waguet, Paris, 1929, Vol. XI, pp. 270–273. Suger, who was born c. 1081 and died in 1151, was Louis' chief minister.

LOUIS XI (1423–1483), King of France, called the 'Spider'.

Of the elegance and grace of his person there is no need to speak, for, although he had very slender legs, his face had nothing handsome or noble about it. So that if someone met him in the street, not knowing his identity, he would more likely judge him a jester or drunkard, or one of such low degree, than a king or man of similar worth. For this reason, before he died quite a few people asserted that he was a leper. Weight was lent to this by the fact that he did not wear the royal purple, or long and precious clothes as befits great men; more often they were cheap and scarcely long enough to cover his buttocks.

SOURCE: Basin. *Histoire des règnes de Charles VII et Louis XI*, edit. Quicherat, Vol. III, Book VII, Chapter IX, pp. 165–166; quoted O. Mosher, *Louis XI*, Toulouse, 1925, p. 33. Thomas Basin (1412–1491) was Bishop of Lisieux. He hated Louis XI, who seized his temporalities.

LOUIS XIV (1638–1715), King of France. Known as *Le Roi Soleil* because of the splendour of his court, his reign is the longest recorded in European history. He became King at the age of five.

In his walk, his speech, his countenance, in his whole person, there was an air of grandeur, a noble and imposing character, which came from the opinion he had formed of an absolute king, like the Olympian Jupiter shaking the universe with his frown. His face was correctly beautiful, in spite of his age; and his mouth, opened frequently, as if to show his teeth, had not that foolish expression which such a habit often lends to the physiognomy. One would have believed he was always on the point of speaking, and this gave the more value to his rare words, measured and weighed in the balance. Pretty feet and handsome legs are advantages not to be despised; and the King, who was very proud of his, showed them off by the elegance of his shoes and the tightness of his small clothes. His figure had been admirable; but the flesh which he put on in his devout days was beginning to mar the perfection of his contours. He became even too fat ... He was not very careful about his adornment, but although his inward man was of an incredible uncleanliness, it did not appear upon his person.

SOURCE: Cardinal Dubois, *Memoirs*, trans. Ernest Dowson, Leonard Smithers & Co. 1899, Vol. 1, pp. 72–73.

LOUIS XV (1710–1774), King of France.

Though no longer young, he appeared to be very handsome; his eyes were of a deep blue, *royal blue eyes*, as the Prince of Conti said; and his look was the most imposing that can be imagined. In speaking he had a laconic manner, and a particular brevity of expression, in which there was nothing harsh or disobliging; in short, there was about his whole person something majestic and royal, which completely distinguished him from all other men.

SOURCE: *Memoirs of the Countess de Genlis . . . written by Herself*, London, 1825, Vol. 1, p. 194.

At 12 saw the King and Queen go to Mass; the latter carried thro' the apartments in a Sedan. At night saw them sup in public or at a Grande Covert, a Maigre supper, but very sumptuous. When the King or Queen called for a drink it was tasted by two before it was presented . . . The King is a very good looking man; rather short; appears young of his years; great lover of hunting. His Queen looks very old, plain and sickly; their son, the Dauphin, tall, thin and sickly.

SOURCE: Thomas Pennant, *Tour on the Continent 1765*, edit. G. R. de Beer, Ray Society, 1948, pp. 27–28.

LOUIS XVI (1754–1793), King of France.

[In 1774, shortly before he became King.] The Dauphin is very awkwardly made, and uncouth in his motions. His face resembles his grandfather's, but he is not near so handsome, though he has by no means a bad countenance. His nose is very prominent, his eyes are grey, and his complexion is sallow. He seemed cheerful and chatty, and I think his aspect bespeaks a good-natured man . . . He is not yet quite formed as to legs and strength, and has a good deal of that restless motion, first upon one leg and then upon another, which is also remarkable in some members of the English royal family.

SOURCE: Henry Swinburne, *The Courts of Europe at the Close of the Last Century*, H. S. Nichols & Co., 1895, Vol. I, p. 10.

L

Though slender in his younger years, he gradually acquired a healthy robust habit, which was probably increased by the frequent exercise he took in hunting. He was rather above the middle size, inclining to be corpulent, uncouth in his gait, and deficient in what is understood by personal accomplishments. His features were prominent, his countenance open, and it seemed to announce that honesty was inseparable from all his actions.

SOURCE: *Character of the Late King of France*, in *The Britannic Magazine for the Year 1793*.

LOUIS, DAUPHIN (1661–1711), son of Louis XIV and heir to the throne of France until his death; known as 'Le Grand' or simply as 'Monseigneur'.

The *Grand Dauphin*, known by the title of *Monseigneur*, resembled the Queen in features, in manner the King. He was of medium height, elegant in spite of his stoutness; in the manner of his physiognomy, and in his carriage, there was a certain good-nature. The King, his father, who loved him with his accustomed indifference, said that his son had the look of a German prince. His face was pleasant, although it bore the marks of a kick, given him accidentally by the Prince de Conti, when they were both children. His complexion tanned and red like a drunkard's did not go with his hair, of a beautiful blond colour; his dwarfish, deformed feet were an ill termination to his superb legs.

SOURCE: Cardinal Dubois, *Memoirs*, trans. Ernest Dowson, Leonard Smithers & Co. 1899, Vol. I, p. 94.

LOUIS PHILIPPE I (1773–1850), King of the French. Exiled in 1848, he went to England and spent his last years at Claremont House.

Louis Philippe was a man of average height, sufficiently strong, agile and active, moving easily, his head high, but a little awkward because he was long-waisted. He had a large face with regular features, rather handsome on the whole, just right, one would have said, for the great wig of Louis XIV, to whom he bore a striking resemblance . . .

The King's countenance in repose was rather impressive. His eyes, more animated than handsome, had an expression of shrewdness, good will and gaiety. His aquiline nose . . . was the noblest and most royal of all his features. His mouth, expressive and pleasant, was capable of mimicry which would have succeeded in the comedy theatre. His facial expressions reflected his conversation. Vivacity, liveliness, and a certain good-natured roguishness, a joyous and informal animation, and in serious moments, the calm of tested courage rather than the flame of heroism—that is what his features expressed, reinforced by a varied and penetrating accent and by an involuntary and fluent imitation of those about whom he was speaking. His word, gestures and bearing in public had little of majesty, and in moments of stress he did not gain in nobility. One recognised in his conversation, if not a king, at least an important personage, a man whom birth and habits had formed for great situations, although his gravity was perpetually enlivened by outbursts and laughter with which he interrupted his most solemn speeches. The King lacked the very highest qualities of mind. He was not made for profound or sublime matters . . .

SOURCE: Charles de Rémusat, *Mémoires de ma Vie*, edit. Charles H. Pouthas, Paris, Librairie Plon, 1960, Vol. III, p. 493; quoted and trans. Paul H. Beik, *Louis Philippe and the July Monarchy*, Anvil Original Books, 1965, pp. 131–132.

LOUIS-PHILIPPE ALBERT, COMTE DE PARIS (1838–1894), grandson of Louis Philippe I, King of the French.

And on the second day [June 24th, 1886] at two o'clock in the afternoon, the piers were black with people, an English boat, which had hoisted at its mainmast the tri-coloured flag, sailed slowly away from the Tréport quay.

I can still see that scene. The sun was shining brilliantly, and the deck was covered with flowers. On the bridge stood a man, bare-headed, his handkerchief in his hand, his head bent slightly sideways over his shoulder. His figure, which usually had a light stoop, was now erect, making him look taller. It was the Comte de Paris leaving for England, an exile.

SOURCE: Henri Stephan de Blowitz, *My Memoirs*, Edward Arnold, 1903, p. 310.

LOUISA, QUEEN OF FREDERIC V OF DENMARK (1724–1751), fifth daughter of George II of England.

I send you the best picture I can obtain of the Princess Louisa which represents her but very imperfectly ... The real object exceeds this resemblance in every respect as her beauty is enlivened by the moving feaures; when she speaks no picture can express her Grace, any more than the accent of her Voice. The Dignity, Decency and Civility of her behaviour would distinguish her amongst a thousand fine ladies even if she was not a King's daughter.

SOURCE: Lord Carteret to Walter Titley, Chargé d'Affaires in Copenhagen; quoted E. Thornton Cook and Catherine Moran, *Royal Daughters*, Heath Cranton, 1935, p. 75.

LOUISE, DUCHESS OF SAXE-COBURG-SAALFELD (1800–1831), mother of Albert, Prince Consort to Queen Victoria.

The poor little bride was so trembling and overcome when she entered the room, that she could not speak for crying. She is a sweet little thing, not beautiful, but very pretty through her charm and vivacity. Every feature of her face is expressive; her big blue eyes under their long black eyelashes often look so sad, and then she is suddenly a gay, wild child. She has a pleasant voice, speaks well, and is at the same time so friendly and intelligent that one must like her. I hope she is still growing, as she is very small. This afternoon there was a big reception and banquet. Louise, in her heavy, silver-embroidered wedding-dress, and covered with jewels, was more magnificant than pretty; the silver made her look pale ...

IN 1817.

SOURCE: The Dowager Duchess, *Diary*, quoted D. A. Ponsonby, *The Lost Duchess*, Chapman & Hall, 1958, p. 48.

LOUISE, PRINCESS OF BADEN (1779–1826). See Elizabeth Alexieievna, Empress of Russia.

LOUISE, QUEEN OF PRUSSIA (1776–1810). See Augusta Wilhelmina Amelia Louise, Princess of Mecklenburg-Strelitz.

LOYOLA, ST. IGNATIUS OF (1491–1556), soldier, founder of the Society of Jesus which spearheaded the Roman counter-attack on Protestant doctrines; canonised in 1622.

Although allegedly tonsured, he never had his hair cut at the crown as the statutes required; his bright red hair fell curling to his shoulders. He wore a suit of gaudy colours, again contravening the ecclesiastical statutes for the tonsured; his suit was slashed with another bright colour; he had a small scarlet cap, with the insignia of his ancestors and a gay, waving feather. He strode about with his cape slinging open to reveal his tight-fitting hose and boots; a sword and dagger were at his waist. He had been seen to come and go (on visits to his native Azpeitia) with breast-plate, coat-of-mail, sword, dagger, a cross-bow with darts, and every kind of weapon.

AS A YOUNG COURTIER.

SOURCE: The *Monumenta Ignatiana*, Series IV, Vol. I, 1904, pp. 580–597. The *Monumenta Ignatiana* are part of the series *Monumenta Historica Societatis Jesu* and include the testimony of witnesses while the canonisation of Ignatius was being discussed.

And reaching a village before he came to Montserrat he wished to buy pilgrim garb, which he would need for his Jerusalem journey; so he bought some coarse sacking, loosely-woven and with no selvedges; and he gave orders to have a garment made at once, loose and reaching to his feet; he also brought a pilgrim's staff and a gourd which he tied to his saddle, and some rope-soled sandals, of which he wore only one, and this not for appearance's sake, but because one leg was still in bandages and in a rather bad state; so much so that, although he went mounted all the way, each night he found this leg swollen; therefore he thought it necessary to wear a sandal on that foot.

SOURCE: The Saint's autobiography in the *Monumenta Ignatiana*, Series IV, *Fontes Narrativi de S'Ignatio de Loyola*, Vol. I, 1943, p. 384.

We were walking along on the homeward journey, all together, and chatting a little, when, just as we neared the little chapel of the Apostles, a poor beggar dressed all in sacking such as pilgrims wear, came out towards us [i.e. Ignatius]. He was not very tall; his skin was white and his hair red; he was good-looking, if somewhat serious, and kept his eyes fixed on the ground ... He walked very wearily and with a limp in the right foot ... He asked my mother if she knew of any hospital nearby where he could find lodging. She noted that he looked a good and honourable person whose glance moved one to devotion and piety; she also noticed that he was beginning to go bald. She told him that the nearest hospital was three leagues away in Manresa, from which town she had come and towards which she was now returning; she added that, if he wished to accompany or follow our group, she would endeavour to secure accommodation for him. Thanking her in Christian and honourable words, he decided to follow us, we all going slowly because of his lameness, so that he could come along in our company ...

SOURCE: *Monumenta Ignatiana*, Series IV, Vol. II, 1918, pp. 82ff.

The continual interior devotion of Our Father showed itself in a great peace and composure of countenance. Neither for any news told him, nor for anything else that might happen, joyful or sad, spiritual or temporal, did any interior change show itself by facial expression or bodily gesture. When he went to meet someone to whom he wished to show kindness his face used to light up with such joy that he really seemed to receive that person into his innermost soul . . . He had bright eyes, with a penetrating glance that read one through and through, but his modesty seldom allowed him to raise them. They were sunken in the sockets and in his later years his eyelids were so wrinkled from the tears he shed at Mass and when praying that when he went about with his eyes cast down one would think they were the eyes of a dead man.

IN LATER LIFE.

SOURCE: Father de Camara, in *Monumenta Ignatiana*, Series IV, Vol. I, 1904, p. 323.

All the above quotations are included in Mary Purcell, *The First Jesuit*, Dublin, M. H. Gill & Son Ltd., 1956, pp. 23–24, 70, 81–82, 323.

LUISA ISABEL (c. 1710–1742), daughter of Philip, Duke of Orleans, she married Luis I of Spain (1707–1724); she was sent back to France on her husband's death because of her disorderly conduct.

She was fat, not seventeen, gluttonous, ate with both hands; the two men attendants carried her off swinging in their arms, like a fat spirit in Henry 8th; her feet did not touch the ground till she landed in the third room, and then she fell a-boxing them: she never reads or works; seldom plays cards, and crops her hair like an English schoolboy.

SOURCE: Letter from Lord Percival to D. Dering (1726), Historical Manuscripts Commission, Vol. VI, Report 7, App. 248c; quoted Sir Charles Petrie, *The Spanish Royal House*, Geoffrey Bles, 1958, p. 66.

LULLY, JEAN BAPTISTE (1632–1687), French composer.

A very ugly little man, and extremely careless in his dress. One scarcely saw his small red-lidded eyes, and they, too, scarcely saw anything, but their sombre fire expressed great intelligence and a great deal of mischief; his whole face was in fact grotesque, bizarre.

SOURCE: a contemporary account quoted by Mary Hargrave, *The Earlier French Musicians (1632–1834)*, Kegan Paul, Trench, Trübner & Co. Ltd., 1917, p. 33.

LUTHER, MARTIN (1483–1546), one of the first movers of the Reformation in Europe.

When I saw Martin in 1522, in his forty-first year, he was moderately fleshy, so upright in carriage that he bent backward rather than forward, with face raised towards heaven, and with deep brown-black eyes, flashing and sparkling like a star, so that you could not easily bear their gaze . . . By nature he was a friendly and affable man, but not given to fleshy lust or unseemly pleasures, while his earnestness was so mingled with joy and kindliness that it was a pleasure to live with him.

SOURCE: John Kessler, a Swiss and author of a book on the Reformation; quoted Arthur Cushman McGiffert, *Martin Luther, the Man and his Works*, T. Fisher Unwin, 1911, pp. 240–241.

Because it was Sunday, the crazy man wore his best clothes, consisting of a gown of dark camel's hair, with sleeves trimmed with satin, and a rather short coat of serge, bordered with fox skin. He had a number of rings on his fingers, a heavy gold chain around his neck, and a cap on his head such as priests wear . . . He has a rather coarse face, but he tries to give it as soft and sensitive appearance as possible. His speech is moderately rapid and not much roughened by German . . . He confessed himself his unfamiliarity with Latin, but claimed he knew well how to talk in his mother tongue. His eyes are wide open, and the more I looked at them, the more I felt they were like the eyes of a possessed person I once saw, fiery and restless, betraying the fury and delirium within.

IN 1535.

SOURCE: Pietro Paolo Vergerio, Papal Legate, a letter to a friend; quoted Arthur Cushman McGiffert (see above), p. 354.

MACHIAVELLI, NICOLÓ (1469–1527), Florentine statesman and political writer; author of *The Prince*.

A glimpse given by Machiavelli himself, written in exile on his small property at San Casciano, after being dismissed from office, imprisoned and put to the torture:

The evening being come, I return home and go to my study; at the entrance I pull off my peasant clothes, covered with dust and dirt, and put on my noble court dress; and thus becomingly re-clothed I pass into the ancient courts of the men of old, where, being lovingly received by them, I am fed with that food which is mine alone; where I do not hesitate to speak with them, and to ask for the reason of their actions, and they in their benignity answer me; and for four hours I feel no weariness, I forget every trouble, poverty does not dismay, death does not terrify me; I am possessed entirely by these great men.

SOURCE: letter to Francesco Vettori, December 13, 1513; quoted *The Prince*, Everyman edition, trans. W. K. Marriott, J. M. Dent & Sons, 1908, Introd., p. xv.

MAGELLAN, FERDINAND (1480–1521), Portuguese circum-navigator.

. . . his appearance was not greatly in his favour, since he was of small stature.

SOURCE: Herrera: quoted (footnote) F. H. H. Guillemard, *The Life of Ferdinand Magellan*, George Philip & Son, 1890, p. 61.

This is one of the scant references to the first circumnavigator's appearance. It is also known that he was rather lame, from wounds received in Africa.

MAGON, CHARLES-RENÉ DE (1763–1805), Rear-Admiral. Third in command of the Combined Fleet at the Battle of Trafalgar, where he was killed.

I have it from Lauriston, afterwards a marshal and peer of France, then aide-de-camp to Napoleon, who was in Ville-neuve's fleet that on the day after this battle [the indecisive encounter with the English Admiral Sir Robert Calder off Cape Finisterre, July 22nd, 1805] Rear-Admiral Magon was a prey to such violent indignation when the first signal was given by the admiral to let the English Fleet go, that he stamped and foamed at the mouth, and that whilst he was furiously pacing his own ship, as that of the admiral passed in its retreat, he gave vent to furious exclamations, and flung at him in his rage whatever happened to be at hand, including his field-glass and even his wig, both of which fell into the sea; but Villeneuve was not only too far off for these missiles to reach him, but was entirely out of hearing.

SOURCE: De Ségur, one of Napoleon's aides-de-camp; quoted Edward Fraser, *The Enemy at Trafalgar*, Hodder & Stoughton, 1906, pp. 73–74.

MAHLER, GUSTAV (1860–1911), Austrian composer and conductor.

I met him at Trient, but when he got out of the train I failed to recognise him. Wishing to look his best he had gone to the barber at Toblach before he left, and he had been given a close crop while he read the newspaper without giving a thought to what was going on. The sides of his head were shorn as close as a convict's and his excessively long, thin face, deprived now of all relief, was unrecognizably ugly. I could not get used to the transformation and after two days he sadly departed again.

Mahler was quite without vanity about his personal appearance. He grew a beard in his early years to give him an older look. He also had enormous horn-rimmed spectacles made for him, 'so as to see in all directions.' The lenses were round and gave him a very menacing appearance. Later on, at Maiernigg, he used to let his moustache grow because he found shaving a nuisance.

SOURCE: Alma Mahler, trans. Basil Creighton, *Gustav Mahler, Memories and Letters*, John Murray, 1946, p. 128.

He is a kind of legendary type of German musician, rather like Schubert, and half-way between a schoolmaster and a clergyman. He has a long, clean-shaven face, a pointed skull covered with untidy hair, a bald forehead, a prominent nose, eyes that blink behind his glasses, a large mouth and thin lips, hollow cheeks, a rather tired and sarcastic expression, and a general air of asceticism. He is excessively nervous, and silhouette caricatures of him, representing him as a cat in convulsions in the conductor's desk, are very popular in Germany.

SOURCE: Romain Rolland, *Musicians of To-day*, Kegan Paul, Trench, Trübner & Co., n.d., p. 219.

MALTESE WOMEN, EARLY NINETEENTH CENTURY

. . . little, with beautiful hands and feet. They have fine black eyes, though they sometimes appear to squint owing to their always looking out of one eye, half the face being covered with a sort of veil made of black silk, called a *faldetta*, which they twist about very gracefully and arrange with much elegance . . . They are extremely fond of gold and silver ornaments and the peasants are often loaded with trinkets of these metals. Their dress consists of a short shift, a linen or cotton under-petticoat, a coloured upper one, generally blue and open on one side, and a corsage with sleeves. The back part of their neckerchief is fastened up to the head, and their hair which is smooth, well-powdered and pomatumed is dressed in front in the form of a sugar-loaf, much in the style of the *toupées à la grecque*, so long worn by the men. They ornament their necks with gold and silver chains; sometimes indeed with necklaces of precious stones. Their arms are loaded with bracelets, and their ear-rings are in general more expensive than elegant. The shoe buckles are extremely large and always either of gold or silver.

SOURCE: L. de Boisgelin, *Ancient and Modern Malta*, London, 1804; quoted Roderick Cavaliero, *The Last of the Crusaders*, Hollis & Carter, 1960, p. 76.

MANET, ÉDOUARD (1833–1883), French impressionist painter.

At that moment the glass door of the café grated upon the sanded floor, and Manet entered. Although by birth and art essentially a Parisian, there was something in his appearance and manner of speaking that often suggested an Englishman. Perhaps it was his dress—his clean-cut clothes and figure. That figure! those square shoulders that swaggered as he went across a room, and the thin waist; and that face, the beard and nose, satyr-like shall I say? . . . He sits next to Degas, that round-shouldered man in a suit of pepper-and-salt. There is nothing very trenchantly French about him either, except the large neck-tie; his eyes are small, and his words are sharp, ironical, cynical.

SOURCE: George Moore, *Confessions of a Young Man*, 1888; quoted Dorothy Carrington, *The Traveller's Eye*, Pilot Press, 1947, p. 36.

MANFRED (c. 1232–1266), King of Sicily, illegitimate son of the Emperor Frederick II. Played an important part in the struggle between the Papal partisans (Guelfs) and the Hohenstaufen supporters (Ghibellines) in thirteenth-century Italy. Chroniclers of both factions praise him.

Nature endowed him with all the graces, and fashioned all parts of his body in such well-accorded beauty that there was no part that could be bettered.

SOURCE: a chronicler of the Ghibellines (his own party).

He was proficient in the liberal arts, the first among the nobility in courage and diligence, and he was handsomer and more gifted than his brothers; he might well be called the Lucifer of his family.

> A handsome cavalier, knightly and wise was he,
> With all good qualities endowed, and courtesy;
> He had no lack, except one single thing,
> —True faith—an ugly fault in count or king.

SOURCES: a Guelf chronicler and a Guelf poet.

All the above quotations are included in H. D. Sedgwick, *Italy in the Thirteenth Century*, Constable & Co., 1913, Vol. I, pp. 388–389.

MARAT, JEAN PAUL (1743–1793), French revolutionary; assassinated by Charlotte Corday.

Physically, Marat had the burning, haggard eye of a hyena. Like a hyena's his glance was always anxious and in motion. His movements were rapid and jerky, his features were marked by a convulsive contraction which affected his way of walking. He did not walk, he hopped.

His countenance, toadlike in shape, marked by bulging eyes and a flabby mouth . . . Open sores, often running, pitted this terrible countenance.

SOURCE: both quoted from contemporary sources in Stanley Loomis, *Paris in the Terror*, Jonathan Cape, 1964, p. 92.

MARGHERITA (late fourteenth century), a slave girl in Italy.

A slave of about twenty ran away from us this eve, of dark hair and eyes and a meet figure, that is, neither fat nor thin. She is small and her face not much like a Tartar's, but more like our fashion here, and she speaks our language not too incorrectly. Her name is Margherita . . . She ran away from Marignolle, and took with her all her clothes, to wit, a bluish skirt, quite fresh, and a gown and a towel and other such trifles, and an old lambskin skirt with a black belt, and she is wont to wear a little cap.

SOURCE: Letters from Franco Sachetti, the writer, to a Pisan merchant; quoted Iris Origo, *The Merchant of Prato*, Jonathan Cape, 1957, p. 197.

MARGUERITE (MARGOT) DE VALOIS (1553–1615), Queen of Navarre; famous for her beauty.

[Marguerite commonly wore a blond wig as her naturally black hair was not considered to harmonise well with her complexion.] Nevertheless, I have seen this magnificent princess wear her own hair without any additional contrivance in the shape of a wig; and in spite of its being black, like that of her father, King Henri, she knew so well how to curl, frizzle, and arrange it, in imitation of her sister, the Queen of Spain (who always wore her own, which was black like a Spaniard's), that such head-dress became her as well, or better, than any other she could invent.

SOURCE: Brantôme, *Dames illustres*. Brantôme was an enthusiastic admirer of Marguerite and further records:

I remember (for I was present), that when the Queen-Mother took the Queen her daughter to her husband, the King of Navarre, she passed through Cognac and abode there some days. While they were there, came divers great and honourable ladies of the neighbourhood to see them and do them reverence, who were all amazed at the beauty of the princess and could not praise her enough to her mother, she being lost in joy. Where-upon, she prayed her daughter to array herself most sump-tuously in the fine and superb apparel that she wore at Court for great and magnificent pomps and festivities, in order to give pleasure to these worthy dames. And this she did to obey so good a mother, appearing robed superbly in a gown of silver tissue and dove-colour, *à la Boulonnoise*, with hanging sleeves, a costly head-dress, and a white veil, neither too large nor yet too small, the whole accompanied by such noble majesty and perfect grace that one would have judged her rather a goddess of heaven than a princess of earth . . . I saw her in the procession [Palm Sunday 1572] so beautiful that nothing in the world could be seen so fair; because, besides the beauty of her face and form, she was most superbly and most richly adorned and apparelled. Her lovely fair face, which resembled the heavens in their sweetest and calmest serenity, was adorned about the head by so great a quantity of large pearls and costly jewels and, in particular, by sparkling diamonds worn in the form of stars, that people declared that the serenity of the face and the arrangement of the jewels resembled the sky when it is very starry. Her beautiful body, with its full tall form, was robed in a gown of crinkled cloth-of-gold, the richest and most beautiful ever seen in France . . . She wore it all day, although its weight was very great; but her beautiful, full, strong figure supported it well and aided her greatly, since had she been a little dwarf of a princess or a dame only elbow-high, as I have seen some, she would assuredly have died under the weight, or else had been forced to change her gown and take another. Nor is this all, for, being in the procession, walking according to her high rank, her face uncovered, so as not to deprive the people of its kindly light, she seemed more beautiful still, by bearing everywhere in her hand a palm-branch, as our queens of all time have been wont to do, with royal majesty, with a grace, half-proud, half-sweet, and in a manner little common and so different from all the rest that whosoever had never seen her and known her would have said: 'Here is a princess who is above the run of all others in the world!' And we courtiers went about declaring with one voice boldly: 'This beautiful princess does well to bear a palm in her hand, since she bears it away from all others in the world, and surpasses them all in beauty, in grace, and in every perfection.'

On other occasions Brantôme remarks on Marguerite's dresses of 'shimmering white satin', and 'rose coloured Spanish velvet, covered with spangles'.

The passages from Brantôme are included in H. Noel Williams, *Queen Margot*, Harper & Brothers, 1907, pp. 29–30, 65–66.

MARIA AMELIA AUGUSTA (b. 1752), wife of King Frederick Augustus I of Saxony (q.v.).

The reigning Electress . . . Maria Amelia Augusta, is of the house of Deux-Ponts, and was born in 1752. Her person is tall, elegant, and dignified, though perhaps she cannot strictly be termed handsome, as her face is marked with the small-pox. She has fine hair in prodigious quantity, a fair complexion, eyes by no means destitute of expression, and an interesting countenance. Her manner, which impresses at first with the idea of distance, and reserve, becomes on nearer acquaintance, easy, affable, and pleasing. In conversation she is lively and communicative; without possessing either superior talents, or a very cultivated understanding. Her life, like that of Princesses in general, is uniform and destitute of gaiety or variety. She goes indeed regularly to the comedy, to the chace, and to the country but the Elector commonly accompanies her on these occasions, which can scarcely be denominated parties of pleasure. The Electress has little taste for sedentary amusements; a circumstance the more to be regretted, as she passes many of her private hours in solitude or seclusion, without company of any kind. Music and painting form her principal resources. Over her husband she is supposed to possess no political influence; and their marriage, which hitherto has not been productive of issue, may be considered rather as an alliance of state, than as a union of mutual inclination.

IN 1778.

SOURCE: N. W. Wraxall, *Memoirs of the Courts of Berlin, Dresden, Warsaw, and Vienna*, London, 1799, Vol. II, pp. 188–189.

MARIA LUISA, QUEEN OF SPAIN (1751–1819), the wife of Charles IV and mistress to Manuel de Godoy (q.v.).

Many confinements, several illnesses and what is perhaps the germ of a more or less hereditary disease have completely wrecked her. Her skin is greenish, and the loss of several teeth, replaced by false ones, has given the coup de grâce to her outward appearance. The King himself has noticed it, and often tells her, jokingly it is true, that she is ugly and getting old.

SOURCE: Zinovieff; quoted Jacques Chastenet, trans. J. F. Huntingdon, *Godoy*, The Batchworth Press, 1953, pp. 49–50.

MARIE ANTOINETTE (1755–1793), Queen of Louis XVI of France; executed October 16th, 1793, by revolutionaries.

In the Summer of 1776, when I quitted France, Marie Antoinette may be said to have reached the summit of her beauty, and of her popularity . . . Her personal charms consisted more in her elevated manner, lofty demeanour, and graces of deportment, all of which announced a Queen, than in her features, which wanted softness and regularity. She had besides weak or inflamed eyes: but her complexion, which was fine, aided by youth and all the ornaments of dress, imposed on the beholder.

AGED 21.

SOURCE: Sir N. William Wraxall, *Historical Memoirs of My Own Time*, 1815, Vol. I, p. 116.

An account of the Queen during her imprisonment in the Conciergerie:

In the morning when she got up, the Queen used to put on a pair of little slippers with trodden-down heels, and every other day I used to brush her lovely black velvet shoes with St. Huberty heels two inches high . . . I took the greatest care in preparing her food. Madame, who was always spotlessly clean and most particular, looked at my well-washed white linen and her eyes seemed to thank me for showing her this consideration . . . I admired the beauty of her hands, which were indescribably graceful and white. Without moving the table, she always placed herself at meal-time between the table and the bed. I was thus enabled to admire the elegance of her features, which showed up very clearly in the light from the window. One day I noticed a few very faint traces of small-pox. These were almost imperceptible and invisible from a few steps away.

When Labeau was in charge, Madame did her hair in front of him and me, while I was making her bed and folding her dress on a chair. I noticed patches of white hair on both her temples. She had practically none on her forehead or on the other parts of her head. Her Majesty said it came from the trouble of the sixth of October.

At her execution:

On the previous day knowing that she was going to appear before the public and the judges she had thought it seemly to do her hair higher on her head than usual. She had attached to her linen bonnet with its little pleated fringe the two pinners, which she had kept in the cardbord box, and under these streamers she had put on a piece of black crape, the whole making a very becoming widow's head-dress.

M

But to go to her death she had only kept the simple linen bonnet without streamers or other signs of mourning. As she had only a single pair of shoes she kept on her black stockings and shoes of prunella which she had not spoilt or rendered shapeless during the seventy-six days she was with us.

SOURCE: a chambermaid, Rosalie Lamorlière, *Account of Marie-Antoinette's captivity in the Conciergerie*, Paris, 1897; quoted Georges Pernoud and Sabine Flaissier, *The French Revolution*, trans. Richard Graves, Secker & Warburg, 1961, pp. 213–214, p. 219.

MARIE LESZCINSKA (CATHERINE-SOPHIE FÉLICITÉ)
(1703–1768), became Queen of France and wife of Louis XV. She was the daughter of the King of Poland.

This princess is small, it is held however that she is a little taller than the young Duchess d'Orléans; her figure is well proportioned and slender, her carriage graceful and unembarrassed in her movements, walking well, her head well set on, her hair bordering on chestnut, her temples well shaped, her forehead high, her eyebrows well shaped and arched, the eyes deep set, not large but lively and bright, the cheeks full enough with a natural colour, the nose a little long but neither fat nor red nor parrotlike, otherwise well shaped enough, the mouth neither large nor small, the lips full and red; the contour of the face fairly good looking when the eyes are cast down, the complexion good, and fresh; fresh water, and sometimes snow water are her only paints, and she certainly never puts on rouge or white; her air is smiling and gracious, her voice sweet and agreeable, her eyes not large and well formed, her arm round but rather thin because this princess has lost her plumpness, her hand neither pretty nor ugly, and both white . . . She takes much after her father both in appearance and in humour and wit. She has had smallpox with which she is not marked. She has a supple mind which will take the form and fashion desired. I have had the honour of seeing her work, walk, dance, of speaking to her and seeing her in bed . . .

I omitted to say that her neck is well proportioned, her shoulders well placed and broad enough, a high breast white like her throat. This princess without being beautiful is loveable for her gentleness, her wit, her wisdom, her behaviour. She is a combination of all the virtues.

IN 1725, SHORTLY BEFORE HER WEDDING TO LOUIS.

SOURCE: A message to the Duke of Bourbon from his emissary, Lozillière, who styled himself *Chevalier 'de Méré'*; quoted E. Rede Buckley, *A Lily of Old France*, H. F. and G. Witherby, 1926, pp. 26–29. For Marie Leszcinska see also under Thomas Pennant's description of Louis XV.

MARX, KARL HEINRICH (1818–1883), German Socialist and philosopher and head of the International Working Men's Association.

Marx was then still a young man, about 28 years old, but he greatly impressed us all. He was of medium height, broad shouldered, powerful in build, and energetic in his deportment. His brow was high and finely shaped, his hair thick and pitch black, his gaze piercing. His mouth already had the sarcastic line that his opponents feared so much. Marx was a born leader of the people. His speech was brief, convincing and compelling in its logic. He never said a superfluous word.

SOURCE: Friedrich Lessner; quoted *Reminiscences of Marx and Engels*, Foreign Languages Publishing House, Moscow, 1959, p. 153.

He was, in fact, of powerful build, more than average height, broad-shouldered, deep-chested, and had well-proportioned limbs, although the spinal column was rather long in comparison with the legs, as is often the case with Jews. Had he practised gymnastics in his youth he would have become a very strong man.

SOURCE: Paul Lafargue, Marx's son-in-law; quoted ibid., p. 76.

MARY OF BURGUNDY, DUCHESS (1457–1482), heiress of Charles the Bold, last of the great Dukes of Burgundy (q.v.), and wife of the Emperor Maximilian I.

I have a lovely good virtuous wife . . . She is small of body, much smaller than 'die Rosina' [a former mistress of Maximilian], and snow-white. Brown hair, a small nose, a small head and features, brown and grey eyes mixed, clear and beautiful. Her mouth is somewhat high, but pure and red.

SOURCE: Letter of Maximilian to Sigismud Prüschenk (December 8th, 1477), included in V. von Kraus, *Maximilians I, vertraulicher Briefwechsel mit Sigismund Prüschenk*, p. 30, and quoted R. W. Seton-Watson, *Maximilian I*, Archibald Constable & Co. Ltd., 1902, p. 14.

MASSÉNA, ANDRÉ, PRINCE D'ESSLING (1756–1817), Marshal of Napoleon I.

He was of a hardy constitution, and an indefatigable character; night and day on horseback amongst rocks and mountains, the warfare peculiar to which he was particularly acquainted with. He was resolute, brave, intrepid, full of ambition and pride . . . His conversation was uninteresting; but on the report of the first cannon, amongst balls and dangers, his ideas gained strength and clearness. If defeated, he began again as if victorious.

SOURCE: Napoleon I, *Memoirs*, edit. Somerset de Chair, Faber & Faber, 1948, pp. 72–73.

MAXIMILIAN I (1459–1519), Holy Roman Emperor from 1493. Son of Frederick III.

Mounted on a large chestnut horse, clad in silver armour, his head uncovered, his flowing locks bound with a circlet of pearls and precious stones, Maximilian looks so glorious in his youth, so strong in his manliness, that I know not which to admire most—the beauty of his youth, the bravery of his manhood, or the promise of his future.

AT HIS MARRIAGE IN 1477.

SOURCE: Letter of Wilhelm v. Hoverde, August 23rd, 1477, quoted Janssen, *Gesch. des deutschen Volkes*, Vol. I, p. 592, and R. W. Seton-Watson, *Maximilian I*, Archibald Constable & Co., Ltd., 1902, p. 14.

MAZARIN, JULES (1602–1661), French Cardinal, chief minister of Louis XIV.

On the steps of the throne from which the hard and terrible Richlieu had destroyed rather than governed men, there was a gentle kind successor, who was so very sorry that his cardinal's dignity prevented him from humiliating himself so much as he would have wished to everybody, who drove through the streets with only two little footmen behind his carriage . . .

His strength was to listen . . . He had brains, an insinuating manner, cheerfulness, style, but his shabby mind spoilt it all.

SOURCE: Cardinal de Retz, *Memoirs*; quoted P. J. Helm, *History of Europe 1450–1660*. G. Bell & Sons, 1961, pp. 257–258.

Mazarin's features had nothing vulgar about them; they were rather agreeable than imposing. His was a lofty forehead, and an air of gentleness seemed stamped upon his face. It was difficult to approach him, because his door was besieged by a number of petitioners. This first obstacle once overcome, he was found to be extremely affable. He could so thoroughly control both his features and his words that at the very moment when he was most concealing his thought, he seemed to express it with the greatest sincerity . . . He readily forgave those who had offended him, and many persons were astonished at seeing his late enemies now attached to his person, sharing his pleasures and anxieties . . . His clemency was always disarmed by suspicion, nor did he even punish obstinacy in rebellion. His natural sagacity was perfected by work; he slept little and was sparing of leisure. All important affairs were treated by him immediately, and without the help of any intermediate agent. . . . He had so thorough a command over his outward appearance that he never seemed to offend anyone . . . He had neither vanity nor haughtiness. Whether in prosperity or in adversity, his features were equally impassible; but not so his soul. If he was great during the epoch of his power, he appeared still more so when struck down by misfortune . . .

SOURCE: Priolo, *De rebus Gallicis*; quoted Gustave Masson, *Mazarin*, S.P.C.K., 1886, pp. 277–279.

MAZZINI, GUISEPPE (1805–1872) Italian patriot and founder of the Young Italy movement which aimed to liberate Italy from foreign or domestic tyranny, and unify it under a republican form of government.

Mazzini's personal appearance has often been described. It was striking and peculiar. When I first saw him in 1864 (January), he was 58 years old. His appearance altered little from that time to February 1871, when I took leave of him, thirteenth months before his death. Mazzini was of the middle height, but appeared taller, because of his slenderness and noble carriage; his features were regular and beautiful; his face a fine oval, his complexion a very clear olive; his hair had been extremely dark, but when I knew him it was mixed with grey, though it never became white; it was always abundant, though he had a very high forehead, so that it did not grow low down or at his temples. His eyes were the most remarkable features of his face. They were extremely large, luminous, of a velvet darkness, and full of fire and passion; every emotion was expressed in them; but their habitual expression was that of a grave, tender, brooding melancholy. In conversation his face was most animated; it was mobile and full of expression, from the most humorous to the most profound, conveying the impression of a soul above the common level of humanity. He had a delicate moustache and beard.

Mazzini's dress was also peculiar to himself. Early in life he determined to wear mourning for his country, and throughout his life he wore nothing but black. He wore always a black velvet waistcoat, buttoned high up to the throat, and leaving no shirt front visible, and round his throat a black satin stock or scarf instead of a collar. Although this costume was singular it was not at all eccentric; on the contrary, it was becoming and suitable, and seemed a part of himself. Indeed it seemed like the habit of a priest, inseparable from his calling; and there was, in his whole appearance and manner, the dignity and sanctity of an Apostle.

SOURCE: Mrs. Hamilton King, *Letters and Recollections of Mazzini*, Longmans, Green & Co., 1912, pp. 114–115.

MEDICI, CATHERINE DE (1519–1589). See Catherine de Medici.

MEDICI, FERDINAND I DEI (1549–1609), a Cardinal from the age of fourteen, he never took holy orders, but succeeded his brother as ruler of Florence in 1587; he retained the Cardinal's purple until his marriage.

This Ferdinand, having given up his Cardinal's hat, possessed the Dukedom when I was in Florence, being of a mean stature, corpulent and fat with great legs, one eye a little squinting or some such way blemished, his visage broad and full with a great chin and a brown beard, not thick of hair and kept short. He seemed to me to have nothing in his apparel, furniture or train to draw men's eyes upon him. His cloak was of black cloth with one silk lace, his breeches were round of black velvet without any the least ornament, he wore leather stockings and a leather sheath to his sword, his coach was lined with green velvet, but worn till it was threadbare, neither was it drawn with brave horses but such as seemed to come from the plough, and those that went on foot by his coach spoke to him with their heads covered, only the Bishop of Pisa sat in the coach with him on the same side, and on his right hand, who was his chief favourite. He was said to be of good and sound judgement, affable and mercifully disposed, and in matters of love to desire the first gathering of the Rose, but never after to care for the tree.

SOURCE: Charles Hughes, edit., *Shakespeare's Europe* (*Unpublished Chapters of Fynes Moryson's Itinerary*), Sherratt & Hughes, 1903, p. 96. For a note on Moryson, see under Bellarmine, Roberto.

MEDICI, LORENZO DEI (1449–1492), called 'the Magnificent'. He ruled Florence from the death of his father, Piero, 'the Gouty', in 1469; he was a patron of philosophers and artists, including Michelangelo, and was himself a considerable poet and prose writer.

Lorenzo was a man rather above middle height, broad in the shoulders, with a body solid and robust. In agility he was second to none, and though in exterior bodily gifts Nature had proved herself a stepmother to him, yet in inward qualities of the mind she had indeed shown herself a benignant mother. He had an olive complexion, and though his features were deficient in beauty, yet there was a dignity about him which compelled the respect of the beholder. His sight was weak, and his nose stunted, and he was entirely without the sense of smell. This, however, did not trouble him: on the contrary, he was accustomed to say that he was much indebted to Nature, seeing that there are many more things which offend the sense of smell than things which give pleasure to it.

SOURCE: Filip Valori, *Life of Lorenzo*; quoted E. L. S. Horsburgh, *Lorenzo the Magnificent*, Methuen & Co., 1908, p. 99.

MELANCTHON, PHILIP (1497–1560), German Lutheran theologian and reformer.

Philip was rather small in size, but not remarkably so, since it was not far different from the common size of masculine bodies. The set of his limbs was very neat, the forehead broad and high, remarkable for a vein which protruded in it, hair rather thin, neck long, throat remarkably hollow, eyes fine, and their brightness wonderfully clear, the chest quite broad, the belly and flanks rather narrow. But the shape of all parts of the body was entirely appropriate and in harmony. All senses were keen in a body weighed down by no mass of flesh and of such a kind that, while it was easily affected because of its thinness, it was capable of great endurance, and not easily very tired. And he himself used to say that whenever he came from Tübingen to Stuttgart . . . as he often did, and drank these heavier wines, pains in the limbs immediately began to attack him, and so he desired the quicker to return to Tübingen.

SOURCE: *De Vita Philippi Melancthonis, Joachimi Camerarii Narratio,* first published 1566, republished in *Vitae Quatuor Reformatorum . . . Melancthonis a Camerario . . . nunc iunctum editae, Praefatus est A. F. Neander,* Berolini, 1841, p. 29.

MENDEL, GREGOR JOHANN (1822–1884), botanist, whose work was the basis of modern genetic theory; his experiments were largely conducted in the garden of the Augustinian monastery of Brünn, Moravia, where he was the Abbot.

I still seem to see him as he walked back to the monastery through the Bäckergasse, a man of medium height, broad-shouldered, and already a little corpulent, with a big head and a high forehead, his blue eyes twinkling in the friendliest fashion through his gold-rimmed glasses. Almost always he was dressed, not in a priest's robe, but in the plain clothes proper for a member of the Augustinian order acting as schoolmaster— tall hat; frock-coat, usually rather too big for him; short trousers tucked into top-boots.

SOURCE: Herr Breit, an old acquaintance.

No doubt there are many who can still remember the Professor Mendel of those days [1860], a rather stocky, healthy looking, cheerful kind of cleric, contemplating the world and life through his gold-rimmed spectacles, and never disposed to give any one the cold shoulder . . . His countenance, somewhat roughly hewn by nature as sculptor, was beautified and irradiated by a fine, a noble spirit, for his goodness won all hearts. I can fancy that I see him now standing in front of his pupils, looking at them in most friendly fashion; I see his brown curls;

I hear the cordial tones of his voice, and smile as I recall the slightly provincial burr of his utterance.

SOURCE: Inspector Langer of Vienna's contribution to the *Brünner Tagesbote*, on the occasion of the Mendel centenary festival.

I recall his dear, loyal face, his kindly eyes which often had a roguish twinkle, his fair, curly head, his rather squat figure, his upright gait, the way he always looked straight in front of him; and I hear the sound of his clear voice, note his strong Silesian accent.

SOURCE: School Inspector Budař, in the *Mährische Korrespondent*.

All the above descriptions are included in Hugo Iltis, *Life of Mendel*, trans. E. and C. Paul, George Allen & Unwin Ltd., 1932, pp. 88–89.

MENDELSSOHN-BARTHOLDY, JAKOB LUDWIG FELIX (1809–1847), German composer.

Personally he was of middle height, and of slender frame, but possessed of strong muscular power; for Mendelssohn was a good gymnast, swimmer, rider, walker and dancer; and yet his outward and inner nature was one of extraordinary sensitiveness . . . He would invariably have a leaf of paper and pen or pencil at hand when conversing, to sketch down whatever occurred to him. To spend any time in mere talk caused him to look frequently at his watch, by which he sometimes gave offence; his impatience was only satisfied when something was being done, such as music, reading, chess etc.

When not irritated or annoyed by some 'common person' as he would say, his manners were most pleasing. His features, of the real Jewish, oriental type, were decidedly handsome; a high, thoughtful forehead, depressed at the temples; large, expressive dark eyes, with drooping lids, and a peculiar veiled glance through the lashes; this however sometimes flashed distrust or anger, sometimes happy dreaming and expectancy. His nose was arched, and of delicate form; still more so the mouth, with its short upper and full under lip, which was slightly protruded, and hid his teeth, when, with a slight lisp, he pronounced the hissing consonants.

SOURCE: William Spark, *Musical Memories*, W. Reeves, third edition, pp. 27–28.

METTERNICH, KLEMENS LOTHAR WENZEL, PRINCE
(1773–1859), Austrian statesman.

When Metternich laughs, his face goes to pieces. An enormous mouth opens in a circle; his eyebrows rise unevenly towards his forehead, and seem to come apart. There is something devilish in this grimace, and as soon as he begins to joke, the Prince's voice, normally rather a drawl, at once loses its character and becomes harsh and squeaky.

SOURCE: Sir Thomas Lawrence; quoted John Fisher, *Eighteen Fifteen, an End and a Beginning*, Cassell, 1963, p. 41.

METTERNICH, PRINCESS PAULINE (1836–1921), grand-daughter of Prince Clement Metternich and wife of Richard Metternich, Austrian Minister to Dresden, Ambassador to Paris, etc.

Pauline Metternich, as she was in the days when Winterhalter painted her, slender and glowing with youth and high spirits, certainly not beautiful with that large, badly formed mouth, the turned-up nostrils, and yet with the dark eyes full of secret, provocative laughter, with the small head poised on the long graceful neck, so radiantly animated and alive, that one can almost fancy that the smile, lingering in the eyes and on the painted lips, mocks at the shocked consternation caused by one of her audacious *risqué* remarks.

AGED ABOUT 21.

One evening at the ball at the Kinsky Palace . . . I saw my mother beckoning to me from across the room, and knew by her bright eyes and flushed cheeks that she had once more met a friend from the days of her youth in Vienna. 'Be quick', she whispered urgently as I obeyed her summons, 'I want to introduce you to Princess Metternich.'

Could this stout old lady in the silver grey satin dress be the fabulous Pauline Metternich of whom I had heard so much, I wondered. And then, as I dropped the customary curtsy, and felt my hand held in the soft little jewelled fingers, I looked up at the heavily powdered face, at the large mouth, painted an almost startling crimson, and met the wise eyes in the brilliant dark eyes, I felt the indescribable power and attraction of a magnetic personality.

AGED ABOUT 73.

SOURCE: Meriel Buchanan, *Victorian Gallery*, Cassell & Co., 1956, pp. 4, 23.

MEZZOFANTI, JOSEPH CASPAR (1774–1849), Cardinal of the Roman Church and notable linguist; he spoke approximately fifty languages.

I saw Cardinal Mezzofanti for the first time in July 1841. He was then in his sixty-seventh year; but, although his look and colour betrayed the delicacy of his constitution, his carriage, as yet, exhibited little indication of the feebleness of approaching age. He was below the middle stature, and altogether of a diminutive, though light, and in youth most active frame. His shoulders, it is true, were slightly rounded, and his chest had an appearance of contraction; but his movements were yet free, tolerably vigorous, and, although perhaps too hurried for dignity, not ungraceful. His hair was plentifully dashed with grey; but, except on the crown, where the baldness was but partially concealed by the red *zuchetto* [skull cap], it was still thick and almost luxuriant . . . His countenance was one of those which Madame Dudevant strangely, but yet significantly, describes as 'not a face but a physiognomy'. Its character lay far less in the features than in the expression. The former, taken separately, were unattractive, and even insignificant.

The proportions of the face were far from regular. The complexion was dead and colourless, and these defects were made still more remarkable by a small mole upon one cheek. There was an occasional nervous winking of the eyelids, too, which produced an air of weakness, and at times even of constraint; but there was, nevertheless, a pervading expression of gentleness, simplicity, and open hearted candour, which carried off all these defects, and which no portrait could adequately embody ... The great charm of Cardinal Mezzofanti's countenance was the look of purity and innocence which it always wore. I have seldom seen a face which retained in old age so much of the simple expression of youth. I had almost said of childhood; although with all this gaiety and light-heartedness, there was a gentle gravity in his bearing which kept it in perfect harmony with his years and character. He had acquired, or he possessed from nature, the rare and difficult characteristics of cheerful old age.

SOURCE: C. W. Russell, *The Life of Cardinal Mezzofanti*, Longman, Green, Longman, Roberts & Green, 1863, pp. 398–400.

MICHELANGELO (1475–1564), Florentine painter, sculptor, and architect; his full name was Michelagniolo di Lodovico Buonarroti-Simoni.

Michelangelo is of a good constitution; his body rather sinewy and large-boned, than fat or fleshy; above all healthy, both by nature, and as a consequence of the physical exercise he has taken, and his moderate and frugal habits; although as a boy he was sickly and ailing, and he has had two illnesses in later life ... He has always had a good colour in his face; and as regards his stature, he is of medium height, broad in the shoulders, and the rest of his body in proportion, though rather slender than otherwise. The shape of the head in front is round, so that above the ears it makes one-sixth more than half a circle. Thus the temples project somewhat beyond the ears, the ears beyond the cheeks, and then beyond the rest; insomuch that the head in proportion to the face cannot but be called large. The forehead from this point of view is square; the nose somewhat flattened, not by nature, but because when he was a boy, one named Torrigiano de' Torrigiani . . . with a blow of his fist, crushed the cartilage of the nose, so that he was brought home like one dead . . . the nose, however, flattened as it is, is in proportion to the forehead and the rest of the face. The lips are thin, but the lower one is slightly thicker than the other, so that, when seen in profile, it slightly projects . . . The forehead in profile almost overhangs the nose . . . the eyes may be called small rather than otherwise, and are the colour of horn, but changing and scintillating with flashes of yellow and blue; the ears are well proportioned, the hair and beard black, except that at his present age of seventy-nine they are both plentifully sprinkled with grey; and the beard is four or five inches long, divided and not very thick.

SOURCE: Ascanio Condivi, *Vita da Michelangelo Buonarroti*, trans. S. Elizabeth Hall; Kegan Paul, Trench & Trübner, 1905; pp. 79–80.

Now talking of his adventures, he [Piero Torrigiani] fell to speaking of Michel Agnolo Buonarroti, led to this by a drawing I had made from a cartoon of that most divine master . . . Torrigiani . . . holding my drawing in his hand, spoke thus: 'Buonarroti and I, when we were lads, used to go to the church of the Carmine to study in the chapel of Masaccio. Now Buonarroti had a habit of teasing all the rest of us who were drawing there; and one day in particular he was annoying me, and I was more vexed than usual; so I stretched out my hand and dealt him such a blow on the nose that I felt the bone and the cartilage yield under my fist as if they had been made of crisp wafer. And so he'll go with my mark on him to his dying day.'

SOURCE: *Memoirs of Benvenuto Cellini*, trans. Anne Macdonell, J. M. Dent & Sons, Everyman's Library, 1907, pp. 17–18.

> I've grown a goitre by dwelling in this den—
>   As cats from stagnant streams in Lombardy,
>   Or in what other land they hap to be—
>   Which drives the belly close beneath the chin:

My beard turns up to heaven; my nape falls in,
    Fixed on my spine: my breast-bone visibly
    Grows like a harp: a rich embroidery
    Bedews my face from brush-drops thick and thin.
My loins into my paunch like levers grind:
    My buttock like a crupper bears my weight;
    My feet unguided wander to and fro;
In front my skin grows loose and long: behind,
    By bending it becomes more taught and strait;
    Crosswise I strain me like a Syrian bow:
        Whence false and quaint, I know,
    Must be the fruit of squinting brain and eye;
    For ill can aim the gun that bends awry.
        Come then, Giovanni, try
    To succour my dead pictures and my fame;
    Since foul I fare and painting is my shame.

SOURCE: poem written by Michelangelo to Giovanni da Pistoia
while working on the ceiling of the Sistine Chapel, 1509; quoted
Richard Friedenthal, *Letters of the Great Artists, from Ghiberti to
Gainsborough*, Thames & Hudson, 1963, pp. 78–79.

MICKIEWICZ, ADAM (1798–1855), Polish poet.

These are the noble features which the sculptor David [d'-
Angers] immortalized at Goethe's behest, these are the dreamy
eyes that reflect the glow of a heart fired with pure love. But
these eyes shine only momentarily . . . The gravity of the time is
expressed in every line of its representative's face. The furrows
recount to the observant eye the oppressive days outfaced. The
damp breath of the dungeon vault at Wilno may have bleached
your hair, O worthy friend of the noble Thomas Zan, but
neither Senator Novosiltsov's cross-questioning nor the flattering promises of the affable courtiers in St. Petersburg could
compromise your true heart's steadiness. There is something of
marble in this famous Pole's expression. His voice is hoarse. He
pronounces French very harshly, almost brokenly. There is no
insinuation in his delivery, no expressive pantomime, no lively

gesticulation. Here one sees nothing of the carefully chosen costume of the younger French lecture-desk heroes, none of that striving for effect, that seeking for applause. Completely enveloped in his simple dark brown coat, the earnest man sits motionless before the closely packed crowd of listeners, only now and again smoothing back from his forehead his bushy gray hair, grown low and thick, whose former shining black still appears in places. The words that struggle from lips so expressive of energy and steadfastness lose none of their spirit for all their simplicity. Often he is at a loss for the precise expression and must search for it—but he finds it.

SOURCE: an article in the *Beilage zur Allgemeinen Zeitung*, March 9th, 1843, by an unidentified L. A. Z. who attended Mickiewicz's course in the *Collège de France*; quoted Manfred Kridl, edit., *Adam Mickiewicz, Poet of Poland*, Columbia University Press, 1951, pp. 183–184.

MIRABEAU, HONORÉ-GABRIEL RIQUETI, COMTE DE
(1749–1791), French revolutionary and orator.

My son, whose body grows, whose prattle increases, and whose face grows incredibly ugly, is moreover ugly by choice and predilection; and, in addition, interminably oratorical.

SOURCE: his father, le Marquis de Mirabeau, in a letter to a friend; quoted in Antonina Vallentin, *Mirabeau, Voice of the Revolution*, Hamish Hamilton, 1948, p. 20, trans. E. W. Dickes from *Mirabeau avant la Révolution* and *Mirabeau dans la Révolution*, Paris, 1946 (2 volumes).

He walked more or less between the nobility and the Third Estate, the last of the nobles. His piercing eye roved over the crowd of spectators, and he seemed to be interrogating the multitude with his provocative gaze. He carried his head high and thrown back. He rested his right hand on the pommel of his sword, and held under his left arm a hat with a white feather. His thick hair, brushed up above his broad forehead ended in thick curls at the level of the ears. The rest of it, collected behind his head was brought into a big black taffeta bag, which hung above his shoulders. There was something imposing about his ugliness.

SOURCE: the recollection of an eleven-year-old boy, son of a lawyer named Portalis, who watched the procession that preceded the opening of the provincial Estates in 1789; quoted ibid, pp. 288–289.

MOLIÈRE (1622–1673), the assumed name of Jean Baptiste Poquelin, French actor and dramatist.

Molière was neither too fat nor too thin; his stature was large rather than small, his carriage was good, and he had a well made leg. He walked thoughtfully, he had a very serious air, a big nose, a large mouth, thick lips, a brown complexion, and the different movements that he gave to them made him look extremely comical. As regards his character he was kind, desirous to please and generous. He was very fond of speaking in public, and when he read his plays to the actors he liked them to bring their children, to draw his own impressions from their natural emotions.

SOURCE: *Mercure de France*, May 1740; quoted Henry M. Trollope, *The Life of Molière*, Archibald Constable & Co., 1905, p. 21. Trollope notes that the whole article in the *Mercure de France* was previously attributed to Angélique du Croissy, later known as Mlle. Poisson, who retired from the stage in 1694, and died in 1756, aged 99. More recently it has been asserted (by M. Arthur Desfeuilles in the second edition of *Extraits des Mémoires publiés dans le Mercure de France par Madame Paul Poisson*) that the only part of these extracts actually written by Mlle. Poisson is the portrait of Molière.

MOLTKE, HELMUTH CARL BERNHARD, COUNT VON (1800–1891), Prussian field marshal; for 30 years chief of staff of the Prussian army.

The Field-Marshal was a tall and lean old man, whose head was quite bald, and who used to wear a wig—which could not

N

possibly be taken for anything else—mainly in order to prevent himself from catching cold. Moltke himself was the driest man I ever met in my life. His thoughts resembled a mathematical problem. He has been called in France 'le grande silencieux', and in a certain sense he deserved the appellation. But he was something more than that; he was a great thinker, inexorable in his decisions, never giving his attention to anything else save what he considered to be his duty.

SOURCE: Princess Catherine Radziwill, *Memories of Forty Years*, Cassell & Co., 1914, p. 164.

MONET, CLAUDE (1840–1926), French impressionist painter.

When he first came to the school the other students were jealous of his well-dressed appearance and nicknamed him 'the dandy'. My father, who was always so modest in his choice of clothes, was delighted with the spectacular elegance of his new friend. 'He was penniless, and yet he wore shirts with lace at the cuffs!'

SOURCE: Jean Renoir, *Renoir My Father*, trans. Randolph and Dorothy Weaver, Collins, 1962, pp. 101–102.

MONGOLS, THE, THIRTEENTH CENTURY. A description of the warriors who, under Jenghis Khan (1162–1227), conquered Central Asia, invaded Russia and, later, Western Europe.

They are inhuman and beastly, rather monsters than men ... dressed in ox-hides, armed with plates of iron, short and stout, thickset, strong, invincible, indefatigable, their back unprotected, their breasts covered with armour ... They have one-edge swords and daggers, are wonderful archers, spare neither age, nor sex, nor condition. They know no other language than their own, and no one else knows theirs.

SOURCE: Matthew Paris, *Chron. Maj.*, iv. 76ff.; quoted R. H. C. Davis, *A History of Medieval Europe*, Longmans, 1950, p. 404.

MONTAIGNE, MICHEL DE (1533–1592), French essayist and
philosopher.

My height is rather below the average. This defect hath not
only the drawback of ugliness, but, in addition, that of incon-
venience . . . A beautiful figure, in truth, is the only beauty
allowed to men . . . For the rest, my figure is strong and well-
set, my face not fat but full, my complexion—between the
jovial and melancholy—showeth moderately sanguine and of
tempered heat. For my health, it is steady and gay.

SOURCE: Montaigne, *Essais*, ii, 17: 'De la Présomption'; quoted
   Edith Sichel, *Michel de Montaigne*, Constable & Co., 1911, p. 13.

In music or singing, for which I have a very unfit voice, or to
play on any sort of instrument, they could never teach me
anything. In dancing, tennis, or wrestling, I could never arrive
to more than an ordinary pitch; in swimming, fencing, vaulting,
and leaping, to none at all. My hands are so clumsy that I
cannot even write so as to read it myself, so that I had rather
do what I have scribbled over again, than take upon me the
trouble to make it out. I do not read much better than I write,
and feel that I weary my auditors: otherwise, not a bad clerk.
I cannot decently fold up a letter, nor could ever make a
pen, or carve at table worth a pin, nor saddle a horse, nor
carry a hawk and fly her, nor hunt the dogs, nor lure a hawk,
nor speak to a horse. In fine, my bodily qualities are very well
suited to those of my soul; there is nothing sprightly, only a full
and firm vigour.

SOURCE: ibid, trans. Charles Cotton, *Michel Eyquem de Montaigne*,
   The Essays, Encyclopaedia Britannica Inc., 1952, p. 312.

MOZART, LEOPOLD (1719–1787), violinist and composer; he
   was the father of Wolfgang Amadeus (q.v.).

I look like poor Lazarus. My dressing-gown is so ragged that if
someone rings in the morning I must run and hide. My flannel
jerkin, which I have been wearing day and night for so many
years, is so torn that it will scarcely stay on, and I cannot have

a new dressing-gown or jerkin made. All the time that you two have been away I have not had a pair of shoes made. I no longer have any black silk stockings. On Sundays I put on old white stockings, and all week long I wear the black woollen Berlin stockings that I bought for 1 gulden 12 kreutzer . . . We cannot even consider plays and balls. Such is our life: cares within and cares without. And on top of all this I have neither my wife nor my son, and God knows whether or when we will see each other again.

SOURCE: a letter from Leopold to Wolfgang; quoted Erich Schenk, *Mozart and his Times*, Secker & Warburg, 1960, p. 230.

MOZART, WOLFGANG AMADEUS (1756–1791), Austrian composer; Mozart was an infant prodigy and astonished the courts of Europe from the age of five.

Then I was at Thun's, where the boy from Salzburg and his sister played clavier. The poor little fellow plays wonderfully. He is intelligent, lively, utterly sweet. His sister is a little master. He clapped applause for her. Fräulein von Gudenus, a good clavier-player herself, gave him a kiss, whereupon he wiped his mouth.

AGED ABOUT 6.

SOURCE: Count Karl Zinzendorf's journal; quoted Erich Schenk, *Mozart and his Times*, Secker & Warburg, 1960, p. 44.

Among the rest, whom should I spy there but the celebrated little German, Mozart, who 3 or 4 years ago surprised everybody in London so much by his premature musical talents. I had a great deal of talk with his father. I find they are at Prince Pallavicini's. The little man is grown a good deal but still a little man—he is engaged to compose an Opera for Milan.

SOURCE: Cedric Howard Glover, edit. *Dr. Charles Burney's Continental Travels, 1770–1772*, Blackie & Sons Ltd., 1927, p. 43.

I never shall forget his little animated countenance, when lighted up with the glowing rays of genius; —it is as impossible to describe it as it would be to paint sunbeams . . . I remember at the first rehearsal of the full band [i.e. in *Marriage of Figaro*], Mozart was on the stage with his crimson pelisse and gold-laced cocked hat, giving the time of the music to the orchestra. . . . Those in the orchestra I thought would never have ceased applauding, by beating the bows of their violins against the music desks. The little man acknowledged, by repeated obeisances, his thanks for the distinguished mark of enthusiastic applause bestowed upon him.

SOURCE: *Reminiscences of Michael Kelly*, London, 1826; quoted Erich Schenk, *Mozart and his Times*, Secker & Warburg, 1960, pp. 373–374.

MURAT, JOACHIM (1767–1815), Marshal of France and King of Naples.

Murat himself was the conspicuous figure, and well pleased to be so. Tall and masculine in person; his features well formed, but expressing little beyond good nature and a rude energy and consciousness of physical power; his black hair flowing in curls over his shoulders; his hat gorgeous with plumes; his whole dress carrying an air of masquerade.

SOURCE: Sir Henry Holland, *Recollections of Past Life*, Longmans, Green, 1872; quoted Joanna Richardson, *The Disastrous Marriage*, Jonathan Cape, 1960, p. 95.

NAPOLEON I (1769–1821), Emperor of the French; finally exiled after the Battle of Waterloo in 1815.

I was strangely surprised by his appearance; nothing was further from the picture I had formed of him. In the midst of a large general staff, I saw an extremely thin man of less than average height. His powdered hair, cut in an unusual manner well below the ears, fell to his shoulders. He was dressed in a single breasted suit buttoned to the neck and decorated with narrow gold embroidery, and in his hat he wore a tri-coloured plume.

At first sight his face did not appear to me to be handsome, but the pronounced features, a lively and inquisitive eye, and an animated and lively gesture revealed an ardent soul; and the broad and anxious forehead a profound thinker. He had me sit near him. His speech was brusque and at that time very incorrect.

IN 1796.

SOURCE: Count Miot de Mélito, *Memoirs*; quoted in Maximilian Vox, *Napoleon*, Evergreen Books Ltd., 1960, pp. 10–11.

He was dressed in a plain green coat with silver buttons (each having a different device on) with an upright green velvet collar, on his left side was a large emblazoned star, the imperial eagle in the centre. Nankeen breeches and white silk stockings with large gold buckles in his shoes. He wears a large cocked hat not mounted—the picture of Isabey with a full length portrait of Napoleon in the gardens of Malmaison with his arms folded has some resemblance, the best of any I have seen certainly, but this is not half stout enough for him, unless, since the painting of that, he has greatly increased in corpulency— he is what we generally say of such stature a little thick set man with a corporation—a most inactive appearance, with a large head, large mouth, the eyes deeply arched and his teeth apparently very good. On approaching him he surveys you from head to foot and then fixes his eyes sternly at you for a few minutes—while speaking he takes his snuff box from his pocket and at every pause, takes a copious pinch.

SOURCE: Diary of William Kershaw; quoted in A. Ponsonby, *More English Diaries*, Methuen, 1927, p. 185 onwards. Kershaw was a purser in the Merchant Navy, and visited St. Helena during a voyage home.

NAPOLEON III (CHARLES LOUIS NAPOLEON BONAPARTE) (1808–1873) Emperor of the French.

He is extremely short; but with a head and bust which ought to belong to a much taller man . . . His profile is good; the eyes are light blue, deep set and very peculiar, with a melancholy cast. An expression mild and gentle, as well as determined. His hair is rather lighter than ours, not at all grey, neither is he bald. He has no whiskers, but great moustaches, with very long straight ends to them, like the poor Duke of Genoa's, and a long *royale*. The manners are particularly good, easy, quiet, and dignified, as if he had been born a king's son, and been brought up for the palace.

SOURCE: Queen Victoria, *Leaves from a Journal*, André Deutsch, 1960, pp. 30, 48.

NERI, PHILIP, SAINT (1515–1595), Italian churchman; one of the outstanding figures of the Counter Reformation.

In his side Philip felt so great a heat, that it sometimes extended over his whole body, and for all his age, thinness, and spare diet, in the coldest nights of winter it was necessary to open the windows, to cool the bed, to fan him while in bed, and in various ways to moderate the great heat. He felt it so much in his throat, that in all his medicines something cooling was mixed to relieve him. Cardinal Crescenzio, one of his spiritual children, said that sometimes when he touched his hand, it burned as if the Saint was suffering from a raging fever; the same was also perceived by abbot Giacomo, the Cardinal's brother, himself tenderly beloved by Philip. In winter he almost always had his clothes open and his girdle loose, and sometimes when they told him to fasten it lest he should do himself some injury, he used to say he really could not because of the excessive heat which he felt. One day at Rome, when a great quantity of snow had fallen, he was walking in the streets with his cassock unbuttoned . . . In the time of Gregory XIII, when the order was given that all confessors should wear surplices in the confessional, the Saint went one day to the pope with his waistcoat and cassock unbuttoned: his holiness, marvelling very much, asked him the reason of it: 'Why', said Philip, 'I really cannot bear to keep my waistcoat buttoned, and yet your holiness will have it that I shall wear a surplice besides.' 'No, no', replied the pope, 'the order was not made for you; do as you please...'. His characteristic hatred of everything like ostentation appeared in his clothes, which were generally like those of other people, without any affectation either of fineness or of plainness. He never used silk, or any sort of clothes of delicate material, or showy; he generally wore a serge cassock, with a cloak of Bergamascan stuff; thick and wide shoes, and the collar large; and he did not allow any of his shirt to be seen about his wrists. He was a great lover of cleanliness, and held dirt in special abomination, particularly dirty clothes.

SOURCE: Father Bacci's life of St. Philip, published as *Life of St. Philip Neri*, London, Thomas Richardson & Son, 1847, from the corrected edition by Marini, Rome, 1837. Volume I, pp. 24–25, 266–267.

NICEPHORUS II PHOCAS (c. 912–969), Emperor at Constantinople.

On June 7th, Whit-Sunday, in what is known as the Hall of Garlands, I had audience of Nicephorus, a man of strange aspect, a pygmy in stature, with eyes that looked almost as small as a mole's. He was further disfigured by a short, broad, grizzled beard which hid his throat. His long, thick hair makes him resemble a pig, and his skin is as dark as an Ethiopian's. Not at all the sort of man you would like to meet unexpectedly at midnight.

He also has a swollen belly, is lean in the loins, with short thighs but long shanks, and disproportionately large heels and feet. He was dressed in a robe which must, to begin with, have been costly, but it was old, evil-smelling, and faded. Shameless in speech, foxy by disposition, he is a very Ulysses for lies and false oaths. You, my Lords and Emperors, have always seemed to me handsome; but now much handsomer, now that I have seen Nicephorus. Always splendid, but how much more splendid now. Always mighty, but now much mightier. Always kind-hearted, but now far more so. Always virtuous, but now more virtuous still. To his left, but much further back, were seated the two little Emperors, once his masters, now his subjects.

SOURCE: Liudprand of Cremona's account of his embassy to Constantinople on behalf of Otto I of Germany; quoted Helen Diner, *Emperors, Angels and Eunuchs*, trans. E. C. Paul, Chatto & Windus, 1938, p. 246.

The king of the Greeks has long hair and wears a tunic with long sleeves and a bonnet; he is lying, crafty, merciless, foxy, proud, falsely humble, miserly and greedy; he eats garlic, onions and leeks, and he drinks bath water.

SOURCE: Liudprand of Cremona, *Works*, trans. F. A. Wright, The Broadway Medieval Library, Routledge & Sons, 1930, p. 259. Liudprand (Liutprand, Luitprand) as Otto's ambassador is a biased but none the less highly important source for this period.

NICOLI, NICOLAO (d. 1437), Italian writer.

To describe Nicolao, he was of handsome presence, lively, with a smile usually on his face, and pleasant manner in conversation. His clothes were always of fine red cloth down to the ground; he never took a wife so as not to be hindered in his studies. He had a housekeeper to provide for his wants, and was one of the most particular of men in his diet as in all else, and was accustomed to have his meals served to him in beautiful old dishes; his table would be covered with vases of porcelain, and he drank from a cup of crystal or of some other fine stone. It was a pleasure to see him at table, old as he was.

AGED MORE THAN 65.

SOURCE: Vespasiano da Bisticci, *Vespasiano Memoirs*, trans. William George and Emily Waters, George Routledge & Sons, 1926, p. 403. For a note on Vespasiano see under D'Arezzo, Lionardo.

NICHOLAS I (1796–1855), Emperor of Russia.

The Tsar of that period, Nicholas I, was a most imposing personage, and was generally considered the most perfect specimen of a human being, physically speaking, in all Europe. At court, in the vast rooms filled with representatives from all parts of the world, and at great reviews of his troops, he loomed up majestically, and among the things most strongly impressed upon my memory is his appearance as I saw him, just before his death, driving in his sledge and giving the military salute . . . Colossal in stature; with a face such as one finds on a Greek coin, but overcast with a shadow of Muscovite melancholy; with a bearing dignified, but with a manner not unkind, he bore himself like a god. And yet no man could be more simple or affable, whether in his palace or in the street.

SOURCE: Andrew Dickson White, *Autobiography*, Macmillan & Co., 1905, Vol. I, pp. 451, 470; quoted Nicholas V. Riasanovsky, *Nicholas I and Official Nationality in Russia, 1825–55*, University of California Press, 1959, p. 2.

The Tsar is deserving of all the praise I have heard of him. He is one of the handsomest men I ever saw, six feet three inches at least in height, and 'every inch a king'. His figure is robust, erect and stately, and his features are of great symmetry, and his forehead and eye are singularly fine. 'The front of Jove himself, the eye like Mars to threaten and command.' In short he is a regular-built Jupiter.

SOURCE: John Motley, letter to his wife, St. Petersburg, Dec. 25th, 1841, in *Correspondence*, Vol. I, p. 86; quoted ibid.

NIETZSCHE, FRIEDRICH (1844–1900), German philosopher.

He had a small, rather than middle-sized form. The head was set deeply in the shoulders above the thick-set yet delicate body. Owing to his glistening convex spectacles and the long hanging moustache, his face lost that intellectual expression which often imparts to men of insignificant height something imposing. Still, his whole personality by no means indicated any indifference to outward appearance. He presented no such spectacle as Jacob Burckhardt with his close-cropped hair, his coarse linen and the well-worn suit, bordering on shabbiness, and hung in so slovenly a manner upon the powerful figure of that smiling stoic.

No, Nietzsche had adapted himself to the mode of the day. He wore light-coloured trousers, with a short jacket, and round his collar a daintily-knotted cravat, likewise of some delicate colour. Not that there was anything loud about this attire. Nietzsche had no desire to pose as a Dandy—when has the German professor ever succeeded in that?—but strove to attain something artistic in his appearance; witness the strands, rather than locks of long hair which framed his pale face.

Yet how removed from artistic Bohemianism was all that this man's art denoted in other respects! The small daintily-shod feet carried him with heavy, almost weary steps up to the professor's chair. Sitting there, his form was concealed behind the barrier, only his head remaining visible.

The rushing of the Rhine was like an organ Fortissimo, and I was anxious to ascertain whether the lecturer's voice could make itself audible, even with the windows closed. But that was the very experience which captivated and bewildered me: Nietzsche had a voice! Not the full tone of the orator, nor the sharply articulated but in the main ineffective modulation which characterises the pathos of many a university teacher—Nietzsche's voice, quiet and unaffected, as it issued from his lips had but one thing in its favour—it came from the soul . . . He only half knows Nietzsche, who has never experienced the interpreting melody of his spoken words.

IN 1869.

SOURCE: Ludwig von Scheffler; quoted M. A. Mügge, *Friedrich Nietzsche, his Life and Work*, T. Fisher Unwin, 1908, pp. 35–36.

NOBEL, ALFRED BERNHARD (1833–1896), Swedish chemist and engineer; the bulk of his fortune was left in trust for the establishment of the prizes named after him.

Alfred Nobel made a very favourable impression. In his advertisement he had called himself 'an elderly gentleman' and we had imagined him to be grey-haired and full of quirks and pains. But that was not the case. He was then only forty-three, was somewhat below average height, wore a dark full beard; his features were neither ugly nor handsome; his expression was somewhat gloomy, but was relieved by the kindly blue eyes; his voice alternated between a melancholy and a satirical tone. He met me at the hotel where I was staying, and, thanks to the letters we had exchanged, we did not feel like strangers. Our conversation soon became lively and absorbing.

SOURCE: Bertha von Suttner, the Austrian writer, who had just been engaged as Nobel's private secretary; quoted in *Nobel, the Man and his Prizes*, edit. Nobel Foundation, Elsevier Publishing Co., 1962, p. 7.

ORANGE, WILLIAM IV HENRY, PRINCE OF (1711–1751).
See William IV Henry, Prince of Orange.

ORLEANS, ELIZABETH CHARLOTTE, DUCHESS OF (1652–1722), daughter of the Elector Palatine, in 1671 she married Philip, Duke of Orleans. She was most commonly known by the title of 'Madame'.

The Princess did not strike me as so ugly as I had been told; she was a German beauty, without grace or delicacy, her fresh and ruddy complexion, fat cheeks, buxom figure, and plump arms did honour to her robust health; her eyes were fine enough and her long, white teeth did not spoil her mouth. In the distance, 'tis true, the red patch where her eyebrows should have been, damaged the general effect of her face. I have since had occasion to remark her awkward gait, which made her seem deformed.

SOURCE: Cardinal Dubois, *Memoirs*, trans. Ernest Dowson, Leonard Smithers & Co., 1899, Vol. I, pp. 37–38.

ORLEANS, LOUIS, DUKE OF (1372–1407), younger son of the French King, Charles V. His quarrel with his uncle, Philip II, Duke of Burgundy, was a dominating factor in the affairs of France at that period.

A young and handsome knight, very clever and enterprising and well cut out to make of himself an exalted prince.

SOURCE: Marquis de Saluzzo.

Good and devout people he loves, and readily listens to their instruction—as appears by his daily and prolonged frequenting of the Church of the Celestins . . . To the poor he gives willingly and liberally—daily with his own hand at the season of our Lord's passion . . . he visits the hospital of the sick poor, distributes alms himself, and visits the holy places . . . The prince loves gentlemen and heroes . . . To him, for his fair youth and from expectation of his kindnesses, they come from all parts; and he receives them lovingly . . . In his boyish ways, and in all else, he is very attractive: fair he is in body, and has a very sweet and good countenance: is gracious in his disport: holds himself becomingly on horse back: looks well in his rich and comely garments: knows what to wear at a fête, and dances very well: he is playful in courteous manner: laughs and amuses himself winningly among the ladies . . . So natural a judgment has he, as to be surpassed therein by none of the same age: stately and gracious in his demeanour, he is calm and temperate in his utterance: wickedness or cruelty there is none in him. Sweet and amiable are his replies to all who have to do business with him; and, among his other graces, in fine language adorned with natural eloquence none excels him . . . Of women he likes not to hear what is dishonourable spoken, nor evil talk of any man . . . Enough could I say of this prince, wise in his youth. Much has he striven to bring peace to the Church. Should he live to old age, he will be a prince of great excellence —by whom much good will be done.

SOURCE: Christine de Pisan (a strong supporter of the royal dukes). Both the above quotations are included in F. D. S. Darwin. *Louis D'Orléans* (*1372–1470*), John Murray, 1936, pp. 139–141.

OSCAR II (1829–1907), King of Sweden and Norway; he succeeded his brother, Charles XV, in 1872.

Any day after your arrival in Stockholm you may be passing over *Norrbro* (North-bridge). Your companion may whisper suddenly to you, 'There comes the King!' You see a tall, handsome, elderly gentleman approaching. You cannot stare at him, barefacedly. You do not care, certainly, to be more rude towards a King than to any other stranger, and so you give him a passing glance, and almost lose your opportunity of seeing royalty at home. But other such opportunities crowd upon you. You may chance to see his Majesty riding in the royal park of Stockholm, at a concert, at the theatre (if you are a theatre-goer), or at the Royal Chapel in his box-like little room, looking down on church and chancel, and able by an attentive ear to hear prayer and preaching. You may even meet the King in a shop, buying something peculiarly beautiful or magnificent for a birthday gift at the palace, or looking at some unusual importation from foreign parts. Such casual views of royalty without state will not long satisfy you. Having seen the man, you want to see the monarch . . .

The King enters last, magnificent in his gold-embroidered red cloak, his ermine cape, and the insignia of the princely order of the Seraphim. His mantle, that has been so carefully borne up, is thrown over the back of the silver chair, and those of the princes are also disposed behind them.

His Majesty speaks sitting, reading from a paper in his hand. In his rich, strong voice, he begins in the old way: 'Good gentlemen, and Swedish men'. You forget to use your eyes, and strain your ears to listen and understand.

SOURCE: Mrs. Woods Baker, *Pictures of Swedish Life*, Hodder & Stoughton, 1894, pp. 46–49.

OTTO I (912–973), Roman Emperor, called 'The Great'.

The king of the Franks, on the other hand [the contrast is with Nicephorus Phocas, q.v.] is beautifully shorn, and wears a garment quite different from a woman's dress and a hat; he is truthful, guileless, merciful when right, severe when necessary, always truly humble, never miserly, he does not live on garlic, onions and leeks nor does he spare animals' lives so as to heap up money by selling instead of eating them.

SOURCE: Liudprand of Cremona, *Works*, trans. F. A. Wright, The Broadway Medieval Library, Routledge & Sons, 1930, p. 259. For a note on Liudprand see under Nicephorus.

PADEREWSKI, IGNACE JAN (1860–1941), pianist, composer and Prime Minister of Poland.

He stood proud, with a belly like a pregnant kangaroo, the kind that begins south of the belly button and hangs like a bag, and he had everything a caricaturist demands of a virtuoso: long hair, polka-dotted flowing tie, large-brimmed hat, and gray morning coat. I watched him squinting nervously and sketched that special blend of forms I was later to note frequently in the faces of musicians; fragility in harmony with bullish masculinity. In Wagner, Listz, Verdi, Gershwin, a weak upper jaw is matched with a solid impressive lantern jaw. In Paderewski's case the chin was puny, but the forehead was ruggedly royal.

SOURCE: Emery Kelen, *Peace in Their Time*, Victor Gollancz, 1964, p. 126.

PAOLI, PASQUALE (1725–1807). Corsican general and patriot; ceded island to England, 1794–1796, and retired to England after conquest of Corsica by Napoleon.

I saw him soon after his arrival, dangling at Court. He was a man of decent deportment, vacant of all melancholy reflection, with as much ease as suited prudence, that seemed the utmost effort of a wary understanding, and so void of anything remarkable in his aspect, that being asked if I knew who it was, I judged him a Scottish officer (for he was sandy-complexioned and in regimentals) who was cautiously awaiting the moment of promotion. All his heroism consisted in bearing with composure the accounts of his friends being tortured and butchered, while he was sunk into a pensioner of that very Court that had proclaimed his valiant countrymen and associates rebels.

SOURCE: Horace Walpole, *Memoirs*, revised edition, Matthew Hodgart, *Memoirs and Portraits*, B. T. Batsford, 1963, pp. 213–214.

PARACELSUS (c. 1490–1541); the name assumed by Theophrastus Bombastus von Hohenheim, Swiss-born physician and alchemist.

... As to Paracelsus, he has been dead for a long time and I should hate to speak against the spirit of his death (as the saying goes). While he was living I knew him so well that I should not desire again to live with such a man. Apart from his miraculous and fortunate cures in all kinds of sickness, I have noticed in him neither scholarship nor piety of any kind. It makes me wonder to see all the publications which, they say, were written by him or left by him but which I would not have dreamt of ascribing to him. The two years I passed in his company he spent in drinking and gluttony, day and night. He could not be found sober, an hour or two together, in particular after his departure from Basle. In Alsace, noblemen, peasants and their women folk adulated him like a second Aesculapius. Nevertheless, when he was most drunk and came home to dictate to me, he was so consistent and logical that a sober man could not have improved upon his manuscripts. I had to translate them into Latin and there are several books which I and others thus translated. All night, as long as I stayed with him he never undressed, which I attributed to his drunkenness. Often he would come home tipsy, after midnight, throw himself on his bed in his clothes wearing his sword which he said he had obtained from a hangman. He had hardly time to fall asleep when he rose, drew his sword like a madman, threw it on the ground or against the wall, so that sometimes I was afraid he would kill me. I would need many days to tell what I had to put up with ...

... He was a spendthrift, so that sometimes he had not a penny left, yet the next day would show me a full purse. I often wondered where he got it. Every month he had a new coat made for him, and gave away his old one to the first comer: but usually it was so dirty that I never wanted one ...

In the beginning he was very modest, so that up to his twenty-fifth year, I believe he never touched wine. Later on he learned how to drink and even challenged an inn full of peasants to drink with him and drank them under the table, now and then putting his finger in his mouth like a swine.

SOURCE: A letter by Oporinus, at one time Paracelsus's amanuensis; quoted Henry M. Pachter. *Paracelsus*, Henry Schuman, New York, 1951, pp. 145–156.

PASCAL, BLAISE (1623–1662), French scientist and writer on religious subjects, 'a man whose genius gives him a unique eminence among modern thinkers' (Jean Orcibel).

He made his bed himself, brought his dinner out of the kitchen into his room and carried the remainder back again thither, and in short made no other use of his domestics than to dress his victuals, go on errands, and do such other things as he could by no means do himself... He had by nature such a gift of eloquence that it empowered him to express himself just as he pleased with most surprising facility ... his discourse never failed of having the effect he desired from it ... He wore ... an iron girdle full of sharp points, which he put on next to his skin, and when any idle thought came into his head, or when he took any pleasure in the place he was in, or when any other thing of this kind happened, he would give himself blows with his elbows to make the prickings of this girdle more violently painful, and oblige himself by this means to call his duty to remembrance. This practice appeared to him of such use that he kept to it till his death, even to those last days of his life when perpetual pains afflicted him. As he was not able to read or write he was under the necessity of being idle, and of only walking about.

o

SOURCE: Madam Perier, *Life of Mr. Paschal* [sic], trans. W.A. in
Life of Mr. Paschal with his letters, London, 1744, volume I, pp.
i–xxviii. Madam Perier was Pascal's sister.

PASTEUR, LOUIS (1822–1895), French chemist and micro-
biologist.

He minutely inspected the bread that was served to him [at the
dinner table] and placed on the table-cloth everything he
found in it; small fragments of wool, of roaches, of flour worms.
Often I tried to find in my own piece of bread from the same
loaf the objects found by Pasteur, but could not discover
anything. This search took place at every meal, and is perhaps
the most extraordinary memory that I have kept of Pasteur.

SOURCE: Adrien Loir; quoted Rene J. Dubos, *Louis Pasteur*,
Gollancz, 1951, p. 80.

PELÉVÉ, MADAME CHARLOTTE (in 1783, according to Mrs.
Sherwood, she 'owned to being forty years of age; as her father
had been dead forty years, it was impossible for her to pretend
she was younger'.) Madame Pelévé was an Englishwoman who
had married an official in the household of the Duke of Orleans—
'Egalité'—who was guillotined in 1793. The description below is
included for its vivid account of costume absurdity.

Never shall I forget the arrival of Madame de Pelévé at Stanford . . . She arrived in a post-chaise with a maid, a lap-dog, a
canary bird, an organ, and boxes heaped upon boxes till it was
impossible to see the persons within. I was, of course, at the door
to see her alight. She was a large woman, elaborately dressed,
highly rouged, carrying an umbrella, the first I had seen.
She was dark, I remember, and had most brilliant eyes. The
style of dress at that period was perhaps more preposterous and
troublesome than any which has prevailed within the memory
of those now living. This style had been introduced by the ill-
fated Marie Antoinette, and Madame Pelévé had come straight
from the very fountain head of these absurdities. The hair was
worn crisped or violently frizzed about the face in the shape of a
horse-shoe, long stiff curls, fastened with pins, hung on the neck,

and the whole was well pomatumed, and powdered with different coloured powders. A high cushion was fastened at the top of the hair, and over that, either, a cap adorned with artificial flowers and feathers to such a height as sometimes rendered it somewhat difficult to preserve its equilibrium, or a balloon hat, a fabric of wire and tiffany, of immense circumference. The hat would require to be fixed on the head with long pins, and standing, trencherwise, quite flat and unbending in its full proportions. The crown was low, and, like the cap, richly set off with feathers and flowers. The lower part of the dress consisted of a full petticoat generally flounced, short sleeves, and a very long train; but instead of a hoop, there was a vast pad at the bottom of the waist behind, and a frame of wire in front to throw out the neckerchief, so as much as possible to resemble the craw of a pigeon.

Such were the leading articles of this style of dress, and so arranged was the figure, which stepped forth from the chaise at the door of the lovely and simple parsonage at Stanford. My father was ready to hand her out, my mother to welcome her, and what would have alarmed most other persons in her appearance, was set down by them only as a result of a long residence in Paris, where it was well known that people did over-dress, and were almost compelled to wear rouge. The band-boxes were all conveyed into our best bed-room, whilst Madame had her place allotted to her in our drawing room, where she sat like a queen, and really, by the multitude of anecdotes she had to tell, rendering herself very agreeable. Whilst she was with us she had never concluded her toilet before one or two in the day, and she always appeared either in new dresses or new adjustments.

SOURCE: *The Life of Mrs. Sherwood (Chiefly Autobiographical)* . . . *edited by Her Daughter, Sophia Kelly*, 1854, pp. 49–50.

PESTALOZZI, JOHANN HEINRICH (1746–1827), Swiss educational pioneer and theorist.

By the moral struggles which he sustained, his health was occasionally impaired, but his iron constitution could not be undermined by transient fits of nervousness which had their origin more in the too free indulgence of his strong and acute feelings than in any defect in his physical organisation. His stature was short, and by a tendency of his head to sink in between his shoulders, his deportment, even in his younger years, uncomely. His eyes beaming with benevolence and honest confidence, soon dispelled any unpleasant impressions which the ruggedness of his appearance was calculated to produce; while his wrinkled countenance, which attested in every feature the existence of a soul to whom life was more than a thoughtless game, commanded, with irresistible power, that reverence which his figure could never have imposed. His entire neglect of his person and dress increased the natural disadvantages of his exterior . . .

Mrs. Pestalozzi was in company with some other ladies enjoying the promenades of a watering place . . . when her husband, who came travelling on foot, to pay her a visit, was perceived at a distance by one of the company; and the singularity and unattractiveness of his appearance having affected the sensibilities of his fair beholder, to whom he was personally quite unknown, she exclaimed, addressing Mrs. Pestalozzi: 'Ah! je vous en prie Madame, regardez donc, quel monstre!' 'C'est mon mari, Madame', was Mrs. Pestalozzi's proud reply.

SOURCE: E. Biber, *Henry Pestalozzi and His Plan of Education*, Charles H. Law, 1858, pp. 87–88.

PETER I (1672–1725), 'the Great'; Emperor of Russia from 1682.

You know that the Sovereign is very tall, but he has one very unpleasant trait: he has convulsions, sometimes of the eyes, sometimes in his arms and sometimes in his whole body. At times he rolls his eyes so much that only the whites can be seen . . . Then he also has spasms of his legs so that he can hardly stand still in one place. For the rest he is well built, dressed as a sailor, very simple in his tastes, and he wishes for nothing else than to be on the water.

AGED 26, ON A VISIT TO LONDON.

SOURCE: Jacob Lefort, a brother of Peter's favourite, Franz Lefort; a letter cited in M. M. Bogoslovsky, *Materials for a Biography*, Leningrad, 1940–1948, Vol. 2, p. 350; quoted in Ian Grey, *Peter the Great*, Hodder & Stoughton, 1962, p. 123.

The Czar Peter had a bearing and countenance as rigid and icy as the climate of his kingdom, he had a colossal frame, admirably proportioned, in spite of its leanness; his face was terrible, with his savage gaze, his piercing eyes, his bushy eyebrows, thick lips, his oiled black locks, and tawny skin. Excessive indulgence in strong liquors had given him a nervous affliction which was perpetually contorting his physiognomy. His movements were abrupt, his carriage haughty, and it was all of a piece. His voice had ever a tone of anger, and the majesty he affected took a savage and uncouth character. I know no man more anxious to learn, or endowed with greater intelligence. It was sufficient for him to see, in order to understand, and I have known him to correct explanations given him by artists and men of science. Wit he possessed, but it was steeped in the snows of his Russia.

SOURCE: Cardinal Dubois, *Memoirs*, trans. Ernest Dowson, Leonard Smithers & Co., 1899, Vol. II, p. 78.

The Czar was a very tall man, exceedingly well made; rather thin, his face somewhat round, a high forehead, good eyebrows, a rather short nose, but not too short, and large at the end, rather thick lips, complexion reddish brown, good black eyes, large, bright, piercing, and well open; his look majestic and gracious when he liked, but when otherwise, severe and stern, with a twitching of the face, not often occurring, but which appeared to contort his eyes and all his physiognomy, and was frightful to see; it lasted a moment, gave him a wild and terrible air, and passed away. All his bearing showed his intellect, his reflectiveness, and his greatness, and was not devoid of a certain grace. He wore a linen collar, a round brown wig, as though without powder, and which did not reach to his shoulders; a blue coat tight to the body, even, and with gold buttons; vest, breeches, stockings, no gloves or ruffles, the star of his order over his coat, and the cordon under it, the coat itself being frequently quite unbuttoned, his hat upon the table, but never upon his head, even out of doors. With this simplicity, ill-accompanied or ill-mounted as he might be, the air of greatness natural to him could not be mistaken.

SOURCE: *Memoirs of the Duke of Saint-Simon*, trans. Bayle St. John, Allen & Unwin, 1913, Vol. III, p. 93.

PETER III (1728–1762), Emperor of Russia (Charles-Peter-Ulrich of Holstein); husband of Catherine II (q.v.).

There [in Eutin in 1739] I met for the first time the Grand Duke, who was good looking, well mannered and courteous. In fact this boy of eleven whose father had just died, was considered a prodigy. He was pale and looked delicate; his trouble was that his entourage tried to make this child behave as an adult and forced him to a strict discipline, thus developing in him deceitfulness and hypocrisy.

SOURCE: *Memoirs of Catherine the Great*, edit. D. Maroger, trans. Moura Budberg, Hamish Hamilton, 1955, p. 33.

PETRARCH, FRANCESCO (1304–1374), Italian poet and humanist; personal glory was one of his greatest ambitions and in 1341 he was presented with the poet's crown on the Capitol at Rome.

... tall and handsome—with a round face and complexion between fair and dark, but inclining to swarthiness; with glance grave, yet cheerful and denoting keen intelligence; with a gentle manner and graceful gestures. He has an engaging smile, but never bursts into loud and senseless laughter; his gait is modest, his speech placid and humorous. He rarely speaks unless addressed, and then answers his questioner in so weighty a manner as to attract even the ignorant.

IN 1341.

SOURCE: Boccaccio, *Life of Petrarch*; quoted E. H. R. Tatham, *Francesco Petrarca*, Sheldon Press, 1926, Vol. II, p. 141. Boccaccio's description of Petrarch dates from the poet's crowning as Laureate and before Boccaccio knew him personally. But he may well have been present at the ceremony and probably heard Petrarch speak in public.

In my early days my bodily frame was of no great strength, but of much activity. I cannot boast of extreme comeliness, but only such as in my greener years would be pleasing. My complexion was lively, between fair and dark, my eyes sparkling, my sight for a long time very keen [until it failed me unexpectedly after my sixtieth year, so that to my disgust I had to have recourse to glasses. Old age at length attacked a body that had always been most healthy, and beseiged it with the usual array of diseases].

SOURCE: Petrarch, *Epistle to Posterity*; quoted E. H. R. Tatham (see above), Vol. II, p. 418. Tatham concludes that the first draft of the *Epistle* was probably written around 1355 at Milan; in c. 1371–1373 it was revised by Petrarch, and the bracketed portion added.

PHILIP II (1527–1598), King of Spain. Husband of Mary I of England. Sent Great Armada against Elizabeth, 1588.

He was a Prince who fought with gold rather than with steel, by his brain rather than by his arms. He has acquired more by sitting still ... than his father did by armies and by wars ... Profoundly religious, he loved peace and quiet. He displayed great calmness and professed himself unmoved in good and bad fortune alike ... He held his desires in absolute control and showed an immutable and unalterable temper ... No one ever saw him in a rage, being always patient, phlegmatic, temperate, melancholy.

SOURCE: The Venetian Ambassador; quoted P. J. Helm, *History of Europe 1450–1660*, G. Bell & Sons, 1961, p. 171.

... the living image, the faithful portrait, of the Emperor his father [i.e. Charles V] he resembles him altogether, in complexion, in appearance, in features; he has the same mouth, the same pendant lip, with all his other physical characteristics; but he is of less stature, that of the Emperor being medium while his is small. At the same time, he is very well made and very fit, as far as those can judge who have seen him in tourneys, with or without arms, on foot or on horse-back.

IN ABOUT 1557.

SOURCE: Giovanni Michieli, Venetian Ambassador, from Gachard, *Rélations des Ambassadeurs vénitiens sur Charles-Quint et Philippe II*, Brussels, 1855; quoted Jean H. Mariéjol, *Master of the Armada*, trans. Warre B. Wells, Hamish Hamilton, 1933, p. 34.

Small of stature, but he is so well made, so well proportioned, and dresses with such good taste and chooses his clothes so cleverly that one could not imagine anything more perfect . . . the constitution of this Prince is very delicate, and accordingly he lives with great regularity, and habitually nourishes himself with very substantial meats, eating neither fish, nor fruit, nor anything which might engender ill humours. He sleeps a great deal, takes little exercise, and his pastimes are all quiet.

SOURCE: ibid., Ambassador Michael Soriano.

. . . favoured like his father [see entry for Charles V] but not so pock-marked, great lips, his hair auburn, polled, and his beard white and auburn, with a felt hat and white feather.

SOURCE: *Description of the faces and visages of moste of the Princes of Christendome in the time of K.H.8 . . .* , 1552; MS. at College of Heralds.

PHILIP V (1683–1746), King of Spain. He was the grandson of Louis XIV and constantly intrigued to secure the succession to the throne of France; in 1724 he abdicated but resumed the throne a few months later on his son's death.

The King of Spain is very hunch-backed, and is not in other respects well made, but he is bigger than his brothers. He has the best mien, good features, and fine hair. What is somewhat singular, although his hair is very light, his eyes are quite black; his complexion is clear red and white; he has an Austrian mouth; his voice is deep, and he is singularly slow in speaking. He is a good and peaceable sort of a person, but a little obstinate when he takes it in his head. He loves his wife above all things, leaves all affairs to her, and never interferes in anything. He is very pious and believes he shoud be damned if he committed any matrimonial infidelity . . . The good gentleman ought to be surrounded by competent persons, for his own wit would not carry him far; but he is of a good disposition, and is one of the quietest men in the world. He is a little melancholy, and there is nothing in Spain to make him gay.

SOURCE: Duchess Elizabeth Charlotte D'Orleans, *Memoirs of the Court of Louis XIV* (edit. from her German correspondence), London, 1824, pp. 304–305.

PHILIP, DUKE OF BURGUNDY (1396–1467), known as 'the Good'; Duke from 1419.

In stature he was moderately tall, and his body was well proportioned to his height; his limbs were rather slender; he was uncommonly handsome of figure, well-formed, as straight as a reed, and strong in his arms and in his back, his neck was in proportion to his body, his hands were slim and his feet lean; he had more bone than flesh, and his veins were broad and full of blood. He had the family face with long, dignified features; his complexion was swarthy and dark; his nose was long, not aquiline; his brow was full, ample and far from bald. His hair was between fair and dark, and was smooth and even; his beard and eyebrows matched his hair, but he had heavy, bushy eyebrows, the hairs of which rose like horns in his anger. His mouth was well-proportioned, with full and florid lips. His eyes were bright and sometimes proud and penetrating, but usually friendly in expression; his inmost heart was shown in his face, the lines of which matched his whole being. His inner and outer selves were one; his visage and his character bore equivalent testimony, one to another; his heart did not contradict his countenance, nor his countenance his heart . . . His very appearance proclaimed him an emperor and by his natural grace he deserved to wear a crown ... Had he stood in a cow-shed, he would have seemed like a god in a temple; he adorned his surroundings wherever he might be ... In his aspect he had the celestial gift that not even an enemy could behold him without delight; this was proved time and time again.

He was solemn of walk, noble in demeanour, and handsome in his bearing; he sat but little and would stand for a long time; he dressed modestly but richly, changing his garb with the times, as did other men; he was strong on foot and most agile on horseback; he liked the bow and handled it very well, and he was skilful at tennis, his one out-door pastime was the diversion of hunting, in a grand and lavish manner; he spent a long time at meals, and was the best served of all living men; he was mod-est at table and straight forward in his converse; in silence he would look at people and looking at them would hestitate to address them; wherever he was he would speak only with due cause; there was no emptiness in his words; he would speak in a moderate tone of voice, never raising it through passion; he was a kindly listener, treating all people alike and kindly in his reply; he was slow to make promises, and still slower to become angry; but once roused he was an enemy. He uttered no oaths nor other vile words, nor insults towards any man, nor did he recall any man's shame; he spoke of good men with favour, and of bad men with pity. He was accommodating, most generous in serving, quiet in all his ways and diligent in business ... He was as true as fine gold and a man of perfect integrity.

SOURCE: Georges Chastellain, *Oeuvres*, Vol. VII, edit. Baron Kervyn de Lettenhove, Brussels, 1865, pp. 219–221.

PHILIP NERI, SAINT (1515–1595). See Neri, Philip, Saint.

PIUS VII (1740–1823), Pope from 1800; quarrelled with Napoleon and was imprisoned at Avignon in 1809. Later he was moved to Fontainebleau, and only returned to Rome in 1814.

By Mon Signor Doria, the little Master of the Ceremonies, we [see note below] were led thro' a narrow passage-room into that in which the Pope was standing, in his white cloth habit buttoned up to the chin and his shoes of scarlet velvet, embroidered with gold flowers. He received us most courteously and we formed a circle before him—said much of the Inglese— that he was now too old to travel that he would rather have gone to England than where he did go—that he was going to receive some English ladies in the Garden—To each of whom he gives a rosary—When we knelt to kiss his hand, he seemed distressed, and made many efforts as if to assist us to rise. His manners however were very simple, his courtesy equal to the most refined, and the sort of hysteric laugh half subdued with which he spoke generally to us, as we were named to him, discovered a modesty and anxiety to please which were engaging. It lasted about five minutes.

IN 1815.

SOURCE: Samuel Rogers, *Italian Journal*, edit. J. R. Hale, Faber & Faber, 1956, p. 230.

Samuel Rogers was a renowned arbiter of taste and frequently acted as host to all the great literary and artistic figures of his day. In this extract from his *Journal*, inconsistencies of punctuation, etc. are Rogers's own. His companion here was the Abbé Taylor, it being customary at that time for English visitors to be presented by a Scots or Irish ecclesiastic resident at Rome. (Taylor was an Irishman.)

PIUS X (GUISEPPE SARTO) (1835–1914), Pope from 1903. Proclaimed a saint in 1954.

In build the Pope is short and thickset, with heavy limbs, which causes him to walk rather awkwardly. His face, marked with the wholesome crudities of a peasant, was a dull olive in tone.

Far from being Italian in type, it bore the impress of a purely Teutonic origin. The hands of His Holiness, singularly large and powerful, are not unlike those of a farm labourer, accustomed to heavy work.

Physically he is as unlike Pope Leo XIII [q.v.] as Cromwell was unlike Richelieu. Leo gave one the impression of intellectual dignity and austerity, whilst the characteristics of Pius X are homely benevolence and simple religion.

In repose the face is sad, almost stern; but when it lights up with a pleasant smile, the radiance of the expression obliterates all traces of sadness, and beautifies the actual plainness of the features.

I understood later that the set stern expression was contemporary with his new responsibilities, which he accepted so unwillingly, and found such a heavy burden to carry.

SOURCE: H. J. Thaddeus, *Recollections of a Court Painter*, The Bodley Head, 1912, pp. 320, 321.

PLATO (1737–1812), Archbishop of Moscow, and author of numerous religious works; his real name was Pierre Befchin.

Upon our arrival at the convent, we were told he was then walking in a small garden, the care of which constituted his principal pleasure; and the employment characterised the simplicity and innocence of his life. As we entered the garden, we found him seated on a turf bank, beneath the windows of the refectory, attended by a bishop, an old man his vicar, the *abbé* of the monastery and some others of the monks. I could scarcely believe my eyes when they told me it was Plato; for though I had often seen him in his archiepiscopal vestments, his rural dress had made such an alteration, that I did not know him. He was habited in a striped silk bed-gown, with a night-cap like the silk nets which hang down the back, as commonly seen on the heads of Italian postilions, and a pair of woollen stockings, with feet of coarse linen, fastened on with twine in an uncouth manner. He was without shoes, but a pair of yellow slippers laid at some distance. By his side, on the bank, was placed his broad-brimmed hat, such as is worn by the shepherdesses of the Alps; and in the hat-band, to complete the resemblance, was stuck a bunch of withered flowers. His white beard, and that mildness and animation of countenance which distinguished him, gave to his features a most pleasing expression.

IN 1800.

SOURCE: Edward Daniel Clarke, *Travels in various countries of Europe, Asia and Africa,* 1810 edition, Vol. I, pp. 150–151.

POINCARÉ, RAYMOND (1860–1934), French Prime Minister and President.

He was an angry, yapping little schauzer for whom the Versailles Treaty had not enough fangs in it. His profusion of grey hair had deserted the top of his head and camped entirely around the biting area; a light brown spot in the centre marked the place where the onion soup made its entrance. He had deep bone-sheltered eyes like cinders in a pit, and his forehead toppled over his brow as if placed by a drunken angel. He was pedantic in grooming as in everything else. Every gesture and word of his was clipped to the right size, and he had the defiant bearing of a provincial trial lawyer prosecuting someone for having swiped *Le Coq Gaulois.*

SOURCE: Emery Kelen, *Peace in Their Time,* Victor Gollancz, 1964, pp. 91–92.

POMPADOUR, JEANNE ANTOINETTE POISSON LE NORMANT D'ÉTOILES, MARQUISE DE (1721–1764), courtesan; mistress of Louis XV.

Le Marquise de Pompadour was above the average in height, slim, of easy bearing, supple, elegant; her face and figure were well matched; face a perfect oval, beautiful hair, light chestnut rather than fair, eyes fairly large, framed by beautiful eyebrows of the same colour as the hair; and a most delightful smile, with the most beautiful complexion in the world, gave to her features the greatest animation. Her eyes had a particular charm which they owed perhaps to the uncertainty of their colour; they had neither the bright sparkle of black eyes, nor the tender languor of blue eyes, nor the finesse which is peculiar to grey eyes; this uncertainty of colour seemed to make them fit for all kinds of bewitching enticement and to express in turn all the impressions of a very changeable spirit; also the play on the countenance of Madame de Pompadour was of infinite variety, yet one never perceived a discordance among the features of her face; all concurred to the same end, which presupposed a mind in full control of itself; her movements accorded with the rest and the *ensemble* of her person seemed to mark the transition between the last degree of elegance and the first degree of nobility.

SOURCE: Leroy, Lieutenant of hunting of the park of Versailles; quoted Margaret Trouncer, *The Pompadour*, Hutchinson, 1956, p. 52.

POQUELIN, JEAN BAPTISTE (1622–1673). See Molière.

POTEMKIN, GRIGORI ALEKSANDROVICH, PRINCE (1739–1791), Russian field-marshal; favourite of Catherine II.

I here behold a Commander in Chief who looks idle and is always busy; who has no other desk than his knees, no other comb than his fingers, constantly reclined on his couch, yet sleeping neither at night nor in the day time ... Trembling for others, brave himself, stopping under the hottest fire of a battery to give his orders, yet more an Ulysses than an Achilles; alarmed at the approach of danger, frolicsome when it arrives; bored in the midst of pleasure, unhappy in being too fortunate, surfeited with everything; easily disgusted, morose, inconstant, a profound philosopher, an able minister, a sublime politician, or a child of ten years old ... concealing under the appearance of harshness kindness of heart; whimsical in matters of time, meals, and inclination; wanting to have everything as a child, or as a great man knowing how to do without anything; sober though seemingly a glutton, gnawing his fingers, or it may be apples, or it may be turnips; scolding or laughing, mimicking or swearing; engaged in wantonness or in prayers; singing or meditating; sending for twenty aides-de-camp and saying nothing to any of them; withstanding heat better than any man,

while he seems to think of nothing but the most voluptuous
baths; not caring for cold, though he seems unable to exist
without furs; always in a shirt without pants or in rich regimentals embroidered at the seams; barefoot or in slippers embroidered with spangles; wearing neither hat nor cap; it is thus
I saw him once in the middle of a musket fire; sometimes in a
nightgown, sometimes in a splendid tunic with his three stars,
his orders, and diamonds as large as a thumb round the portrait of the Empress . . . crooked and almost bent double when
he is at home; and tall, erect, proud, handsome, noble, majestic
or fascinating when he shows himself to his army, like Agamem-
non in the midst of the monarchs of Greece.

SOURCE: Prince de Ligne, in a letter to le Comte de Ségur;
quoted Harold Nicolson, *The Age of Reason*, Constable, 1960, pp.
178–179.

PROUST, MARCEL (1871–1922), French novelist.

Proust was beginning to be lionised. He would lie in bed all day
in his stuffy darkened room, and in the evening he would put
on his elaborate evening clothes (those white kid-gloves
clasping an opera hat) and attend the receptions given to
members of the Peace Conference. He appeared like Beethoven
at the Congress of Vienna. He would flit about looking like a
Goanese bridegroom.

SOURCE: Harold Nicolson, *Some People*, Constable & Company,
1927, new edition, 1958, p. 101.

RACINE, JEAN (1639–1699), French tragic dramatist.

No-one possessed a greater talent or a more agreeable mien.
There was nothing of the poet in his manners: he had the air
of a well-bred and modest man, and at last of a good man.

SOURCE: *Memoirs of the Duke of Saint-Simon*, trans. Bayle St John,
Allen & Unwin, 1913, Vol. i, p. 137.

RANCÉ, ARMAND JEAN LE BOUTHILLIER DE (1626–1700), French founder of the Trappist Cistercians.

He was in the flower of his age, not being more than about twenty-five years old; his height was above medium, well set up and well proportioned. His physiognomy was happy and spiritual, he had a high forehead and his nose was large and long, without being aquiline; his eyes were full of fire, his mouth and all the rest of his face harmonised as well as one could wish in a man. All this united to produce a certain air of gentleness and grandeur, which augured happily, and which caused him to be both loved and respected. For the rest, he had such a delicate constitution that the least wind was enough to give him a cold; it was difficult to understand how he could stand up to the fatigue of hunting and of study; But it was much more surprising, when after his conversion, in spite of his continual austerities and the labours of a penitence almost without precedent in recent centuries, he yet survived to a good old age— clear proof that we lack courage much more than physical strength, that nothing is impossible to grace, and that it is sufficient to love God as much as he has loved us in order to undertake great things for him.

SOURCE: L'Abbé Marsollier, *La Vie de Dom Armand-Jean Le Bouthillier de Rancé*, Paris, 1703, pp. 15–16.

RASPUTIN, GREGORY EFIMOVITCH (1871–1916), Russian monk, notorious for his debauched life, and for the power he possessed over the Tsarina.

When my father arrived in St. Petersburg for the first time, he was wearing the simple dress of a wandering *moujik*: full linen smock, wide trousers and high peasant's boots. He was a tall man of exceptional strength, very broad-shouldered and with those magnetic eyes, set in black circles, the disturbing fixity of which had so often been described. My father was then nearly forty . . .

From the first they began to present a distorted picture of

my father, exaggerate his simplicity, saddle him with a reputation for vulgarity and coarseness he in no way deserved. Because his hands were big and horny, they said they were dirty; because he wore a brown beard, thick and slightly curling and long hair divided by a parting in the middle of his head with two wisps sometimes hanging over the forehead, they said he was ill-kempt and slovenly.

SOURCE: Marie Rasputin, trans. Arthur Chambers, *The Real Rasputin*, John Long Ltd., 1929, pp. 41–43.

Last night at a restaurant over on the island where I had stopped for a time on my way back from dinner, at the house of a friend, I saw Rasputin. He was in the company of a few friends and sycophants and of one or more of the wretched men in public life who fawn on him in the expectation of preferment through his influence. He is a strange and rather striking looking man. The most noticeable feature about him is the eyes. They are large, observant eyes, shifting or steady at his will, and I could quite fancy their having a disconcerting effect on a person on whom they rested for a while with calm assurance. They are what we would be apt to call the hypnotic eye. They are certainly what the Italians would call the evil eye.

SOURCE: George T. Marye [American ambassador to Russia, 1914–1916], *Nearing the End in Imperial Russia*, Selwyn & Blount, Ltd., 1929, p. 444.

REMBRANDT (REMBRANDT HARMENSZ VAN RIJN)
(1606–1669), Dutch painter.

He was a most temperamental man and despised everyone. The ugly and plebeian face by which he was ill-favoured, was accompanied by untidy and dirty clothes, since it was his custom, when working, to wipe his brushes on himself, and to do other things of a similar nature. When he worked he would not have granted an audience to the first monarch in the world, who would have had to return and return again until he had found him no longer engaged upon that work. He often went to

P

public sales by auction; and here he acquired clothes that were old-fashioned and disused as long as they struck him as bizarre and picturesque, and those, even though at times they were downright dirty, he hung on the walls of his studio among the beautiful curiosities which he also took pleasure in possessing, such as every kind of old and modern arms—arrows, halberds, daggers, sabres, knives and so on—and innumerable quantities of exquisite drawings, engravings and medals, and every other thing which he thought a painter might ever need.

SOURCE: *Life of Rembrandt* by Filippo Baldinucci, who died in 1696; quoted Ludwig Goldscheider, edit., *Rembrandt, Paintings, Drawings, Etchings*, Phaidon Press, 1964, p. 23. Though Baldinucci was not strictly a contemporary of Rembrandt he tells us that most of his information was supplied by the Danish painter Bernhardt Keil (1625–1687), a pupil of Rembrandt for eight years, so there is good reason for regarding this description as authentic.

RENAN, ERNEST (1823–1892), French historian and biblical scholar.

I see him a fat, squat, broad-shouldered old man, looking like a benevolent toad, who rolls into a crowded little lecture-room, seats himself at the end of a table, where he opens an old Hebrew Bible, and then with a look round his audience of professors, students, and ladies of fashion, pours out a stream of vivid, malicious and melodious French to the accompaniment of intermittent chuckles of delight from his enthralled audience . . . It was not zeal for the Hebrew Bible which packed the lecture-room, but the fame of the lecturer. 'Le Père Renan' was a Parisian mode, but not altogether a senseless one, for though he spoke on abstruse themes he spoke in a way which all might appreciate. His *causeries*, poured out from a full mind with an air of artless meditation, were of so subtle and exquisite a texture, and fell upon the ears with such seductive melody that even the profane were compelled to enjoy and admire.

SOURCE: H. A. L. Fisher, *An Unfinished Autobiography*, Oxford University Press, 1940, pp. 66–67.

RENOIR, PIERRE AUGUSTE (1841–1919), French impressionist
  painter.

What struck strangers at first meeting were his eyes and his
hands. His eyes were a light brown, bordering on amber, and
they were sharp and penetrating . . . As for their expression,
they had a look of tenderness mixed with irony, of merriment
and sensuousness. They always seemed to be laughing, per-
ceiving the odd side of things . . . his hands were terribly
deformed. His rheumatism had made the joints stiff, and caused
the thumbs to turn inwards toward the palm and his fingers to
bend towards the wrist. Visitors who were not prepared for
this could not take their eyes off this deformity. Though they
did not dare to mention it, their reaction would be expressed by
some such phrase as, 'It isn't possible! With hands like that,
how can he possibly paint those pictures? There's some mystery
somewhere . . .'

  His hair, which had once been light brown, had turned white,
but was still quite thick at the back of his head. On top, however, he was completely bald, a feature which was not visible
since he always wore a cap, even indoors. His nose was aquiline
and gave him an air of authority. He had a beautiful white
beard, and one of us always kept it trimmed to a point for him.
Curiously enough, it curved slightly to the left, owing to the
fact that he liked to sleep with the bedclothes tucked well up
under the chin.

  As a rule he dressed in a jacket with a button-up collar and
long, baggy trousers, both of striped grey cloth. His Lavallière
cravat, royal blue with white polka dots, was carefully knotted
round the collar of his flannel shirt. My mother used to buy his
cravats in an English shop, because French manufacturers have
gradually let their blue turn to a slate colour . . . In the evening, except in summer, a little cape was put around his shoulders. He wore high, grey-checked felt carpet slippers, or else
plain dark brown ones with metal clasps. Out of doors he was
shielded from the sun by a white linen hat. In the house, he
preferred a cloth cap with ear-flaps, of a type advertised by a
'novelty store' at the beginning of the century as 'chauffeurs'

caps.' He did not look like a man of our times, but made us think of some monk of the Italian Renaissance.

SOURCE: Jean Renoir, *Renoir My Father*, trans. Randolph and Dorothy Weaver, Collins, 1962, pp. 31–32.

RETZ, JEAN FRANÇOIS PAUL DE GONDI, CARDINAL DE (1614–1679), French churchman and political conspirator; leader of the 'Fronde' before he went over to the Court party in exchange for his Cardinal's hat.

As we stood together, there came to us a little swarthy man, with eyes as quick as lightning, albeit near-sighted:—it was Coadjutor De Retz. He lamented that his profession hindered him from dancing.

SOURCE: *Journal of Lady Beatrix Graham, Sister of the Marquis of Mentrose*, Bell & Daldy, 1871, pp. 35–36.

RICHELIEU, ARMAND EMMANUEL SOPHIE SEPTE-MANIE DE PLESSIS, FIFTH DUKE (1766–1822), French statesman.

His astonishing resemblance to his grandfather struck all those who had known the Marshal in his youth. He was tall, lanky, very thin, a little bent. At the age of fifteen his face was charming, and it remained pleasing to the end of his life. Its chief ornament was a pair of large dark eyes full of fire, which gave the face an expression both of wit and piquancy. He was of very dark complexion, with curly and intensely black hair, which turned grey very early.

SOURCE: The Comte de Langeron, a lifelong friend from his Vienna days; quoted Cynthia Cox, *Talleyrand's Successor*, Arthur Baker Ltd., 1959, pp. 23–24.

ROBERT II (c. 970–1031), King of France from 996; known as 'the Pious'.

He was tall with fine, soft hair, neatly arranged; he had modest eyes, and a pleasant, gentle mouth for giving the holy kiss of peace; his beard was full and his shoulders high . . . When he mounted his royal horse (an admirable creature), his toes bent round almost to touch his heel, which in that century was regarded by those who saw it as a miracle. He prayed to God frequently and continually, genuflected an immeasurable quantity of times, and, to use the terms of Aurelius Victor, and speak the language of men, he was a man who had arrived at the highest rank by his merits in all fields. When he sat in the council chamber, he readily admitted to being under the authority of the Bishops. Never did an injury lead him to revenge; he loved simplicity, and spent his time in conversation, walking, and always ate his meals in company; he studied the holy scriptures so much that day never passed in which he did not read his psalter, nor pray out loud to God and Saint David. He was kind, friendly, of a pleasant and courteous character, preferring helpful deeds to flattery.

SOURCE: Helgaud [his chaplain], *Vie du Roi Robert;* published in M. Guizot, *Collection des Mémoires relatifs à L'Histoire de France*, Paris, 1824, pp. 365–366.

ROBESPIERRE, MAXIMILIEN FRANÇOIS MARIE ISO-DORE DE (1758–1794), French Revolutionary leader, member of the Committee of Public Safety.

There was something singularly strange and fantastic in this extraordinary man, at least, so it appeared to me. He smiled with an affected look of kindness; but there was something sardonic and demoniac in his countenance, and deep marks of the small pox added to the repulsive character of his physiognomy. He appeared to me like a bird of prey—a vulture; his forehead and temples were low and flattened; his eyes were of a fawn colour, and most disagreeable to look at; his dress was careful, and I recollect that he wore a frill and ruffles, that seemed to me of valuable lace . . . there was much of the *petit-maître* in his manner and appearance, strangely contrasting with the plebeian taste of the times.

SOURCE: J. G. Millingen, *Recollections of Republican France*; quoted J. M. Thompson, *English Witnesses of the French Revolution*, Blackwell, 1938, p. 254. For a note on J. G. Millingen, see under Danton, Georges.

Robespierre came slowly forward. He was one of the few men who at this time [i.e., in 1793, when he was addressing the Jacobin Club] still wore the vogue before the Revolution. His hair was dressed and powdered in the old style. He resembled a tailor of the *ancien régime* more than anything else. He wore spectacles which probably served to conceal the twitchings of his pallid face. His delivery was slow and measured. His phrases were so long that every time he stopped to raise his spectacles one thought he had nothing more to say, but after looking slowly and searchingly over the audience in every quarter of the room he would readjust his glasses and then add some more phrases to his sentences which were already of inordinate length.

SOURCE: an onlooker named Fievée; quoted Stanley Loomis, *Paris in the Terror*, Jonathan Cape, 1964, p. 276.

RODIN, (FRANÇOIS) AUGUSTE (RENÉ) (1840–1917), French sculptor.

Auguste Rodin is in person a man of middle height, with an enormous head upon a massive torso. At first sight one sees nothing of him but this leonine bust, the head with its strong nose, flowing grey beard, and small, keen, light-coloured eyes, slightly veiled by short sight and by a gentle irony. The impression of power is accentuated by the rolling gait, the rocky aspect of the troubled brow under the rough brush of hair, the bony thickness of the aquiline nose and the ample curls of beard. But the first impression is partly contradicted by the reticent line of the mouth, the quick look, penetrating, simple and arch (one of the most composite glances I have ever seen), and especially by the voice, which is hollow, not easily modulated, with deep inflections and sudden returns to a dental pronunciation, and of which the meaning and intention are further modified by certain very expressive tossings of the head. He appears simple, precise, reserved, courteous and cordial, without liveliness. Little by little his shyness gives place to a calm and remarkable tone of authority. He is neither emphatic nor awkward, and would seem rather dispirited than inspired. An immense energy breathes in his sober and measured gestures.

SOURCE: Camille Mauclair, *Auguste Rodin*, trans. Clementina Black, Duckworth & Co., 1905, pp. 101–102.

ROLAND DE LA PLATIÈRE, JEANNE-MARIE (1754–1793), French Girondist.

Our common misfortune had brought me in contact with Mme. Roland, the Egeria of the Girondins. Her arrival at the Conciergerie was an event and I was anxious to make the acquaintance of this woman, unknown fifteen months before, who had in so short a space made numerous friends, more numerous enemies, and acquired a high position and great celebrity, leading only to chains and death. Mme. Roland was aged between thirty-five and forty. Her face did not possess the regularity of beauty, but was very attractive to look at, with her lovely fair hair and large blue eyes. She had a graceful figure and perfectly formed hands. Her look was expressive and even in repose her face had a noble and winning quality. One suspected that she was witty before she began to speak, but no woman ever spoke with more purity, grace and elegance . . . To a musical voice she added gestures full of nobility and truth and a glance that acquired animation as she spoke. Every day I experienced a fresh delight in listening to her, less, perhaps, for what she said than for the magical way in which she said it. Such was my impression of Mme. Roland against whom I was prejudiced before I knew her . . .

Detached from the Revolution, Mme. Roland was a different person. No one fulfilled better than she the ideal of a wife and a mother or was able to show more eloquently that it is only in the accomplishment of her sacred duties that a woman can achieve happiness . . .

On the day which Mme. Roland was to appear before the court . . . she waited at the barrier for her name to be called. She had dressed herself with care and was wearing an English style costume of white muslin trimmed with net and gathered up with a black velvet sash. She had done her hair carefully and wore a simple but elegant bonnet, from beneath which her beautiful hair flowed on to her shoulders. Her face seemed more animated than usual, her complexion was brilliant and her lips wore a smile. With one hand she was attending to the train of her skirt, while she made over the other to a crowd of women who clustered round her to kiss it . . .

SOURCE: Comte Beugnot, *Memoirs of Comte Beugnot (1785–1815)*, Paris, 1866; quoted George Pernoud and Sabine Flaissier, *The French Revolution*, trans. Richard Graves, Secker & Warburg, 1961, pp. 259–261.

My complexion is vivid rather than clear, and it is of a dazzling colour. My mouth is a bit large, but it would be difficult to find a smile that is sweeter or more engaging than mine. Though my hand is not small, it is very elegant because of its long slender fingers, which indicate cleverness and grace. My teeth are white and well placed and I enjoy the fulness of excellent health. Such are the treasures with which nature has endowed me.

SOURCE: a self-description from Madame Roland's *Mémoirs* quoted Stanley Loomis, *Paris in the Terror*, Jonathan Cape, 1964, p. 183.

ROMANOFFS, THE (1903). A picture of the last representatives of the House that ruled Russia from 1613 to 1917.

In February 1903 there were two famous costume balls where all the guests appeared in fourteenth-century Russian dress, the first one being given in the Hermitage. Although no foreigners had been invited, the daughters of Sir Charles Scot, the British Ambassador, were allowed seats in the gallery to watch the brilliant scene in the hall below as the Emperor [Tsar Nicholas II] and Empress [Alexandra], in the dress of the

Tsar Alexis Michaelovitch and his second wife, led the polon-
aise, followed by the Imperial family and all the members of
the nobility.

A lot has been written about the Romanoffs, and they have—
perhaps not always unjustly—been severely criticised, but
nobody, even their bitterest enemy, could deny their good looks;
always, on any state occasion, when one saw them following the
slight figure of the Emperor, one was struck anew by the magnificence of these tall, splendid men, and the upright dignity
of their bearing, and on that night in the glittering brocades and
velvets of the old Boyar costumes, they must indeed have been a
spectacle of almost incredible splendour. There were many
beautiful women among them too. The Empress herself in a
dress and overmantle of gold embossed brocade, embroidered
with pearls and diamonds; the Emperor's sister, the Grand
Duchess Xenia, small and slender, with her rather wistful face
and great dark eyes, her halo-shaped head-dress encrusted
with diamonds and emeralds; the Grand Duchess Serge in a
dress of silver tissue and an overmantle of her favourite blue-
green brocade; the Grand Duchess Vladimir in rose and gold,
Princess Orloff, Princess Belloselsky, Princess Troubetzkoie,
and Princess Yousoupoff in a dress of silver brocade, topped by a
short crimson and silver jacket, trimmed with sable, her head-
dress blazing with rubies and diamonds, with the great diamond
called the Polar Star set in the centre.

SOURCE: Meriel Buchanan, *Victorian Gallery*, Cassel & Co., 1956,
pp. 182–183.

ROSSETTI, GABRIELE PASQUALE GIUSEPPE (1783–1854),
Italian poet and author, the father of the more famous Dante
Gabriel Rossetti.

As might be expected of one possessing so many accomplishments, and whose career had been marked by so much courage,
the Professor was a man of striking character and aspect; so that,
when I was introduced to him in 1848 and his grand climac-
teric was past, and (as with most Italians) a life of studies told
upon him heavily, I could not but be struck with the noble

energy of his face, and by the high culture his expression attested, while a sort of eager, almost passionate resolution seemed to glow in all he said and did. To a youngster, such as I was then, he seemed much older than his years; and, while seated reading at a table with two candles behind him, and (because his sight was failing) with a wide shade over his eyes, he looked a very Rembrandt come to life. The light was reflected from a manuscript placed close to his face, and, in the shadow which covered them, made distinct all the finesse and vigour of his sharply moulded features. It was half lost upon his somewhat shrunken figure wrapped in a student's dressing-gown, and shone fully upon the lean, bony, and delicate hands in which he held the paper. He looked like an old and somewhat imperative prophet, and his voice had a slightly rigorous ring, speaking to his sons and their visitors.

SOURCE: F. G. Stephens, a monograph entitled *Dante Gabriel Rossetti*, 1894; quoted *Dante Gabriel Rossetti, His Family Letters*, edit. with a memoir by William Michael Rossetti, Ellis & Elvey, 1895, Vol. I, pp. 19–20. W. M. Rossetti himself notes (ibid., p. 14):

In person Gabriele Rossetti was rather below the middle height, and full in flesh till his health failed; with a fine brow, a marked prominent nose and large nostrils, dark-speaking eyes, pleasant mouth, engaging smile, and genuine laugh. He indulged in gesticulation, not to any great extent but of course more than an Englishman. His hands were rather small—not a little spoiled by a life-long habit of munching his nails. As to other personal habits, I may mention free snuff-taking without any smoking; and a hearty appetite while health lasted, with more of vegetable diet than Englishmen use. In his later years teeth and palate had failed, and all viands tasted like hay.

ROSSINI, GIOACHINO ANTONIO (1792–1868), Italian composer.

Rossini has been for some time a resident in Paris; and whenever he receives, every one is anxious to be admitted to his soirées, where good music is sure to be heard, or to his dinner-table where excellent macaroni is as certain to be served up. The master looks in perfect health, and has more of the English-man that the Italian in his personal appearance. The photographs that are sold of him are perfect of their kind, and express the good-nature and sly humour for which he is remarkable.

SOURCE: *Reminiscences and Recollections of Captain Gronow*; first published 1862–1866; abridged edit. by John Raymond, Bodley Head, 1964, p. 282.

ROUSSEAU, JEAN JACQUES (1712–1778), French writer and philosopher; author of *Le Contrat social* (1762), which proclaimed the principles of national sovereignty and universal suffrage, and which exerted considerable influence on the French Revolution.

I must confess, that nothing ever appeared to me so odd and fantastical as his figure and appearance, which I merely considered as a masquerade. His coat, his *marron*-coloured stockings, his little round wig, the whole of his costume, his manners and deportment, seemed to me a scene of comedy most ludicrous, and perfectly well acted ... I never knew a literary character more agreeable or with less affectation. He spoke simply of himself and without spite of his enemies ... His eyes were small, and though deep set, were very piercing, and as if they would penetrate and pry into the very soul of the individual he was interrogating. It seemed to me that he would instantly have discovered a falsehood or evasive reply ... He had a most agreeable smile, full of mildness and *finesse*, was talkative, and, as far as I found, very gay.

SOURCE: *Memoirs of the Countess de Genlis, Illustrative of the History of the Eighteenth and Nineteenth Centuries*, written by herself, London, 1825, Vol. 2, pp. 4–8.

He is very complimentary without being polite, or at least without seeming to be so. He appears to be ignorant of the usages of society; but it is easy to see that he is exceedingly intellectual. He has a dark complexion; his features are lighted up by eyes full of fire. When he has spoken and one looks at him, he seems nice-looking; but, when one recalls him to mind, it is always as an ugly man. It is said that he is in ill-health, but that he carefully conceals his sufferings from some motive of vanity; it is apparently this which, from time to time, makes him seem shy.

SOURCE: Madame D'Epinay, *Memoirs*, trans. J. H. Freese, H. S. Nichols, 1899, Vol. I, p. 174.

RUBINSTEIN, ANTON GRIGORIEVICH (1829–1894), Russian pianist and composer.

By jinks, it was a mixtery! He fetched up his right wing, he fetched up his left wing, he fetched up his center, he fetched up his reserves ... He opened his cannon—round shot, shells, shrapnels, grape, canister, mines and magazines—every living battery and bomb a-going at the same time. The house trembled, the lights danced, the wall shuck, the sky split, the ground rocked—heavens and earth, creation, sweet potatoes, Moses, ninepences, glory, tenpenny nails, Sampson in a 'simmon tree— Bang! ! ! !...

With that bang! he lifted himself bodily into the air, and he came down with his knees, fingers, toes, elbows and his nose, striking every single solitary key on the pianner at the same time.

SOURCE: A recitation by George Bagby, *Jud Brownin Hears Ruby Play*, popular all over America during Rubinstein's tour of 1873; quoted Harold C. Schonberg, *The Great Pianists*, Victor Gollancz, 1964, p. 261.

Anton Rubinstein was very much like Beethoven in appearance, and some people even supposed he was a reincarnation. His hands were enormous, Hofmann said that his little finger was 'as thick as my thumb ... his fingers were square at the end, with cushions on them.'

RUDOLPH II (1552–1612), Roman Emperor from 1576, son of the Emperor Maximilian II: a notable patron of scientists, and the greatest collector of his age. His agents ransacked Europe for rare works of art.

Rodolphus the Emperor was of middle stature, somewhat

corpulent, with a ruddy but sour countenance, a short thick beard, and brown coloured hair. At that time mourning for his dead sister, he wore black garments of small price; he was said to love solitariness and to exercise the Arts of Alchemy and Painting. He was most easy of access, and very affable, so as every man spake to him with small reverence . . . He was esteemed sparing of speech and liberal in his nature.

SOURCE: Fynes Moryson, *An Itinerary*, *1605–17*, James Mac-Lehose & Sons, 1908, Vol. IV, p. 253.

RUSSIAN MAN (A) IN 1557.

The Russian is apparelled in this manner; his upper garment is of cloth of gold, silk, or cloth, long, down to the foot, and buttoned with great buttons of silver or else laces of silk, set on with brooches, the sleeves thereof very long, which he weareth on his arm, ruffled up. Under that he hath another long garment buttoned with silk buttons, with a high collar standing up of some colour, and that garment is made straight. Then his shirt is very fine, and wrought with red silk, or some gold, with a collar of pearl. Under his shirt he hath linen breeches, upon his legs a pair of hose without feet, and his boots of red or yellow leather. On his head he weareth a white Colepecke with buttons of silver, gold, pearl or stone, and under it is a black fox cap, turned up very broad.

When he rideth on horseback to the wars or any journey he hath a sword of the Turkish fashion, and his bow and arrows of the same manner. In the town he weareth no weapon, but only two or three pair of knives, having the hafts of the tooth of a fish, called the morse.

IN 1557.

SOURCE: Anthony Jenkinson's account of his first voyage from London to Russia in 1557; quoted Richard Hakluyt, *Principal Navigations, Voyages etc.*, J. M. Dent & Sons, 1927, Vol. I. pp. 417–418.

SAINT-ÉVREMOND, CHARLES DE MARGUETEL DE SAINT-DENIS SEIGNEUR DE (1610–1703), French soldier and satirical writer; served in Thirty Years' War, reaching rank of Field Marshal; exiled to England; received with favour by Charles II and buried in Westminster Abbey.

St. Évremond had blue, lively and sparkling eyes, a large forehead, thick eyebrows, a handome mouth, and a sneering physiognomy . . . His behaviour was civil and engaging, his conversation lively and pleasant, his repartees quick and happy.

SOURCE: Des Maizeaux; quoted T. P. Lathy, *Memoirs of the Court of Louis XIV*, London, 1819, Vol. I, p. 147.

SAINTE-BEUVE, CHARLES AUGUSTIN (1804–1869), French critic and man of letters.

Everything about him displeasing—his scarlet face, his plump cheeks, his spectacles, his forehead, so retreating that the light slipped off it, his complacent manner, his expression of soft self-satisfaction with a hint of acid underneath, his brand new town suit, his horrid gloves, the sheaf of papers in his hand. He was ridiculous from the first moment that he mounted the platform.

SOURCE: M. Henri Boucher, recording Sainte-Beuve's first lecture after he was appointed to the chair of Latin poetry at the College de France, March 9th, 1855. After only a few weeks, he tendered his resignation. Quoted Harold Nicolson, *Sainte-Beuve*, Constable, 1957, pp. 199–200.

A little hook-shaped man, rather uncouth, ugly, still young, but with an ageing, wrinkled face and, in addition to this quite bald. It was even worse when he climbed up on to the platform. We were then treated to a sort of monotonous recitative, an endless canticle, which disappointed the hopes that had been aroused by the arrival of a professor from Paris.

SOURCE: M. Chappuis, a member of the audience at a lecture at the Lausanne Academy; quoted ibid., p. 109.

SAVONAROLA, GIROLAMO (1452–1498), Italian monk and reformer who became unofficial dictator in Florence; conflict with the Pope led to his arrest, torture and hanging.

His body was slight but sturdy; his limbs were so delicately cast that his holy hand seemed translucent. He was always even-tempered, never agitated; and his fine, dark eyes, though they were somewhat small, looked straight at the world with a kindly penetration. His thick, dark beard showed up his broad face and his lively mouth: his nose was slightly aquiline.

SOURCE: Fra Benedetto [one of Savonarola's brethren of S. Marco], *Cedrus Libani*; quoted E. L. S. Horsburgh, *Girolamo Savonarola*, Methuen & Co., 1911, p. 39.

SAVOY, MARIE ADELAIDE OF (1685–1712), later became Duchess of Burgundy and Dauphine of France; she was the mother of Louis XV.

I arrived here before five o'clock; the princess did not arrive until six. I went to the coach to receive her ... At length we reached her room, where there was a crowd and heat enough to kill us. I showed her now and then to those who approached her, and I studied her in every way, in order to write you my impressions of her. She has the best grace and the most beautiful figure that I have ever seen; dressed to paint, and *coiffé* the same; eyes bright and very beautiful, the lashes black and admirable; complexion very harmonious, white and red, all that one could desire; the most beautiful hair, and a great quantity of it. She is thin, as befits her age [only 11]; her mouth is rosy, the lips full, the teeth white, long and ill-placed; the hands well-shaped, but the colour of her age. She speaks little, so far as I have seen, and shows no embarrassment when she is looked at, like a person who has seen the world. She curtseys badly, and with rather an Italian air. She has also something of the Italian in her face; but she pleases; I saw that in the eyes of all present. For my part I am very satisfied with her ... To speak to you, as I always do, I find her all that could be wished; I should be sorry if she were more beautiful. I say it again;

everything is pleasing except the curtsey. I will tell you more after supper, for then I shall remark many things which I have not been able to see as yet. I forgot to tell you that she is short rather than tall for her age.

SOURCE: Louis XIV, letter to Madame de Maintenon, November 4th, 1696; quoted H. Noel Williams, *A Rose of Savoy*, Methuen & Co., 1909, pp. 108–109.

Regularly plain, with pendant cheeks, a forehead too prominent, thick, biting lips; hair and eyebrows of dark chestnut, and well planted; the most eloquent and the most beautiful eyes in the world; few teeth, and those all decayed, about which she was the first to talk and jest; the most beautiful complexion and skin; not much bosom, but what there was, admirable; the throat long, with the suspicion of a goitre, which did not ill become her; a carriage of the head gallant, graceful, majestic, and the manner the same, the smile most expressive; a figure long, round, slender, easy, perfectly shaped; the walk of a goddess upon the clouds—she pleased to a superlative degree.

SOURCE: Saint-Simon, *Mémoires*; quoted ibid., p. 303.

SCARRON, PAUL (1610–1660), French poet, novelist and playwright; though almost paralysed by a spinal complaint, married Francoise d'Arbigné, afterwards Madame de Maintenon.

... I wish I could invent one [i.e., a machine] to buckle my shoe, or to take up a thing from the ground, which I can scarcely do without kneeling, for I can bend my body no further than it is bent by nature. For this reason, when ladies drop a fan or glove, I am not the first to take it up; and often restrain my inclination to perform those little services, rather than expose my spider-like shape. And I hope it will not be construed as pride if I do not always rise from my seat when I ought: for if it is low, I find some trouble in it; and my centre of gravity is so ill-placed, that I am often like to fall back. Things hanging within the reach of others are out of mine; and what they can execute with ease I want strength to perform. I am in danger of being trampled on or stifled in a crowd, where my back is a convenient lodgment for the elbow of any tall person that is near. I can see nothing, and my whole employment is to guard my person. I have forborne to attend his majesty in the house of peers, since I was like to be squeezed to death there against the wall . . . Besides, when I get in, I can never have the pleasure of seeing on the throne one of the best princes who ever sat on it. These, and many others, are the inconveniences continually attending a figure like mine. They may appear grievous to persons not used to them, but they grow easier by habit; and tho' they may a little disturb, they are not sufficient to destroy the happiness of life; of which, at an average, I have enjoyed as great a share as most men.

SOURCE: Paul Scarron; quoted in *On Personal Deformity*, essay in *The Britannic Magazine . . . for the Year 1793*, p. 337.

SCHLEGEL, AUGUST WILHELM VON (1767–1845), German poet, translator and critic.

He was in fact genuinely distinquished in his appearance. Only a few straggling silver-grey hairs still shone on his small, narrow head, and his body was so thin, emaciated, transparent, that he seemed almost a symbol of spirituality.

SOURCE: Heinrich Heine; quoted Max Brod, *Heinrich Heine*, trans. Joseph Witriol, Valentine Mitchell, 1956, p. 79.

SCHLEIERMACHER, FRIEDRICH DANIEL ERNST (1768–1834), German theologian and philosopher.

Then in his holy place and at this solemn hour stood the physically so small and insignificant man, his noble countenance beaming with intellect, and his clear sonorous penetrating voice ringing through the overflowing church. Speaking from the heart, and the clear, full, mighty stream of his eloquence carried everyone along with it. [A sermon to volunteers in the war of liberation which broke out after Napoleon's Russian campaign.]

Q

SOURCE: Bishop Eilert, *Erinnerung aus den Jahren 1813 and 1814*; quoted W. B. Selbie, *Schleiermacher*, Chapman & Hall, 1913, pp. 11–12.

SCHUBERT, FRANZ PETER (1797–1828), Austrian composer.

When I came into closer touch with Schubert he was in the 4th grammar form, a short, sturdy boy with a friendly round face, and strongly marked features. He was not a particular favourite with the clerical professors, yet he was no particular trouble to them by excessive liveliness. He proved that he possessed one of those deep quiet minds which made superficial pedagogues misjudge his silent nature as a sign of little talent. He was even then far in advance of his years mentally, as was proved by a poem written at that period which I kept for a long time but have since lost, and which was written in the style of Klopstock's Odes, hardly comprehended by us pupils, but which had for its theme God's omnipotence in the Universe. ... Schubert had, as long as he was at the Convict, the tiresome task of looking after the music as well as the instruments of the orchestra, to see that they were properly strung, attend to the tallow candle illuminations, give out the parts and place them on the music stands, besides playing the violin.

SOURCE: Anton Holzapfel, a fellow schoolboy of Schubert, in a letter to Ferdinand Luib; quoted Newman Flower, *Franz Schubert*, Cassell & Co., 1928, p. 24.

The figure short, but sturdy, with well-developed solid bones and firm muscles; not angular, but rather rounded. The neck short and strong; shoulders, chest and pelvis broad, finely curved; arms and thighs rounded; hands and feet small; his walk lively and vigorous. The fairly large, round and powerful skull was surrounded by brown, abundantly growing locks. The face, in which the forehead and chin were particularly well developed, showed traits that were not so much actually beautiful as expressive and forceful. The mild eyes, light brown if I am not mistaken, which could flash fire when he was excited, were strongly overshadowed by fairly prominent and bushy brows, and thus seemed smaller than they really were, especially as he often narrowed them, as short-sighted people will. The nose was of medium size, blunt and tilted up a little, and joined by a gentle inward sweep to his full, abundant, firmly set lips, which he generally kept closed. His chin was deeply dimpled. The complexion was pale, but vital, as is usual with genius. The play of his features proclaimed the workings of creative genius, stern when he frowned mightily and compressed his lips, sweet when the eye shone and the mouth smiled. Altogether, Schubert's appearance showed an Olympian, classic expression of harmony between vigour and urbanity.

SOURCE: George Franz Eckel, in a letter to Ferdinand Luib, 1958; quoted Otto Erich Deutsch, *Schubert*, trans. Eric Blom, J. M. Dent & Sons, 1946, p. 926.

SIENESE LADIES (c. 1460).

The ladies of Siena, Italy, were known throughout Europe for their charm and elegance. A poet described them as 'most beautiful and filling all the town' but regretted that all this beauty should be wasted on swine like the Sienese man.

The variety of their head-dresses made them seem to belong to every nation, some looking like angels, others like French or Flemish women, and yet others like Indians, Arabs, or Chaldees.

SOURCE: The Emperor Frederick III, when he travelled through Tuscany in 1460; quoted Iris Origo, *The World of San Bernardino*, Jonathan Cape, 1963, p. 47.

You wear so many vanities upon your head that it is shameful. Some wear battlements, some fortifications and some towers as large as that one [indicating the tower of the Piazza del Campo]. I see upon these battlements the devil's banner . . . I see one woman with a head-dress shaped like tripe, and others like a pancake or a plate. Some fold the rim up and some down . . . Could you but see yourselves, you look like so many owls and hawks . . . O women, you have made a god of your head.

SOURCE: Fra Bernardino of Siena, in a sermon; quoted Iris
Origo (see above), p. 48.

SIGISMUND I (1467–1548), King of Poland from 1506.

The said King of Poland is a handsome figure only slightly
plump; nevertheless he will never be any fatter; a pale face
and body and very white hands, the same height as the *Seigneur
de Berges* . . . but a face more handsome than *Monsieur de Berges*
because it is open and very honest . . . He is, as he told me with
his own mouth, which is fine and red, forty-six years old . . . his
hair is already a little grey . . .

SOURCE: The Emperor Maximilian; quoted Christopher Hare,
Isabella of Milan, Harper & Brothers, 1911, p. 304.

SIGISMUND III (1566–1605), King of Poland (from 1587), and Sweden (from 1594).

Myself did see Sigismund the third and his Queen at the port of
Dantzt [i.e. Danzig, or modern Gdansk] a free City of Prussia,
where thirty ships of Sweden, and one of Holland (in which the
King and Queen passed) were ready to conduct him into his
hereditary kingdom of Sweden, expecting nothing but a fair
wind. He made this voyage to take possession of his father's
kingdom lately dead, which in the mean time was governed by
his Uncle Charles; not without the suspected favour of the
people, he being of the reformed Religion as they were, but the
king being brought up by his mother in the Roman Religion.
The King was tall of stature, somewhat lean of body, with
a long visage and brown complexion, and the hair of his head
was black and short, with a thin, short, and sharp pointed
beard of a yellowish colour. He wore a little black silk bonnet
hanging down about his neck, and plain black garments, he
then mourning for his father.

IN 1593.

SOURCE: Charles Hughes, edit., *Shakespeare's Europe* (*Unpublished chapters of Fynes Moryson's Itinerary*), Sherratt & Hughes, 1903, pp. 78–79. For a note on Moryson see under Bellarmine, Roberto.

SOCRATES (470–399 B.C.), Athenian philosopher.

Later we both served on the expedition to Potidaea and shared the same mess. Socrates proved himself equal to anyone in his ability to endure hardships, not just better than me . . . His endurance of the rigours of winter, and winters there are pretty severe, was equally notable. Once there was a particularly sharp frost when no-one willingly went out of doors at all, or if he had to, he took extraordinary care to wrap himself up and cover his feet in a binding of felt or sheepskin boots. But Socrates used to go out in these conditions wearing the same clothes as usual, and walked barefoot through the snow just as easily as others did fully shod.

SOURCE: Plato, *Symposium*, 219e; trans. B. K. Workman, and included in *They Saw it Happen in Classical Times*, Basil Blackwell, 1964, p. 28.

SOLIMAN I (1494–1566). See Suleiman I.

SOPHIA DOROTHEA (1687–1757), Queen of Prussia; daughter of George I of England, and the mother of Frederick II.

I was seven years at the court of Queen Sophia Dorothea, and was devoted to her with the greatest veneration. She had never been beautiful, but she was stately and distinguished, and she retained all her dignity in her old age. Possibly she had more *esprit acquit* than *esprit inné*, but she was very well educated and well-bred, could converse with everyone, and intercourse with her was delightful. She was uncommonly fond of splendour and society; she liked to have company every afternoon and evening, and to sit a long time at meals, which was sometimes wearisome to us, her ladies-in-waiting. It was beautiful to see what great and respectful tenderness the king had for her.

SOURCE: Countess von Moss, *Neun und sechzig Jahre am Preussischen Hofe*, p. 10; quoted and trans. Gilbert Stanhope, *A Mystic on the Prussian Throne, Frederick William II*, Mills & Boon Ltd., 1912, pp. 40–41.

I shall observe, in addition, that her stature was tall and majestic, and her aspect commanded respect. After becoming a widow, she grew very corpulent; and this propensity increased so much, that it was at length necessary to have chairs made on purpose for her. She was about eighty years of age in the year 1757, at which period she died, having survived her husband seventeen years.

SOURCE: Dieudonné Thiebault, *Original Anecdotes of Frederick II, King of Prussia*; English edition, J. Johnson, 1805, Vol. I, p. 185.

SPINOZA, BENEDICTUS DE (1632–1677), Dutch philosopher.

His Person, and his way of Dressing himself.
As for his person, his size, and the features of his face, there are still many people at the Hague who saw and knew him particularly. He was of a middle size, he had good features in his face, the skin somewhat black, black curled hair, long eyebrows, and of the same colour, so that one might easily know by his looks that he was descended from Portuguese Jews. As for his clothes, he was very careless of 'em, and they were not better than those of the meanest citizen. One of the most eminent Councillors of State went to see him, and found him in a very slovenly Morning-Gown, whereupon the Councillor blamed him for it, and offered him another. Spinoza answered him, that a man was never the better for having a finer gown. To which he added, *It is unreasonable to wrap up things of little or no value in a precious cover.*

SOURCE: Colerus, *Life of Spinoza*, 1706; edit. F. Pollock, in *Spinoza, His Life and Philosophy*, C. Kegan Paul & Co., 1880, pp. 419–420.

STAÉL, ANNE LOUISE GERMAINE NECKER, MADAME DE (1766–1817), French novelist and essayist.

She was a large, masculine-looking woman, rather coarse, and with a thoracic development worthy of a wet nurse. She had very fine arms, which she took every opportunity of displaying, and dark, flashing eyes, beaming with wit and genius. ... Madame de Staël was perhaps at times a little overpowering and totally deficient in those 'brilliant flashes of silence' which Sydney Smith once jokingly recommended to Macaulay.

SOURCE: *Reminiscences and Recollections of Captain Gronow*, edit. by John Raymond, The Bodley Head, 1964, pp. 234–236.

STANISLAUS II AUGUSTUS (1732–1798), King of Poland from 1764 until his abdication in 1795 and at one time the favourite of Catharine the Great of Russia.

The character of Stanislaus is not one of those hard to penetrate, or difficult to delineate. As a man and an individual, he is certainly more amiable, more an object of attachment and respect, than when contemplated in his kingly capacity. His person, from the concurring testimony of all who knew him in his youth, was handsome, graceful, and elegant. Such Count Poniatowski doubtless appeared in the eyes of Catharine the Second, when he first arrived at Petersburgh. But, the graces of that period of his life are fled; and within the last three or four years he is become too lusty, though it would be unjust to say even now that he is at all corpulent. He is of a middle stature, well proportioned, and of a manly figure. His face is open, pleasing, and interesting; the features bold and strongly marked, particularly his nose and chin. Stanislaus's complexion is pale, and he wears his own hair, which is of a deep colour, approaching to black. There is said to be in his cast of countenance, something pensive and melancholy. At first sight, I confess this expression did not strike me; but the oftener I have had opportunities of seeing and studying him, the more visible it becomes: in profile it is particularly apparent. I believe, however, that it is more the result of his actual situation, his past calamities, and his future prospects, than natural and congenial to him. Whether in effect he casts his view backwards, or directs it onwards to the destiny that awaits him, how vast a train of awful and painful reflection must necessarily open on his mind! I have sometimes seen him stand in a thoughtful attitude, musing, silent, and as I could fancy occupied in considering his future fate. It is impossible not to feel for him at such moments, a more than common interest.

SOURCE: N. W. Wraxall, *Memoirs of the Courts of Berlin, Dresden, Warsaw, and Vienna*, London, 1799, Vol. II, pp. 85–87.

STRAUSS, JOHANN (1804–1849), Viennese composer.

All eyes were turned on him, it was a moment of worship. You will ask, I said to myself, the generations of the future will ask: what does he look like, this Johann Strauss? If Napoleon's appearance was classically Roman and calmly antique, if Paganini's was romantic and arresting as moonlight, so that of Maestro Strauss is African and hot-blooded, crazy from the sun, modern, bold, fidgety, restless, unbeautiful, passionate . . .

The man is black as a Moor; his hair is curly; his mouth is melodious, energetic, his lips curl, his nose is snub; if his face were not so white he would be the complete king of the Moors from Ethiopia, the complete Balthazar . . . Typically African, too, is the way he conducts his dances; his own limbs no longer belong to him when the desert-storm of his waltz is let loose; his fiddle-bow dances with his arms; the tempo animates his feet; the melody waves champagne glasses in his face; the ostrich takes a swift run preliminary to beginning his flight . . . the devil is abroad.

SOURCE: Heinrich Laube; quoted Eduard Jacob, *Johann Strauss*, Hutchinson, 1940, pp. 72–73.

STRESEMANN, GUSTAV (1878–1929), German statesman.

Among these surroundings the Foreign Minister in his black

clothes of modern cut was somewhat of an anachronism. He was distinctly a present-day type and essentially Teutonic. Augustus John painted him and, by exaggerating the modelling, produced a caricature, but in no way gave the impression the man himself produced.

His head was round and the planes merged one into the other. Very blond, with light blue eyes, his complexion was inclined to pallor and seemed paler in contrast with the redness of his full lips.

His English was good, though it had a trace of foreign accent.

SOURCE: S. J. Woolf, *Drawn from Life*, Whittlesey House, 1932, p. 201.

SUE, EUGÈNE (1804–1857), French novelist.

Nothing could have been more correct and scrupulously neat than his dress, which was rather dandified, but in good taste, according to the notions of twenty of thirty years ago. He wore always a very broad brimmed hat, of glossy newness, and remarkably tight, light-coloured trousers: which, by the by, were not particularly becoming to a man built in a stout mould; but a Frenchman who cannot diminish the rotundity of his abdomen, generally revenges himself upon his legs, which he circumscribes in the smallest possible compass, giving himself very much the appearance of what we Englishmen are taught to believe to be his national characteristic and prototype —a frog.

Eugène Sue was rather above the middle height, strongly built, with somewhat high shoulders. His hair and brows were very dark, his eyes blue, long and rather closed, and his complexion of a livid paleness. In general society he did not shew off, and preferred rather being treated as a man of the world, than as a distinguished writer.

SOURCE: Captain Gronow, *Reminiscences and Recollections*, edit. John Raymond, The Bodley Head Ltd., 1964, pp. 186–187.

SULEIMAN I (1494–1566), Sultan of Turkey, called the 'Magnificent'; succeeded his father Selim I in 1520.

You will probably wish me to give you my impressions of Solyman.

His years are just beginning to tell on him, but his majestic bearing and indeed his whole demeanour are such as beseem the lord of so vast an empire. He has always had the character of being a careful and temperate man; even in his early days, when, according to the Turkish rule, sin would have been venial, his life was blameless . . . Considering his years (for he is now getting on for sixty) he enjoys good health, though it may be that his bad complexion arises from some lurking malady. There is a notion current that he has an incurable ulcer or cancer on his thigh. When he is anxious to impress an ambassador, who is leaving, with a favourable idea of the state of his health, he conceals the bad complexion of his face under a coat of rouge, his notion being that foreign powers will fear him more if they think that he is strong and well. I detected unmistakable signs of this practice of his; for I observed his face when he gave me a farewell audience, and found it was much altered from what it was when he received me on my arrival.

SOURCE: C. T. Forster and F. H. B. Daniell, *Ogier Ghiselm de Busbecq, Life and Letters*, Kegan Paul & Co., 1881, Vol. I, pp. 159–160.

Ogier Ghiselm de Busbecq was born in 1522 and spent eight years at the Court of Suleiman, from 1555 to 1562.

TALLEYRAND-PÉRIGORD, CHARLES MAURICE DE (1754–1838), French statesman.

He is fattish for a Frenchman; his ankles are weak and his feet deformed and he totters about in a strange way. His face is not at all expressive, except it be of a kind of drunken stupor: in fact he looks like an old fuddled lame village schoolmaster and his voice is deep and hoarse.

SOURCE: John Wilson Croker; quoted John Fisher, *Eighteen Fifteen, an End and a Beginning*, Cassell, 1963, p. 37.

The ball was a most extraordinary one, about four hundred men to forty women ... When I went into the Duke's I found in the first magnificent room about a hundred officers, but soon discovered many well-known bores under these false pretensions; in the doorway I met Talleyrand waddling out; he did not speak to me, so I had only the satisfaction of seeing his dirty, cunning face and long coat for a moment.

SOURCE: Harriet, Countess of Granville, *Letters, 1810–45*; quoted ibid., pp. 198–199.

He frequently gave way to a natural *nonchalance,* but on such occasions spoke but little; but when he at length shook off this mental indolence, his conversation was enchanting. His habitual chit-chat tone was one of graceful levity that skimmed lightly over the surface of every subject, but which, when serious business was the theme, gave way to an extraordinary depth and force of reasoning. It has often been imagined that he lived, as it were, only intellectually, and that his heart found no room for the feelings of affection; but those who were admitted to his intimacy know that his kindness was unequalled, and that its expression not unfrequently penetrated even through the immoveable features which disconcerted so many able negotiators.

SOURCE: *Gentlemen's Magazine*, July, 1838.

TALMA, FRANÇOIS JOSEPH (1763–1826), French actor; friend of Napoleon.

Talma was at that time a heavily built man but very noble in his strength, a man between fifty and sixty. He wore a white silk dressing gown, slackly bound by a foulard scarf which served as a belt. His neck was bare and one could see his swelling throat with prominent muscles and strongly marked veins, signs of a solid frame and virile energy. His face, which everyone knows, was already deeply graven, recalling by its shape and complexion the imperial bronzes of the Byzantine Empire. But this Roman mask, which seemed imposed upon his features when he was on the stage, fell of its own accord when he was *en déshabillé* and let one see only a wide expanse of face, big gentle eyes, a sad finely drawn mouth, cheeks, inclined slightly to fall away and a little flabby, his facial muscles slack like the untensed springs of some tool. The whole effect of his face was imposing, its expression simple and attractive. One sensed a generous nature beneath his wonderful genius. He sought after no effect; he had enough of that on the stage; he relaxed and at home seemed to be resting his eyes. At once I felt at ease and touched to the heart by the kindness of that face, at once commanding and sincere.

SOURCE: Alphonse de Lamartine; quoted Herbert F. Collins, *Talma, A Biography of an Actor*, Faber & Faber, 1964, pp. 302-303.

TAMERLANE (1336-1405). See Timur.

TARTARS, THE (sixteenth century).

For person and complexion they have broad and flat visages, of a tanned colour into yellow and black; fierce and cruel looks, thin haired upon the upper lip ... light and nimble bodied, with short legs, as if they were made naturally for horsemen: whereto they practise themselves from their childhood, seldom going afoot about any business. Their speech is very sudden and loud, speaking as it were out of a deep hollow throat. When they sing you would think a cow lowed, or some great bandog howled.

SOURCE: *Hakluyt's Voyages*, Dent, 1907, Vol. II, pp. 321-322.

TASSO, TORQUATO (1544-1595), the greatest Italian poet of the late Renaissance.

Torquato Tasso was a man of stature so lofty, that, among men of large size, he might have been considered as one of the bulkiest and best proportioned. His complexion had been exceedingly fair, but, first, studies and vigils, and afterwards disasters and infirmities, had made him somewhat pale. The colour of his hair and beard was a medium, between brown and fair; in such a way, however, that the former was somewhat darker than the latter; but that of both was soft, and smooth, and fine. His head was large, and raised both in the forehead, and in the hinder part, which the Greeks call *occiput*; in the middle, however, above each temple, it was rather depressed than round. His forehead was large and square, first rising to the middle, and afterwards inclining to the hair, which latter time had in a great degree removed, and rendered him almost bald. His eye-brows were well arched, dark, scanty, and disjoined. His eyes were large in proportion to his head, round in themselves, but somewhat lengthened in the corners; their pupils were of a moderate size, their colour of a brilliant blue, such as Homer attributes to Pallas; in their gaze and motions, they were grave and staid, and sometimes they were turned upwards, as following the soarings of the mind within, which was generally raised to things celestial. His ears were of a middling size; his cheeks were rather long than round, meagre by nature, and discoloured by indisposition. His nose was large, and inclined towards the mouth, which was also large and leonine; his lips were thin and pale; his teeth white, large, and thickly set; his voice clear and sonorous, and, at the close of sentences, of a sound more grave. Though his tongue was very nimble, his conversation was rather slow than quick, and he was often accustomed to reiterate his last words. He laughed very rarely, and when that happened, gently, without any noise, and somewhat languidly. His chin was square, his beard was thick, and, as I have already mentioned, of a chestnut colour. His neck was well proportioned, his head elevated, his breast and shoulders broad and full, his arms long, free, and sinewy, his hands were very large, but soft and delicate, his fingers such as could easily bend back. His legs and feet were also long, and well proportioned, but more muscular than fleshy; and indeed his whole body was lean, though suitable in thickness to the height of his figure. His whole limbs were so active, that, in exercises of chivalry, he was very expert, and in fencing, riding, or tilting, needed envy no one. All these things, however, he performed with more ability than grace, as the vivacity of his natural, by no means corresponded with that of his animal spirits. For this reason, likewise, in the public orations which he pronounced in different academies, and in the presence of great princes, his sentiments appeared to the audience much more wonderful than the manner in which they were delivered, perhaps, because his mind, collecting, by its continual speculations, the better part of the spirits to the brain, it did not leave a sufficient quantity in the rest of the body to animate and enliven it. Nevertheless, in all his actions, and even when doing nothing, he discovered, to the most careless observer, a manly grace and beauty, especially in his countenance, which was resplendent with such majesty, that it induced every beholder, previous to any knowledge of his merits, to hold him, from his aspect only, in the greatest reverence.

SOURCE: Manso, *Vita di Torquato Tasso*, Venice, 1621, pp. 236 et seq; quoted John Black, *Life of Torquato Tasso*, Edinburgh, 1810, Vol. II, pp. 342–344. We also learn that Tasso chose extremely simple clothes, often black and without ornament, but far from slovenly.

THEODORE I (1557–1598), Tsar of Russia; son of Ivan IV, 'the Terrible'.

The Emperor that now is (called Feodor Ivanowitch) is for his person of a mean stature, somewhat low and gross, of a sallow complexion, and inclining to the dropsy, hawk nosed, unsteady in his pace by reason of some weakness of his limbs, heavy and inactive, yet commonly smiling almost to a laughter. For quality otherwise, simple and slow witted, but very gentle, and of an easy nature, quiet, merciful, of no martial disposition, nor greatly apt for matter or policy, very superstitious and infinite that way . . . He is of thirty-four years old, or thereabouts, and hath reigned almost the space of six years.

SOURCE: Dr. Giles Fletcher, *Of the Russe Common Wealth*, edit.
E. A. Bond, in *Russia at the Close of the Sixteenth Century*, Hakluyt
Society, 1856, p. 144. (Spelling modernised.)

Fletcher visited Russia as Ambassador from Queen Elizabeth I of
England.

THEODORIC II (426?–466), King of the Visigoths; succeeded in
453 after assassinating his brother, Thorismond, and was himself
assassinated by his younger brother, Euric, in 466.

He is a man worth knowing, even by those who cannot enjoy
his close acquaintance, so happily have Providence and Nature
joined to endow him with the perfect gifts of fortune; his way
of life is such that not even the envy which lies in wait for
kings can rob him of his proper praise. And first as to his person.
He is well set up, in height above the average man, but below
the giant. His head is round, with curled hair retreating
somewhat from brow to crown. His nervous neck is free from
disfiguring knots. The eyebrows are bushy and arched; when the
lids droop, the lashes reach almost half-way down the cheeks.
The upper ears are buried under overlying locks, after the
fashion of his race. The nose is finely aquiline; the lips are thin
and not enlarged by undue distension of the mouth. Every day
the hair springing from his nostrils is cut back; that on the face
springs back from the hollow of the temples, but the razor
has not yet come upon his cheek, and his barber is assiduous
in eradicating the rich growth on the lower part of the face.
Chin, throat, and neck are full, but not fat, and all of fair complexion; seen close, their colour is fresh as that of youth; they
often flush, but from modesty, and not from anger. His shoulders
are smooth, the upper and fore-arms strong and hard; hands
broad; breast prominent; waist receding. The spine dividing
the broad expanse of back does not project, and you can see the
springing of the ribs; the sides swell with salient muscle, the
well-girt flanks are full of vigour. His thighs are like hard horn;
the knee-joints firm and masculine; the knees themselves the

comeliest and least wrinkled in the world. A full ankle supports the leg, and the foot is small to bear such mighty limbs.

IN ABOUT 454.

SOURCE: Sidonius Apollinaris, Book I, letter II, to his brother-in-law, Agricola. In edit. O. M. Dalton, *The Letters of Sidonius*, Clarendon Press, 1915, Vol. I, pp. 2–3.

THERESA OF AVILA, SAINT (1515–1582).

In men it is often seen that to those whom the Lord chooses for his sublimest grace and greatest supernatural gifts, he also gives a more perfect and excellent disposition, as is well seen in that he gave to the Mother Teresa de Jesus. She was of very good stature, and in her youth beautiful, and even after she was an old woman of very good seeming, her body large and very white, her face round and full, very well-sized and shaped, her colour white and red, and when she was in prayer, it lit up and became most beauteous, absolutely clear and placid; her hair black and curly, her brow broad, even, and beautiful, her eyebrows of a red colour, somewhat approaching to black, large and somewhat thick, not very much arched but somewhat level. Her eyes black and round and somewhat heavy lidded (papujado), for so they call them, and I know not how better to explain it, not large, but very well placed, and lively, and so merry, that when she laughed, every one laughed with her, and at other times very grave when she was serious. Her nose small, the bridge not very prominent, and the point round, and slightly curved downwards, the nostrils arched and small, her mouth neither large nor small, the upper lip straight and narrow, the lower one thick and slightly pendulous, its shape and colour excellent; her teeth very good, her chin well-shaped, her ears neither small nor large; her hands small and very beautiful. She had three small moles on her left cheek which became her much, one below the bridge of her nose, another between her nose and mouth, and the third below her mouth. These details I have received from those who had more opportunity than I to look at them often. Altogether she was

very comely, and walked gracefully, and was so amiable and
"*apacible*" that she generally pleased every one who looked at
her.

SOURCE: Francis de Ribera's life of Saint Theresa published in
1602. Ribera was a Jesuit monk and scholar, and had been
Theresa's confessor; quoted Gabriela Cunninghame Graham,
Saint Teresa, Adam & Charles Black, 1894, Vol. II, p. 324.

THIERS, LOUIS ADOLPHE (1797–1877), French statesman and
historian.

The firing or testing of the Reffye cannon on the top of the
Honfleur road was at the time one of the pastimes of this seaside
resort [Trouville] . . . M. Thiers nearly every day after lun-
cheon went up to the plateau attended by his military suite . . .
In the distance on the moving water, an old black barge,
pierced with holes like a battle flag, tossing and rocking about,
served as a target. M. Thiers, with his gray hat pushed slightly
back, his big field-glass up to his eyes, his frock-coat buttoned,
and sometimes affecting the traditional pose of Napoleon,
watched the projectiles fly through the air, saw when they
struck, and waved his hat enthusiastically when a straight shot
shook the barge, made it dance about, and hollowed out a
gaping hole in its already perforated hulk . . .

The crowd applauded. M. Thiers raised his hat again,
congratulated the artillerymen who had laid the gun and those
who had fired it, and then rejoined Mme. Thiers and Mdlle.
Dosne, and, followed by an imposing procession, continued his
daily promenade along the sandy road. From the balcony
where I was I could see him lifting his gray hat incessantly,
whilst as he passed the men all took off their hats, and the *vieille
garde*, in brilliant colours, stood aside or bowed like a cornfield
ravaged by the hail and interspersed with daisies, cornflowers,
and poppies.

SOURCE: Henri Stephan de Blowitz, *My Memoirs*, Edward Arnold,
1903, pp. 62–63.

R

TIMUR (1336–1405), Otherwise Timur i Leng or Tamerlane, 'the lame Timur'; Oriental conqueror who waged victorious war from the Irtish and the Volga to the Persian Gulf, and from the Hellespont to the Ganges.

This conqueror was tall. He had a massive head, a high forehead. He was as remarkable for his physical strength as for his courage. And by nature he has been well endowed. His skin was white, and his complexion vivid. He had stalwart limbs, the shoulders large, the fingers powerful. His beard was long, his hand dry. He limped with the right leg, and he had a deep voice.

In middle age his spirit was as firm and his body as vigorous, and his soul as daring as in the past—like enduring rock. He disliked lying and jesting. But he looked for truth even when it was disagreeable to himself. He was not depressed by misfortune, and prosperity did not stir in him any exultation.

He carried for device upon his seal two Persian words, *Rasti Rousti*, that is—Strength is in right. He was very taciturn in conversation, and never spoke of slaughter, of pillage or the violation of women's sanctuaries. He loved brave soldiers.

SOURCE: The chronicle of 'The Arab', Ibn Arabshah, who had been made captive by Timur and who had good reason to hate him. (Timur's skin might well have seemed pale to an Arab.) Quoted Harold Lamb, *Tamerlane, The Earth Shaker*, Thornton Butterworth Ltd., 1929, pp. 153–154.

TIRPITZ ALFRED VON (1849–1930), German admiral; chief builder of German navy at beginning of twentieth century.

Tirpitz remains a calamitous example of the expert invading policy . . . As a man he was bluff, genial, and quite straightforward; with his upright figure, broad chest and immense beard he looked like a sea-captain of the old school.

SOURCE: J. A. Spender, *Fifty Years of Europe*, Cassell & Company, 1936, second and revised edition, p. 284.

TITULESCU, NICOLAS (1883–1941), Rumanian statesman; architect of Little Entente and Balkan Entente; prominent in League of Nations.

Whereas Benes, with his upturned nose, looked unmistakably Czech, Titulescu of Rumania looked like no member of the human race described in any anthropological What's What. He had a small head like a greengage, mongoloid cheekbones, a low forehead, parchment complexion, big baby eyes, and no trace of beard or mustache, but a rich, feminine growth of hair. His fingers were unusually long and doughy, and he gangled in every limb, walking with long, elastic steps, his arms flailing like windmills. He had the shrill voice of a witch.

SOURCE: Emery Kelen, *Peace in Their Time*, Victor Gollancz, 1964, p. 138.

TIUTCHEV, FEDOR (1803–1873), Russian poet.

In my time I have often had the opportunity to speak with and listen to famous conversationalists, but not one of them made such an enchanting impression on me as Tiutchev did. Witty, tender, biting, warmhearted words rolled carelessly from his lips like pearls. He was probably the most worldly man in all Russia, but worldly in the full sense of the word. Every evening he felt a need, like the need for air, of the dazzling light of chandeliers and lamps, the gay rustle of expensive gowns, the laughter and babble of pretty ladies; and yet his exterior corresponded in no way with his tastes. He was ugly, carelessly dressed, clumsy and absent-minded, but all of this vanished when be began to speak, to narrate ... then everyone instantly hushed, and in all the room only Tiutchev's voice could be heard.

SOURCE: Count Sollogub; quoted Richard A. Gregg, *Fedor Tiutchev, The Evolution of a Poet*, Columbia University Press, 1965, p. 16.

TOLSTOY, LEO (LYEV) NIKOLAYEVICH, COUNT (1828–1910), Russian novelist and moral philosopher.

I beheld L. N. Tolstoy for the first time, and, involuntarily, riveted my eyes upon him. He was clad in a dark grey flannel blouse with a wide turn-down collar, displaying his sinewy neck at the curves of the head. He was breathing rather fast from his walk in the cold air, and his grey hair lay in damp tumbled locks upon his temples. He had an alert, wide-awake air, held himself upright, and moved with quick, short steps, hardly bending his knees, which suggested the motion of a man sliding upon ice. He appeared neither older nor younger than his age—he was then sixty-four and produced the impression of a well-preserved, energetic peasant. And his face, also, was a true peasant's face: simple, rustic, with a broad nose, a weather-beaten skin, and thick, overhanging brows, from beneath which small, keen gray eyes peered sharply forth.

But the expression of his eyes was unusual, and involuntarily attracted attention. In them seemed to be concentrated all the vivid tokens of Tolstoy's personality; and he who has not seen those eyes flash and blaze, who has not seen them suddenly acquire a sort of boring and penetrating character, cannot possess a full conception of L. N. Tolstoy's external appearance.

SOURCE: P. A. Sergyeenko, *How Count Tolstoy Lives and Works*, trans. Isabel F. Hapgood, J. Nisbet & Co., 1899, pp. 1–2.

TORRIGIANO, PIETRO (1472?–1522), Italian sculptor; commissioned by Henry VIII to carve an effigy of Henry VII, in Westminster Abbey.

This Torrigiani was singularly handsome, with a bold bearing, and the air rather of a great soldier than of a sculptor, especially having regard to his commanding gestures and his fine sounding voice; while his frown was enough to scare the bravest. And every day he would tell us of his ruffling it with those beasts of Englishmen.

SOURCE: *Memoirs of Benvenuto Cellini*, trans. Anne Macdonell, J. M. Dent & Sons (Everyman's Library), 1907, p. 17.

TURGENEV, IVAN SERGEYEVICH (1818–1883), Russian novelist.

Until the age of fourteen, I was of small stature, obstinate, morose, evil-tempered, and fond of mathematics. At the age of fourteen I fell dangerously ill, was in bed for several months, and when I got up I was almost as tall as you see me now.

SOURCE: Turgenev; quoted *Turgenev*, Avrahin Yarmolinsky, Orion Press, 1959, p. 21.

He lacks even pagan force and loftiness of soul. All he has is spiritual and physical flabbiness, in spite of his huge stature.

SOURCE: Vera Aksakova, quoted ibid., p. 134.

Note: Turgenev was not the only writer who suddenly grew to full height during an illness. W. M. Thackeray records that he was about five feet six inches when he was 15, then, during an illness in 1828, grew to his full height of six feet three.

VAN GOGH, VINCENT WILLEM (1853–1890), Dutch artist; Van Gogh suffered from mental illness and eventually killed himself.

. . . a boy of seventeen, as broad as he was long, his back slightly bent, with the bad habit of letting the head hang; the red blond hair cropped close was hidden under a straw hat: a strange face, not young; the forehead already full of lines, the eyebrows on the large, noble brow drawn together in deepest thought. The eyes, small and deep-set, were now blue, now green, according to the impressions of the moment. But in spite of all awkwardness and the ugly exterior, one was conscious of a greatness, through the unmistakable sign of the deep inner life.

SOURCE: Elizabeth du Quesne van Gogh, *Personal Recollections of Vincent van Gogh*, trans. Katherine S. Dreier, Constable & Co., Ltd., 1913.

VAN RIJN, REMBRANDT HARMENSZ (1606–1669). See Rembrandt (Rembrandt Harmensz Van Rijn).

VENDÉE, LA (fl. 1793—1800). The royalists of western France, composed of nobles, priests and peasants, who took arms against the republicans. One estimate of their losses puts the figure at 337,000, of whom 37,000 were women and children.

As to clothes, there are plenty of them—in the coarse local cloth, in linen, in duck and in Siamese material. There was a great output of red handkerchiefs. Many of these were already produced in the region and a particular circumstance had made them an article of general wear. M. de la Rochejacuelin usually wore one as a turban round his head, another as a scarf round his neck and several round his waist to accommodate his pistols. At the battle of Fontenay the 'blues' were heard shouting 'Aim at the red handkerchief'. That evening the officers begged Henri to change his costume, but he found it suited him and refused to wear anything else. Then they decided to adopt it for themselves, so that it would no longer be a special cause of danger to him. Thus red handkerchiefs became the fashion in the army; everyone wanted to wear them. This form of garb combined with the normal trousers and tunics of officers made them look like brigands, and that is what the republicans called them.

SOURCE: Madame de la Rochejaquelin, *Memoirs*, Paris, 1817; quoted George Pernoud and Sabine Flaissier, *The French Revolution*, trans. Richard Graves, Secker & Warburg, 1961, pp. 300–301.

VENETIAN NOBLEMEN IN THE SEVENTEENTH CENTURY

... when I came from France to Venice I came from boys to men. For here I saw the handsomest, the most sightly, the most proper and grave men that ever I saw anywhere else. They wear always in the town (I speak of the noblemen) a black gown, a

black cap knit, with edging of black wool about it, like a
fringe, an ancient and manly wear, which makes them look
like senators. Their hair is generally the best I saw anywhere;
these little caps not pressing it down as our hats do, and peri-
wigs are here forbid. Under their long gowns (which fly open
before) they have handsome black suits of rich stuffs, with
stockings and garters and Spanish leather shoes neatly made.
In a word, I never saw so many proper men together, nor so
wise, as I saw here walking upon the Piazza of St. Mark.

SOURCE: Richard Lassels, *The Voyage of Italy, or a Compleat
Journey Through Italy*, 1670, Paris; second edition, London, 1698;
quoted Dorothy Carrington, *The Traveller's Eye*, Pilot Press,
1947, p. 45.

VENETIAN WOMEN IN THE SEVENTEENTH CENTURY

As for the women here, they would gladly get the same reputation that their husbands have of being tall and handsome;
but they over-do it with their horrible *cioppini*, or high shoes,
which I have often seen to be a full half yard high. I confess,
I wondered at first, to see women go upon stilts, and appear
taller by the head than any man; and not able to go any whether
without resting their hands upon the shoulders of two grave
matrons that usher them. But at last, I perceived that it was a
good policy, and a pretty ingenious way either to clog women
at home by such heavy shoes (as the Egyptians kept their wives
at home by allowing them no shoes at all); or at least to make
them not able to go either far, or alone, or invisibly.

SOURCE: Richard Lassels, *The Voyage of Italy, or a Compleat
Journey through Italy*, 1670, Paris, second edition, London, 1698;
quoted Dorothy Carrington, *The Traveller's Eye*, Pilot Press, 1947,
pp. 45–46.

VERLAINE, PAUL (1844–1896), French lyric poet.

One felt him to be a man who had never got over the tragedy
of youth. Somewhere behind his immense forehead there dwelt

a soul which could attain the very depths of purity. This drunken vagabond, zig-zagging across the Quartier Latin, this radiant beggar who dragged his feet in the mud, saw nothing but the sky. The horror of being ugly, of being ugly every day, every moment, without respite, even when his heart was dazzled by love for another human being, had, little by little, led him to a profound humility. He had endured all the rebuffs that could possibly come to him . . . [I went] to see Verlaine when I heard that he was gravely ill. I no longer remember the hospital, but ever present in my memory is the poor, ravaged face, the long, trembling hands, which he could hardly lift to take mine; the gleam of the feverish eyes trying desperately to express something which the lips had no longer the strength to utter.

SOURCE: *Two or Three Muses, The Memoirs of Misia Sert,* trans. Moura Budberg, Museum Press Ltd., 1953, pp. 48–49.

VICTOR AMADEUS II (1660–1732), King of Sicily and Sardinia.

This prince was born on the 14th day of May, 1666; and in 1680 entered upon the government of his dominions. He was in possession of the Kingdom of Sicily from the year 1713 to 1718; but in the year 1720 he became king of Sardinia. His person is tall, slender and well-shaped; and even in his advanced age there appears in him an uncommon vivacity and spirit, but tempered with the most engaging mildness and affability. He holds the reigns of government in his own hands, without being swayed or influenced by ministers or mistresses.

IN 1729.

SOURCE: J. C. Keysler, *Travels through Germany, Bohemia, Hungary, Switzerland, Italy and Lorraine,* second edition, London, 1756, Vol. I, p. 197.

VIGNY, ALFRED DE (1797–1863), French novelist and poet.

De Vigny was indeed a singular man—polished, affable, and gentle in his dealings with others—a detachment from earth which, moreover, was admirably in keeping with his interesting face and its delicate spiritual features, framed in long, fair, curling locks, like one of the cherubim whose brother he seemed to be. De Vigny never touched the earth of necessity. When he folded his wings and rested perchance on the summit of a mountain, it was a concession made to Humanity, and because, after all, he found that was the most convenient for the brief dealings he had with us mortals . . . No one had ever come upon De Vigny eating a meal. Dorval, who for seven years of her life passed several hours a day with him, confessed, with an amazement which partook of awe, that she had never seen him eat anything except a radish.

SOURCE: *The Memoirs of Alexandre Dumas (Père)*, selected and trans. A. F. Davidson, W. H. Allen & Co., Calcutta, 1891, pp. 306–307.

VILLENEUVE, PIERRE CHARLES JEAN BAPTISTE SILVESTRE DE (1763–1806), Vice-Admiral; commander-in-chief of the French and Spanish fleets at Trafalgar.

The Admiral was landed on Friday morning at Gosport beach. He was brought on shore by the Commissioner's barge from the Euryalus frigate, lying at Spithead, and walked through the town to the Crown Inn, accompanied only by his second captain, Marchande, and Captain Taylor, of the *Camilla* sloop-of-war. Admiral Villeneuve is well made, and has a manly countenance, appears to be about fifty years of age, and is between five feet eight and nine inches high. He seems melancholy, but not despondent, and is conscious of having done his duty . . . He speaks English but imperfectly.

SOURCE: Contemporary account in the *Hampshire Telegraph*; quoted in Edward Fraser, *The Enemy at Trafalgar*, Hodder & Stoughton, 1906, pp. 377–378. The reporter seems to have misheard the name of Villeneuve's companion. This was Captain Jean Magendie, Villeneuve's flag-captain on the *Bucentaure*.

How well I remember our receiving Villeneuve on board the *Euryalus*, and the Captain of the Fleet, Magendie, to convey them to England. Villeneuve was a thinnish, tall man, a very tranquil, placid, English-looking Frenchman; he wore a long-tailed uniform coat, high and flat collar, corduroy pantaloons of a greenish colour, with stripes two inches wide, half-boots with sharp toes, and a watch-chain with long gold links.

SOURCE: Midshipman Hercules Robinson of the *Euryalus*; quoted Edward Fraser, *The Enemy at Trafalgar*, Hodder & Stoughton, 1906, p. 144.

VOLTAIRE, FRANÇOIS MARIE AROUET DE (1694–1778), the pen name of François Marie Arouet, French poet, philosopher and dramatist; his collected works were published in 70 volumes, 1785–1789.

Voltaire is a long diaphanous body, yet he does not let you easily read the bottom of his thought. His lean, pale and bony face is marked by a look of mockery, all the more perfidious is that it finds expression in fair words. He has a perpetual epigram on his pinched lips, whether he is speaking to a prince or to a lackey.

SOURCE: Cardinal Dubois, *Memoirs*, trans. Ernest Dowson, Leonard Smithers & Co., 1899, Vol. II, p. 162.

He wore on all occasions, grey slippers, grey stockings with rolled tops, a long waistcoat of cotton-twill down to his knees, a big, long wig, and a little black velvet cap. On Sunday he sometimes wore a fine suit of russet silk, all of the same colour, waistcoat and breeches to match, but the waistcoat with big skirts, braided in gold in the Burgundian style, the braid twisted and wired, with big lace ruffles falling to the finger tips, 'for that gave him', he said, 'the air of a nobleman'. Monsieur de Voltaire acted like a tonic on his immediate circle and made them all laugh. He enriched everything he saw and heard.

SOURCE: Prince de Ligne, *Letters and Memoirs*, trans. Leigh Ashton, George Routledge & Sons Ltd., 1927, p. 118.

Thereupon a little door was opened and I found myself face to face with a tall skeleton buried in a large armchair and wearing on his head a huge bearskin cap which covered him down to his eyes. It was Voltaire.

SOURCE: Baron de Frénilly, *Récollections*, edit. Arthur Chuquet, trans. Frederic Lees, William Heinemann Ltd., 1909, pp. 12–13.

During the whole of dinner, M. de Voltaire was very far from being agreeable. He seemed always in a passion with his servants, incessantly crying out to them, and that, too, with such strength of lungs that I often started involuntarily. As the dining-room repeated sounds very strongly, his tremendous voice reverberated in the most alarming manner. I had been told beforehand of this singular foible, which it is so unusual for any one to display before strangers; and, in fact, it was evident enough that it was the mere result of habit, for his servants were not surprised at it or minded it in the least . . .

All the busts and portraits of him that I have seen are extremely like him; but no artist has fully expressed the eyes. I expected to find them keen and full of fire, and they were certainly the liveliest I ever saw; but they also had something indescribably soft and tender in their expression—the whole soul of *Zaire* was expressed in them. His laugh and bitter smile greatly altered the expression of his face. He was much broken down, and his old-fashioned style of dress made him look still older.

SOURCE: *Memoirs of the Countess de Genlis . . . written by herself*, London, 1825, Vol. 2, pp. 249–252.

Voltaire made his appearance out of an adjacent study, and came into the room with more affectation of bodily infirmity than was requisite; not but that he really was as meagre and arid a figure as ever I saw. His dress was a sky blue ratteen coat, lapelled, a blue turned up cap over a long flowing brigadier grey wig, his knees without buckles, his stocking coarse, his shoes thick and large. After a short address on the honor we did a weakly old man, his countenance brightened, his eyes, which were the most brilliant I ever saw, sparkled with pleasure at the attention paid to his fame.

SOURCE: Thomas Pennant, *Tour on the Continent 1765*, edit. G. R. de Beer, Ray Society, 1948, p. 26.

WAGNER, WILHELM RICHARD (1813–1883), German composer.

He would listen with closed eyes to the artists singing to Bülow's pianoforte accompaniment. If a difficult passage went particularly well, he would spring up, embrace or kiss the singer warmly, or out of pure joy stand on his head on the sofa, creep under the piano, jump up on to it, run into the garden, and scramble joyously up a tree, or make caricatures, or recite, with improvised disfigurements, a poem that had been dedicated to him.

SOURCE: Sebastian Röckl; quoted Ernest Newman, *Wagner as Man and Artist*, Victor Gollancz, 1963 re-issue, p. 172.

To look at him was to see turn by turn in the same visage the front face of Faust and the profile of Mephistopheles . . . His manner was no less surprising than his physiognomy. It varied between absolute reserve, coldness, and complete familiarity and sans-gêne . . . When he showed himself he broke out as a whole, like a torrent bursting its dykes. One stood dazzled before that exuberant and protean nature, ardent, personal, excessive in everything, yet marvellously equilibrated by the predominance of a devouring intellect. The frankness and extreme audacity with which he showed his nature, the qualities and defects of which were exhibited without concealment, acted on some people like a charm, while others were repelled by it . . . his gaiety flowed over in a joyous foam of facetious fancies and extravagant pleasantries; but the least contradiction provoked him to incredible anger. Then he would leap like a tiger, roar like a stag. He paced the room like a caged lion, his voice became hoarse and the words came out like screams; his speech slashed about at random. He seemed at these times like some elemental force unchained, like a volcano in eruption. Everything in him was gigantic, excessive.

SOURCE: Edouard Schuré; quoted ibid., pp. 172–173.

In stature Wagner was below the middle size, and like most undersized men always held himself strictly erect. He had an unusually wiry, muscular frame, small feet, an aristocratic feature which did not extend to his hands. It was his head, however, that could not fail to strike even the least inquiring that there he had to do with no ordinary mortal. The development of the frontal part, which a phrenologist would class at a glance amongst those belonging only to the master-minds, impressed every one. His eyes had a piercing power, but were kindly withal, and were ready to smile at a witty remark. Richard Wagner lacked eyebrows, but nature, as if to make up for this deficiency, bestowed on him a most abundant crop of bushy hair, which he carefully kept brushed back, thereby exposing the whole of his really Jupiter-like brow. His mouth was very small. He had thin lips and small teeth, signs of a determined character. The nose was large and in after-life somewhat disfigured by the early-acquired habit of snuff-taking. The back of his head was fully developed. These were according to phrenological principles power and energy. Its shape was very similar to that of Luther, with whom, indeed, he had more than one point of character in common.

SOURCE: Ferdinand Praeger, *Wagner as I Knew Him*, Longmans, Green & Co., 1892, pp. 13-14.

He then [i.e. in 1862] lived at the Hotel Kaiserin Elizabeth, and as my rooms were in that same quarter, it often chanced that I met him on the street going to and from rehearsals, — generally talking to himself, and usually flourishing his great red bandanna. The Master's hair was brown in those days, and he invariably wore a high silk hat and a long frock coat—never by any chance buttoned up.

SOURCE: Angelo Neumann, *Personal Recollections of Wagner*, trans. Edith Livermore, Archibald Constable & Co., 1909, p. 4.

WEBER, CARL MARIA FRIEDRICH ERNST VON (1786–1826), German composer.

Weber's really refined, delicate, and intellectual appearance excited my ecstatic admiration. His narrow face and finely-cut features, his vivacious though often half-closed eyes, captivated and enthralled me; whilst even the bad limp with which he walked, and which I often noticed from the window when the master was making his way home past our house from the fatiguing rehearsals, stamped the great musician in my imagination as an exceptional and almost superhuman being.

SOURCE: Richard Wagner; quoted Percy M. Young, *More Music Makers*, Dennis Dobson, 1955, p. 39.

WEBER, CONSTANZE (1763–1842), became the wife of Wolfgang Amadeus Mozart in 1782; he had previously courted her elder sister, Aloysia.

Now then, who is the object of my love? Do not be alarmed by this, I beg you! Certainly not a Weber? Yes, a Weber, but not Josepha, not Sophie, but Constanze, the middle one . . . She is the martyr among them, and for that very reason perhaps the most sweet-natured, the cleverest, and in a word the best among them. She takes care of everything in the house, and yet they blame her for doing nothing right. Oh, dearest father, I could write pages if I were to describe to you all the scenes that have happened to us both in that house . . . She is not ugly but by no means a beauty. Her whole beauty consists in two small black eyes and in a winsome figure. She is not witty, but has enough sound common sense to enable her to fulfil her duties as a wife and mother. She is not inclined to extravagance. That is an altogether false accusation. On the contrary, she is accustomed to going about poorly dressed. For what little the mother has been able to do for her children has been done for the other two, never for Constanze. It is true that she would like to be neatly and cleanly dressed, but not in the height of fashion. And most of the clothes a woman needs she is able to make her herself. She also does her own hair every day, is a good house-keeper, and has the kindest heart in the world.

SOURCE: a letter from Mozart to his father, Leopold; quoted Eric Schenk, *Mozart and his Times*, Secker & Warburg, 1960, pp. 318–319.

WIELAND, CHRISTOPHER MARTIN (1733–1813), German poet and man of letters.

[In 1777, when Wieland had come to Mannheim for the performance of an opera based on his *Alceste*.] I had imagined him to be quite different from what I found him. He strikes you as slightly affected in his speech. He has a rather childish voice; he keeps on quizzing you over his glasses; He indulges in a sort of pedantic rudeness, mingled occasionally with a stupid condescension. But I am not surprised that he permits himself such behaviour here, even though he may be quite different in Weimar and elsewhere, for people stare at him as if he had dropped from Heaven. Everyone seems embarrassed in his presence, no one says a word or moves an inch; all listen intently to every word he utters; and it's a pity they often have to wait so long, for he has a defect of speech that makes him speak very slowly and he can't say half a dozen words without stopping. Apart from that, he is what we all know him to be, a most gifted fellow. He has a frightfully ugly face, covered with pock marks, and he has a rather long nose. In height he is, I should say, a little taller than Papa.

SOURCE: Wolfgang Amadeus Mozart, the composer; quoted Alfred Einstein, *Mozart, His Character, His Work*, trans. Arthur Mendel and Nathan Broder, Cassell & Co., 1946, p. 19.

WIGNAND, Abbot of Tharisia in the early twelfth century; friend and counsellor of Otto, Apostle to Pomerania.

He was a man of the greatest wisdom and sagacity, whom it was the glory of our order to see and hear. He not only excelled in spiritual grace, but was beloved by all for the beauty of his person and the charm of his character and deportment. Let me try for a moment worthily to portray his venerable appearance and his head which was white like that of Christ. For when he was nearly a hundred years old and was busily engaged day and night in God's work, his eyes shone with a pure light, his steps were firm and swift, his voice penetrating, his teeth numerous and strong, his voice sonorous, his body well set up

and not bent with age, his hoary locks did not harmonize with
his ruddy looks, and his strength was out of proportion to
his age. As in many cases we did not observe any tenacity of
memory, his great age had put an end to this. The cold in his
blood did not chill the keenness of his understanding, his
furrowed brow did not roughen a countenance contracted by
wrinkles, nor did a trembling hand write with irregular curves
on the wax tablet. In him the Lord showed us the beauty of the
future resurrection in order that we might understand concerning sin, for the flesh of others dies while still young, and justly,
but he in a later age was still young, and though we see that
many sinners have that bodily health they use it to go on sin-
ning, whilst he used it to do good.

Having been instructed from his earliest days in the holy
scriptures and having been approved by his pious conversation,
when he was vigorously fulfilling the duty of prior under the
venerable abbot Wulfram, the holy Otto snatched him away
and placed him in charge of the Tharisian monastery. For a
long time, that is for more than twenty years, he ruled with
distinction, and by his honeyed words he scattered on all sides
the sweetness of the heavenly doctrine and incited all men to
love God.

SOURCE: Ebbo's Life of Otto, Apostle of Pomerania, the first
    missionary Tour; in Charles H. Robinson, edit., *The Life of Otto
    Apostle of Pomerania 1060–1139 by Ebo and Hebordus*, S.P.C.K.,
    1920, pp. 98–99.

WILLIAM I (1797–1888), King of Prussia and German Emperor.

His Court, indeed, appeared to be much more convinced of
his advanced age than he was himself. I had heard so much
concerning the precautions which, according to some people of
his Court, he ought to have taken, but to which he obstinately
refused to conform, that I was expecting to see an almost de-
crepit man, borne down by the weight of his years.

I was extremely surprised, therefore, on the first occasion
that I met the Emperor, to find myself in the presence of a man

vigorous and active in his movements, whose blue eyes retained
the vivacity usually associated with youth, and whose walk still
possessed vigour and elasticity. The attitude of the Emperor was
kind in the extreme, his voice expressed sympathy, and it had
an intonation which gave token of rare qualities of heart and
of mind. He had a curious habit when he was talking to anyone
of bending his head in such a manner that it seemed to add to
his height instead of taking away from it. Always very neat in
his dress, he had a certain coquetry in the way in which he
arranged his hair in order to hide his baldness. A long lock from
the back was carried to the front, where it was fastened by
means of a black thread to another coming from his forehead.
This considerably added to the charm of his face. The Emperor
could never have been a handsome young man, but in age he
was imposing.

SOURCE: Princess Catherine Radziwill, *Memories of Forty Years*,
Cassell & Co., 1914, pp. 49, 50.

WILLIAM II (1859–1941), Emperor of Germany.

Memory takes me back to a day at Potsdam in the early
summer of 1907; the Kaiser's birthday, the review of the
Guards, like a scene out of an opera, kindling a real emotion
with—to an English eye—a touch of absurdity, goose-step,
mitred soldiers, etc., but all jollity and glitter under a brilliant
sun. Then lunch on the invitation of the All-Highest in the
Orangery of the Palace, and after lunch the arrival on the green
sward outside of the All-Highest himself in white uniform with
towering helmet and golden eagle perched on top of it, mounted
on an immense horse and surrounded by his staff, also mounted
and in blazing uniforms. Next a summons to the presence and
half an hour standing along by the stirrup while the Imperial
rider poured out his grievances against the English, their dis-
regard of things German, the small number of them that visited
his country and the still smaller number that came to Berlin . . .
 There was a certain bathos in it. Just so might a rich new-
comer who had bought a big house and park in the English

S

country complain that 'the county' did not call on him. But also there was something simple and honest, which was rather attractive. He did not deal in the compliments and platitudes expected of royal personages on such an occasion; he was alive, he was human, he spoke with emphasis and energy, said what occurred to him without reserve or discretion, and incidentally revealed something which it was important to know. If he was old among Kings, he was new among Emperors, and the need to assert himself, to resent slights to his dignity, and to claim his place in the sun and his equality of status was a strong urge explaining much that seemed mere bluster in his own attitude and the policy of his country.

SOURCE: J. A. Spender, *Fifty Years of Europe*, Cassell, 1936, second and revised edition, pp. 278–279.

His undeniable cleverness and versatility, his personal grace and dignity, only aggravated his dangers by concealing his inadequacy. He knew how to make the gestures, to utter the words, to strike attitudes in the Imperial style. He could stamp and snort, or nod and smile with much histrionic art; but underneath all this posing and its trappings, was a very ordinary, vain, but on the whole, well-meaning man, hoping to pass himself off as a second Frederick the Great.

It was my good fortune to be the Emperor's guest at the German army manoeuvres of 1906 and 1908. He was then at the height of his glory. As he sat on his horse surrounded by Kings and Princes while his legions defiled before him in what seemed to be an endless procession, he represented all that this world has to give in material things. The picture that lives most vividly in my memory is his entry into the city of Breslau at the beginning of the manoeuvres. He rode his magnificent horse at the head of a squadron of cuirassiers, wearing their white uniform and eagle-crested helmet. The streets of the Silesian capital were thronged with his enthusiastic subjects . . . What a contrast twelve years would show! A broken man sits hunched in a railway carriage hour after hour, at a Dutch frontier station awaiting permission to escape as a refugee from the execration of a people whose armies he has led through such measureless sacrifices to measureless defeat ...

SOURCE: Winston S. Churchill, *Great Contemporaries*, Thornton Butterworth, 1939, pp. 42, 37–38.

WILLIAM IV HENRY, PRINCE OF ORANGE (1711–1751), hereditary Stadtholder; married Anne, Princess Royal, daughter of George II of England.

Not that he wanted genius, but he was vain and positive, a trifling lover of show, and not master of the great lights in which he stood. The Princess Royal was more positive, and, though passionately imperious, had dashed all opportunities that presented for the Prince's distinguishing himself, from immoderate jealousy and fondness for his person. Yet the Mars who was locked in the arms of this Venus, was a monster so deformed, that when the King had chosen him for his son-in-law, he could not help, in the honesty of his heart, and the coarseness of his expression, telling the princess how hideous a bridegroom she was to expect, and even gave her permission to refuse. She replied, she would marry him if he was a baboon. Well, then, said the King, there is baboon enough for you.

SOURCE: Horace Walpole, *Memoirs of the Reign of King George the Second*, edit. Lord Holland, 1847, Vol. 1, p. 206.

The Prince of Orange's figure, besides his being almost a dwarf, was as much deformed as it was possible for a human creature to be; his face was not bad, his countenance was sensible, but his breath was more offensive than it is possible for those who have not been offended by it to imagine ... The Prince of Orange was a less shocking and less ridiculous figure in this pompous [marriage] procession and at supper than one could naturally have expected such an Æsop, in such trappings and such eminence, to have appeared. He had a long peruke like hair that flowed all over his back, and hid the roundness of it; and, as his countenance was not bad there was nothing very strikingly disagreeable but his stature.

But when he was undressed, and came in his nightgown and nightcap into the room to go to bed, the appearance he made was as indescribable as the astonished countenances of everybody who beheld him. From the make of his brocaded gown, and the make of his back, he looked behind as if he had no head, and before as if he had no neck and no legs.

SOURCE: Lord Hervey, *Memoirs of the Reign of George the Second*, edit. Romney Sedgwick, B. T. Batsford Ltd., 1952, pp. 25, 41. The Memoirs were first edited by John Wilson Croker (1848) from a censored MS. from which Hervey's descendants had removed a number of passages, mainly relating to the royal family. A more complete edition, containing most of the missing material, was published in 1931, from a MS. in the Windsor Castle archives.

XAVIER, SAINT FRANCIS (1506–1552). Spanish Jesuit missionary; called the 'Apostle of the Indies'.

I lived six months with Father Master Francis. He went barefoot, with a poor torn gown, and a kind of hood of black stuff. Every one loved him dearly . . . The *Great Father*, that is the name which has been given to Father Master Francis in these lands . . . Often in that countryside [Travancore] followed by two thousand, three thousand, six thousand people, he would stop, climb up a tree, and from there preach to the people.

SOURCE: a fellow Jesuit missionary; quoted Phyllis Garlick *6 Great Missionaries*, Hamish Hamilton, 1955, p. 33.

XIMENEZ DE CISNEROS, FRANCISCO (1436–1517), Spanish Cardinal and statesman.

He was tall in body, yet strong and thick-set, and his measured gait displayed his innate dignity His voice was manly and firm, such as the poets praise in the heroes; his face was long and lean, his forehead wide and unwrinkled, his eyes of medium size, deep-set rather than prominent—sharp, too, and keen, but moist as though accustomed to weeping. His nose was long and aquiline ... with large, wide nostrils; his teeth were closely set, but the canines were prominent and because of this he was called 'the elephant' in jest by his followers. He had somewhat thick lips which were drawn a little apart because the upper one was slightly raised (but not sufficiently to be considered a deformity). His ears were set very low but were not pendulous; rather, they were perpetually fixed to the joints of his jawbones. The upper part of his whole body was longer than the lower, by a ratio of almost four to three. In the year 1545 ... when a subterranean vault, in which the corpse of Ximenez had been buried, was uncovered, his skull was brought out to the open air. It was joined together without a seam and consisted of continuous bone, as Aristotle once noted is found occasionally in man.

He expressed his thoughts briefly and replied clearly without wandering off the point, for he was very sparing of words, even when he threatened in anger. For when he promised something as a favour he made the favour itself far more generous and ample than his words. And often he used that phrase of Cicero's, that we have not been made by Nature to be esteemed for sporting and jest, but rather for seriousness and certain weightier studies. However, among some of his intimates who were of simple and open nature (for he was very much delighted by men of this kind), he relaxed his mind, fatigued by its burden, in holiday fashion with joking and laughter, but only sparingly and rarely, so that he might be adjudged courteous rather than friendly and affable.

SOURCE: Alvaro Gomez de Castro, *De Rebus gestis Francisci Ximenii*, Lib. VII, 1569 edition, f. 218.

YAKUB KHAN (1849–1923); amir of Afghanistan; proclaimed in 1879 and abdicated in the same year; puppet of the British government.

His appearance, I should say, is decidedly aristocratic. He is of middle height, straight, and well built. His complexion is that of an Italian, and infinitely fairer than that of many of the

bronzed warriors one sees in the British camps. His features
are of the usual coarsely aquiline Afghan type. His expression is
somewhat stern and careworn, but indicates character and
resolution. His beard is short and crisp, and at his age, thirty-
four [he was only thirty years of age at this time] is doubtless
of its natural black colour, undisguised by the cosmetics so
freely used by Afghans when gray hairs appear. The Ameer rode
a well-bitted, light chestnut Turcoman charger, equipped with
European military saddle and bridle. He was dressed in an
Afghan cloak of the finest material of the country, made with
evident attention to a becoming fit, and wore European
trousers fastened under a neat polished-leather boot by chain
straps. His head-dress was a close-fitting cap of Astrakhan wool.
He sat his horse erect and well, and it was easy to fancy him the
gallant soldier and skilful general which in his earlier years he
so often proved himself to be.

SOURCE: *The Times* correspondent, May 9th, 1879; quoted
  D. C. Boulger, *Central Asian Portraits*, London, W. H. Allen & Co.,
  1880, pp. 286–287.

ZOLA, EMILE EDOUARD CHARLES ANTOINE (1840–1902),
French novelist.

Our admirer and pupil Zola came to lunch today. It was the
first time we had ever seen him. Our immediate impression
was of a worn-out *Normalien*, at once sturdy and puny, with
Sarcey's neck and shoulders and a waxy, anaemic complexion,
a strapping young fellow with something of the delicate modelling of fine porcelain in his features, in the line of his eyes, in the
angry planes of his nose, and in his hands. The whole of his
person was built rather like his characters, which he constructs
with two contrary types, mingling male and female in them;
and in his temperament too he offered a certain resemblance
to the natures he creates, with their ambiguous contrasts. The
dominant side of him, the sickly, suffering, hypersensitive side,
occasionally gives you the impression of being in the company

of a gentle victim of some heart disease. In a word, an incomprehensible, deep, complex character; unhappy, worried, evasive, and disquieting. [1868]

Zola came to see me today. He came in with that gloomy, haggard air which is characteristic of his way of entering a room. That man of forty really is a pitiful sight; he looks older than I do. [1880]

At Charpentier's this evening a gentleman came up to me whom I did not recognise at first. It was Zola, but so changed that in the street I should really and truly have passed him without greeting him. He no longer had that resemblance to the portrait by Manet, which he had recovered for a little while; with the hollows under his cheekbones, his hair brushed up from his high forehead, the squalid yellow of his complexion, the nervous contraction of his mouth, and a certain fixity in his gaze, he looked like a ghost with a sickly spitefulness spread all over its face. [1888]

SOURCE: Robert Baldick, edit., *Pages from the Goncourt Journal*, Oxford University Press, 1962, pp. 144, 260, 338.